BLOOM AND BUST

Space and Place

Bodily, geographic, and architectural sites are embedded with cultural knowledge and social value. This series provides ethnographically rich analyses of the cultural organization and meanings of these sites of space, architecture, landscape, and places of the body. Contributions examine the symbolic meanings of space and place, the cultural and historical processes involved in their construction and contestation, and how they communicate with wider political, religious, social, and economic institutions.

BLOOM AND BUST

Urban Landscapes in the East
since German Reunification

Edited by
Gwyneth Cliver and Carrie Smith-Prei

berghahn
NEW YORK · OXFORD
www.berghahnbooks.com

Published by
Berghahn Books
www.berghahnbooks.com

Library of Congress Cataloging-in-Publication Data
Bloom and bust : urban landscapes in the East since German reunification /
edited by Gwyneth Cliver and Carrie Smith-Prei.
    pages cm. -- (Space and place ; volume 13)
    Includes bibliographical references and index.
ISBN 978-1-78238-490-8 (hardback : alk. paper) -- ISBN 978-1-78238-491-5
(ebook)
    1. Germany (East)--Economic conditions--1990- 2. Germany (East)--
Economic conditions--Regional disparities. 3. Cities and towns--Germany
(East)--History. 4. Germany--History--Unification, 1990. I. Cliver, Gwyneth
(Assistant professor) II. Smith-Prei, Carrie, 1975-
    HC290.782.B56 2014
    307.760943'1--dc23
                                                          2014018759

British Library Cataloguing in Publication Data

A catalogue record for this book is available from the British Library

Printed on acid-free paper

ISBN: 978-1-78238-490-8 hardback
ISBN: 978-1-78238-491-5 ebook

Contents

Figures

Acknowledgments

Gwyneth Cliver would like to thank the University Committee on Research and Creative Activity (University of Nebraska at Omaha) for a summer travel grant to do initial research, Deborah Ascher Barnstone for scholarly direction, and Tascha Horowitz and Joseph Marchal for feedback. Carrie Smith-Prei would like to thank the Killam Research Fund (University of Alberta) for funding that led to this volume. Both editors are deeply indebted to Barbara Pausch for her careful reading of early drafts. We would also like to thank Hunter Bivens and Rolf J. Goebel for their intellectual contributions to this project.

Special thanks go to the anonymous readers for Berghahn Books; their critical comments throughout readings of the chapters helped shape the volume in its finals stages. Finally, we thank editor Ann DeVita for her commitment to the project from its early stages, assistant editor Molly Mosher and associate production editor Elizabeth Berg for seeing the volume through production, Mollie Firestone for her careful copyediting, and Marion Berghahn for her support of this volume.

Introduction

GWYNETH CLIVER AND CARRIE SMITH-PREI

> Through combined effort we will soon be able to transform
> Mecklenburg-Western Pomerania and Saxony-Anhalt, Bran-
> denburg, Saxony, and Thuringia into blooming landscapes in
> which living and working are worthwhile.[1]
> —Former German Chancellor Helmut Kohl, July 1990

Anyone familiar with the discourse surrounding the unification process in Germany during the 1990s, and even during the first decade of the
twenty-first century, knows well how central a role concerns about the
built environment in the former German Democratic Republic (GDR)—
architecture, monuments, urban design—have played. Old town centers that had been neglected by the GDR government in favor of new
construction in prefabricated housing complexes became celebrated
loci of historical preservation. A few high-profile demolitions occurred
alongside countless ones of generic residences across the new federal
states. Beloved structures, most famously the Frauenkirche (Church of
Our Lady) of Dresden, were resurrected from a fifty-years status as war
ruins. And empty swaths of land, especially the former No Man's Land
between East and West Berlin, were filled with new construction with
great public fanfare and after passionate debate.

These developments spurred an equally vibrant and often contentious
debate among all branches of German Studies. Literary and cultural
scholars, historians, art and architecture theorists, and anthropologists
alike have grappled with elucidating the significance of this ardent activity and the choices made while demographics were shifting, infrastructure was being improved, the federal government was being reseated,
currencies were being changed and then changed again, and histories
were being written and commemorated in physical form. With archi-

tecture, urban development and shrinkage, and urban design as their objects, scholars have considered and debated the definition of authenticity, the origin and meaning of nostalgia, the fascination with ruins, the relative merits of idealism versus pragmatism, the ephemerality of futurism, and the status of modernism and postmodernism (Hell and Schönle 2010). Further, the built landscape and spaces of the former GDR have become grounds on which the status of unified German identity, shared histories, and mythmaking can be negotiated.

The burden of proof for theories developed during these debates has fallen squarely on the shoulders of a mere handful of prominent cases: the rebuilding of the Frauenkirche in Dresden, the development of No Man's Land in Berlin with a newly designed Potsdamer Platz and Peter Eisenman's Memorial to the Murdered Jews of Europe, the transformation of the Reichstag (German Parliament Building) through Christo's famous wrapping and with Norman Foster's beloved glass cupola, the demolition of the Palast der Republik (Palace of the Republic, headquarters of the GDR) and the reconstruction of the Berliner Stadtschloss (City Palace), the aestheticization of the remnants of the Berlin Wall through their reinvention as the open-air East Side Gallery (Joel 2012). Although discrete studies take other sites into consideration, an undeniable emphasis has been placed on these locations, all but one of which are in the center of the new-again capital. These sites inspire study with their drama, politico-historical significance, and expense, but the emphasis on so small a set of examples deprives scholars of a more nuanced look at changes in the former GDR. They overlook the everyday reality of lived spaces in Magdeburg or Jena for the spectacle of the tourism industry in Berlin. They base aesthetic judgments on projects in which vast sums of public and private funds are invested, but fail to consider the aesthetic significance of sites for which money is scarce or nonexistent. They privilege the public imagination over the public reality.

This volume begins to rectify this oversight by turning attention primarily to cities in the former GDR generally ignored by German Studies. A similar catalog of questions—concerning authenticity, nostalgia, ruin gazing, idealism, futurism, modernism, and postmodernism—arises, but a consideration of spaces that are less celebrated and sometimes also less attractive to gentrification demands these questions be formulated and answered innovatively and with attention to such aspects as individual experience, the power of counterdiscourses, or spatially and architecturally determined affect. The authors of the following chapters, whose scholarly homes are in a diverse array of disciplines within German Studies, investigate, for example, tenacious efforts in Eisenach to maintain a notion of material authenticity in historical preservation that is now considered outdated by professional preservationists, the extent to which unification in 1990 represented a true political and social shift in Erfurt and Frankfurt (Oder), and the signifying power of voids in Hoyerswerda. They take us to Quedlinburg, a small spa town in Thuringia, and the intimate, lived spaces of the Berliner *Kiez* (neighborhood/town-within-a-city). In this way, this volume seeks to challenge the notion that only the highly visible and expensive projects warrant observation, thus heeding Lutz Koepnick's call to "Forget Berlin" and agreeing with Rolf J. Goebel, who asserts that the "Eastern German city has emerged as a formidable counterweight to the centrality of Berlin" (Koepnick 2001; Goebel 2007: 492).[2] This volume builds upon the scholarly discussion by those who have attended to an understanding of the significance of visible symbols in Germany's capital. However, by shifting the focus away from the better known attractions of Berlin to less known, but nevertheless revealing cases, it encourages a rethinking of the popular theories in a number of fields within German Studies, theories concerning physical transformations in the Federal Republic of Germany (FRG) since 1989. Guided by the chapters' emphases, this introduction discusses some of the continuities and departures that surface in such an inclusive examination, thus offering a variegated view beyond notions of historicity, identity, or symbolic production. The following offers a brief excursion to those famous discourse-generating sites intertwined with the cases examined by our contributors to demonstrate how this discourse can develop nuance, offer variations on a theme, or become complicated by new objects of inquiry.

Selling Space: Transformations, Resurrections, and Rejuvenations

An influx of capital from the West during the boom years of the 1990s and early 2000s, significant and fundamental demographic changes, and a shift from an industrial socialist economy to the service-based one characteristic of the capitalism of the last two decades have all contributed to an evolution, both social and physical, in the cities of the former GDR. This evolution is visually discernable in the immediate changes on the surface of cities and towns across the East. The spaces of prominent or historical sites in places like Berlin and Dresden evolved along with less discussed or ahistorical sites in places such as Rostock and Leipzig. Due in part to genuine enthusiasm for the reunion of a long-divided city and visions of a revival of a creative, innovative, and world-class capital as it had been in its Weimar heyday, but amplified by media and scholarly obsession, collective attention has nonetheless remained focused on the capital.

Any tourist of Berlin in the 1990s recalls the flock of mammoth cranes, their long necks crisscrossing and towering over the city and dominating its skyline. The rapid demolition of the Wall left a physical and psychological void patched by a brick scar across the city's face. No Man's Land, for decades lost to the ever-expanding reach of urban development and hence pathologically horizontal and bleak, suddenly and ostentatiously grew into a decidedly vertical and garish visual testament to the dominance of capitalism. Potsdamer Platz, an empty expanse of land between East and West Berlin captured in Wim Wenders's *Wings of Desire* (1987), became famous in the 1990s as Europe's largest construction site with boarded walkways and gaping pits, transforming this East-West intersection into a maze dislocated from time and space. Today, this former Augéian non-place is home to the Sony Center, the Ritz-Carleton Berlin, the Grand Hyatt, and other markers of capitalism and its attendant wealth; Potsdamer Platz has become the shiny and glamorous face of Berlin's new media-savvy culture of elitism (Augé 1995: 34). The Reichstag received its now famous and beloved transparent dome and the chancellor and parliament have new administrative homes. The country has continued its very visible and official *Aufarbeitung der Vergangenheit* (working through of the past) with Daniel Libeskind's evocative and provocative addition to the Jewish Museum and Eisenman's controversial Memorial to the Murdered Jews of Europe. More recently, the city completed the new, and this time truly central train station, standing both practically and symbolically as a final act of unification.

These changes to the built environment inspire or are the result of public—often contentious or heated—discussion, which itself has been read to reveal much about the relationship between space and notions of Germanness, as a self-conscious act of national and political identity reflection (Ruge and Morat 2005). Although the thrust of this volume moves attention away from these high-profile transformations, Christopher Jones's analysis of the crime fiction novel *Potsdamer Platz* examines the role the redevelopment of this square has had on national and individual identity formation. His reading of the detective status of protagonist Tony as a foil to a Benjaminian flâneur, where the latter merely reads instead of writing the urban text but the former achieves both, providing insight into the discourse surrounding these transformations in the 1990s and early 2000s. Residents were eager, even expected, to be involved in discussions and decisions; participating in rebuilding celebrated sites became part and parcel of democracy and the construction of a united German identity in the Berlin Republic.

Potsdamer Platz is a spectacular example because of its sheer size and its placement uniting Berlin's inner core. Further prominent debates on the extensive (re)construction and renovation of spaces in formerly East Berlin have centered on areas historically laden with meaning.[3] A famous example has concerned a valuable tract of land also in the center of Berlin, across from the cathedral and approximately midway between the Brandenburg Gate and the television tower at Alexanderplatz. On this spot, known as the Schlossplatz (Palace Square), the Palast der Republik, a multiuse facility and headquarters of the GDR government, had stood until it was demolished in 2009. In its place, the city is reconstructing the façade of the baroque Stadtschloss, once the main residence of Brandenburg royalty, which had been damaged in World War II bombings and was torn down by the GDR government in 1950. Between its gutting due to necessary asbestos removal and its demolition, the Palast der Republik was a site of protest and temporary art exhibitions. In the years leading up to its removal, a lively and often vitriolic debate raged concerning the proposed demolition. More conservative civic organizations and city planners supported the reconstruction of the Stadtschloss, claiming that only this act could restore the urban harmony of the city, whereas more left-leaning architects, planners, and intellectuals considered the proposal to be a nostalgic and reactionary attempt to deny the contentious history of the twentieth century. After the structure was removed, the debates continued, now focused on the design of the soon-to-be-rebuilt Stadtschloss, known henceforth as the Humboldtforum (Humboldt Forum).[4] The city broke ground on the project in June 2013, and the progress of the construction can be watched around the world on webcam.[5]

A similar, historically driven debate has also captured interested parties in Dresden, where the Frauenkirche, a baroque masterpiece and symbol of the city that had been destroyed by the Allies' firebombing in 1945 and had been left in ruins throughout the GDR period, was rebuilt with extraordinary precision and reopened in 2005 to general approval by the citizens of Dresden and great disdain from many architects and academics. Goebel writes of the impulse to rebuild former structures of the past, such as the Frauenkirche, "In its palimpsest-like topography, the auratic reconstruction of classical monuments promotes the visual enactment of collective memory as a motivating force for post-reunification identity formation in a media-saturated capitalist consumer culture" (2007: 492). For Goebel, the rebuilding of long-vanished past structures represents a sort of capitalism-reinforcing identity formation; Andreas Huyssen similarly discerns a capitalist drive in a nostalgia that is more concerned with the attraction of outsiders as tourists than in the organic and democratic growth of a city at the hands and imagination of its residents (Huyssen 2003). Further examples of contentious reconstruction sites, such as Berlin's Regierungsviertel (government quarter) have received less international attention, but have also generated heated national arguments concerning the relationship between contemporary government buildings and the preservation of structures from both National Socialist and GDR pasts (Costabile-Heming 2011).

Like Jones's discussion of Potsdamer Platz, Rob McFarland and Elizabeth Guthrie's chapter examining the rhetoric of the debate surrounding the reconstruction of Dresden's Frauenkirche does indeed revisit well-trod ground, but their discovery is so novel as to make this ground as new as the phoenix iteration of the church itself. Without making any firm judgment themselves as to the merits of reconstruction, they reveal an inherent contradiction in the academic outrage. Although the dissenters justify their objection to reconstruction by accusing the proponents of nostalgic aura-fetishism, McFarland and Guthrie demonstrate rather convincingly that the replica actually achieves in architectural form Benjamin's overcoming of the aura by means of—here, technical—reproduction.

These transformations and the ensuing debates are known well beyond Germany's borders, and are equally well documented in popular, political, and academic discussions.[6] But similar, and often less glorified metamorphoses have occurred in cities and towns across the former GDR. After more than twenty years of deconstruction, renovation, and (re)construction, built environments across the East—including the rural, industrial, urban, and suburban—have undergone such vast transformations that many locations bear little visual resemblance to their pre-1989 iterations. Gaps from the bombings of World War II have continued to be filled and rubble long left standing cleared, while house façades have received a new coat of paint and modern shopping centers have appeared. Weimar, relatively well preserved as a German and international tourist destination during the years of socialism, has continued to garner attention as the home of German classicism and the birthplace of the Bauhaus, receiving generous funding for the renovations of the city's façades in the period leading up to its 1999 celebrations as the European Capital of Culture. The interest in marketing the renovation and gentrification of space is also present—and contested—in examples on the periphery of public scrutiny. As Susanna Miller, Jennifer Ruth Hosek, et al. discuss in their chapter, the presentation of Prenzlauer Berg on film offers a sense of gentrified cohesion—a resurrection of community as a problematizing counterdiscourse to unification—on the face of residential neighborhoods of Berlin located beyond the tourist destinations. Or as Erika Nelson shows in her analysis of the evolution of the spa industry in the small Thuringian town of Bad Sulza, even hamlets in the former GDR have attempted to capitalize on and subsequently flourish in this scurry to market their structural transformations to tourists.

Thus the resurrection and rejuvenation of spaces across the East work together to establish a capitalist narrative that projects an outward notion of development and growth, presenting as the blooming landscapes of former Chancellor Helmut Kohl's speech, quoted at the outset of this introduction. But a different definition of space as unbuilt environment works against this positivistic and neoliberal promotion of progress, revealing the capitalist manipulation of space to function as a type of "cruel optimism" promising the good life (Berlant 2011). For just as the resurrections and rejuvenations described above occurred in the transformation of space in Berlin, Dresden, or Bad Sulza, gaping cavities— both structural and demographic—yawned from Hoyerswerda to Halle, and the established narrative of transformation and progress is revealed to be one story among many.

That Old Devil Time: Voids, Decline, and Stagnation

Across the East, the face of the landscape has changed as industrial complexes are dismantled, affecting in turn the surrounding towns and small cities.[7] This created new spaces, gaps, and ruins as younger generations fled westward looking for jobs in the face of soaring unemployment rates in the East. In their wake they have left behind empty apartment blocks and have forced entire cities and towns to recalibrate the needs of their infrastructure by demolishing schools and engaging in conscious shrinking, in which cities encourage residents to vacate buildings on the outskirts and populate more centrally located structures in order to reduce the infrastructural burden.[8] With limited resources, these smaller cities work to renovate old construction that had been neglected and update residences built by the GDR, to maintain a quality standard of living for their remaining residents, and to attract businesses. Meanwhile, their populations continue to decrease.

For this reason, an examination of urban change in these cities must constitute either a study of resistance to decline or a study of decline itself. Huyssen speaks of voids; George Steinmetz writes of negative ruins (both 2010). Like existing and populated structures, absent or empty structures communicate the shadow of not only what physically had stood, but also the types of institutions or historical frameworks working within those structures and the people inhabiting or passing through them. In other words, by highlighting absence and decline, these sites are capable of modes of reflection of a different nature to memorials, monuments, tourist attractions, and historical reconstructions, which primarily function as consciously designed memory production.

It is perhaps therefore not surprising that many towns experiencing such regression were highly industrialized during the GDR period. As the factories closed their doors and became wastelands, the living spaces populated by their workers, too, quietly began the process of ruination. Gwyneth Cliver's chapter on the deconstruction efforts in Hoyerswerda addresses the contribution this alternate trend makes to a broader discussion on German identity and the power of symbol in space. In a sense, then, one can read these spaces not only for the traces of lost utopian dreams of a socialist-industrial economy that continue to reverberate in a postindustrial twenty-first-century Germany, but also as a protracted testament to the demise of industrialism as witnessed a couple of decades earlier across the Western world, for instance in the American Midwest.[9]

Further, these sites in decline can also be understood to communicate power and resistance, particularly the failure of a politics of progress to resonate at the level of community. Gil M. Doron calls such voided and empty sites dead zones, which function as an architecture of transgression in the sense that they are, in accordance with critical urban theory, sites of agency for the unseen or the unspoken (2000). While these dead zones differ from the widely publicized discussions surrounding the reconstruction and restoration of well-known structures in the East outlined above to the extent that the emptying out of houses and voiding of infrastructure often resonate only locally, these negative ruins and dead zones are equally charged with national identity-political meaning. They are, in keeping with Doron's claim, transgressive in that they undermine the dominant narrative of progress at the root of bombastic projects of rebuilding and restoration. Instead, they speak a story of decay, collapse, and obsolescence.

This architecture of transgression is also present in Sebastian Heiduschke's chapter on Frankfurt (Oder), in which he speaks to a very different type of subversion or resistance to dominant rhetoric. His examination of architecture and space in three films set in a town on the Polish border shows how the visual portrayal of voided and declining structures illuminates the unemployment, xenophobia, racism, and discontent with unification existing in many towns of the former GDR. The visual rhetoric of architecture can speak a different language of power, one that violently maintains stagnation, emptiness, and division in much of the built landscape of the East. Thus, if official and public rhetoric surrounding the sites of resurrection and rejuvenation discussed above reflects—as well as problematizes—the grand desires of capitalist progress, voids and spaces of decline convey a rhetoric fraught with stagnation and violence, revealing shifts in or the ineffectuality of political power at the community level.

The Effect of Affect: Authenticity and Nostalgia

The notion of aesthetic authenticity lies at the heart of almost all discourse, especially that of a contentious nature, concerning reconstruction and preservation in architecture and urban design. It is, however, an extremely slippery concept. How to define authenticity in architecture has occupied the theoretical concerns of preservationists and planners alike for centuries across national boundaries.[10] Questions such as the following perennially return to plague those troubled with maintaining aesthetic authenticity: Must an authentic preservation rely on original materials and building techniques or can technology that improves soundness and use be incorporated? To what extent do cultural differences determine the notion of authenticity?[11] Must an authentic preservation or reconstruction reflect the original state, or can historical changes be incorporated? When the latter, then how can this be accomplished? What role does authenticity of use play? Of how great an importance is integrity toward contemporary needs and values? For instance, should a medieval structure be made wheelchair accessible and have toilet facilities? How does an authenticity of structure compete with an authenticity of greater environment? For example, should a historical structure be reconstructed if such an action would threaten the integrity of the existing urban culture? Should the authentic evolution of human lifestyles be acknowledged? To what period of history should preservationists, architects, and planners most attend? This last question occupies Germans to an almost obsessive extent, as most notably illustrated by the discourse surrounding the Frauenkirche in Dresden. Parties debated whether an "authentic" cityscape would return the town to the harmonious look of the eighteenth century as made famous by Canaletto's paintings, whether to leave the Frauenkirche in ruins as a reminder of the ravages of war, or whether to demolish the ruins to provide space for new construction that would attest to the forward movement of time and affirm the legitimacy of the present epoch. Claims to authenticity can be made in each case with relative ease; deciding which case's claim to consider most reasonable is anything but easy.[12]

Nostalgia runs as authenticity's emotional undercurrent, and it turns the utopian bent of much official discourse on the authentic away from the future and toward the past (Boym 2001: xiv).[13] Anne Fuchs defines nostalgia as rooted in "experiences of historical dislocation" paved over by a "continuity of longing" (Fuchs 2012: 69). But while nostalgia yearns for a specific past that occurred before that dislocation, it also engenders a deep connectivity of the self to a "bounded locality" (63). Because of this, nostalgia can be a powerful tool for the specificity of place in the debates on authenticity, architecture, and space. Fuchs illustrates this with a discussion of how, in Dresden after World War II, the GDR government's utopian interest in rejuvenating the razed Altmarkt (old market square) for political theater gave way to public nostalgia to rebuild the original structures.

This powerful collision of official city planning with public nostalgia continues to be seen in the discourse on authenticity today. The contributors to this volume investigate how the discourse on authenticity in architecture and planning evolves when lived spaces are the objects under scrutiny, and residents, rather than aesthetic professionals, make the judgments. Heike Alberts reveals the complex relationship among aesthetics, politics, economics, and notions of personal freedom in her account of preservation efforts in Quedlinburg's old town center, a UNESCO World Heritage Site. The desire to preserve the city's rich medieval architectural heritage does not necessarily equate to a straightforward enthusiasm for purity in form and method among residents who, although generally behind the preservation efforts, need to consider comfort, ease, and their own financial wellbeing when their homes and businesses become the objects in question. Jason James's anthropological fieldwork in Eisenach has revealed, in contrast to the results of Alberts's survey in Quedlinburg, a steadfast loyalty to the notion of material precision among residents who promote preservation of the old town, despite the fact that professional preservationists have throughout the past three decades questioned the usefulness of thinking about authenticity solely in terms of material accuracy. The subjects of James's study perceive any concession to pragmatism to be a betrayal of the promises for preserving architectural heritage that were made by politicians during the period of unification.

Fundamental to these discussions on authenticity, then, is the way in which questions surrounding material and visual accuracy collide with either utopian or nostalgic desires and judgments. At work in this collision is the affective response to space due to the personal interaction with the structures in question and an unconscious understanding of locality as part and parcel to individual and national identity. The affective response elicited by plans made by city planners or architectural experts to resurrect or rejuvenate spectacular historical sites, as in the case of the Berliner Stadtschloss or the Dresdner Frauenkirche, uncover collective memory cultures at work. This occurs because these spaces are often seen as symbolic of national identity beyond the immediate locality, or often beyond borders of Germany. The case of Dresden is particularly salient, for as Fuchs notes, it is, along with Hiroshima and Nagasaki, an international symbol of urban destruction in war and personal loss made national narrative (2012: xii). The affective response to the rebuilding of the Frauenkirche is important for a nation wishing to return to a different past, as well as for a people wishing to create a new, old, national identity.

The connection among affect, authenticity, and national identity, however, becomes quite different in everyday spaces, such as homes and business in Quedlinburg, Eisenach, Hoyerswerda, or Prenzlauer Berg. Here, selfhood and history are entangled not in the grand symbolic gestures of national identity, but instead in the quiet emotions of lived experience. Useful here is Ben Highmore's term "social aesthetics," which he uses to describe the "cross-modal investigation" of vectors of emotions and affects, perception, and the senses, particularly in everyday experiences (2010: 120–121). Social aesthetics links "perception, sensorial culture, [and] affective intensities" with their social and cultural contexts (2010: 128). Heiner Stahl's discussion of sound as shaping community and being readable for long-term political turns speaks to this alternative understanding of such everyday experiences and revises the narrative of progress or decline associated with unification. The discourses on resurrection or decline cannot be divided from the social and cultural understanding of living within a space, and this experience is reactive neither to the grand narratives of progress nor the scare tactics of decline—that is, neither the bloom nor the bust—but to the steady movement of life and the long-term slow-drip of political change.

Thus, the affective intensity of authenticity—and the associated nostalgia for the past or a longing for a utopian future—can only be framed in terms of, as Highmore says elsewhere, the "sense of collectivity" that is "central to thinking about the ordinary" (2011: 20, 5). The collective experience, that is the tying together of each singular individual experience of these spaces, generates a cultural and national narrative that can be read. When considered from this perspective, then, the transformations in the former GDR during the last twenty years reveal more historical continuity than we customarily attribute to a period we, for good reason, are in the habit of perceiving as a watershed moment, as the *Wende* (the turn).

Methodology of the Volume

As evinced above, the collection of essays in this book takes a multi-disciplinary and interdisciplinary approach to investigating the evolution of built spaces in the former GDR. For not only is an expansive approach to the type of structures, spaces, and sites across the former East needed to understand better the complexities involved, but more than one discipline must be represented to showcase the diversity in academic approach to these complexities. The volume is multidisciplinary in that the authors call home a variety of disciplines under the umbrella of German Studies. Most are so-called Germanists, who primarily read "texts" (literature, film, cultural phenomena) for their social, political, and cultural significance (Cliver, Heiduschke, Jones, McFarland and Guthrie, Nelson, and Miller, Hosek, et al.), but also included are contributions from a geographer (Alberts), an anthropologist (James), and a historian (Stahl). Among the essays by Germanists, we include literary approaches (Cliver, Jones, and Nelson), film analyses (Heiduschke and Miller, Hosek, et al.), as well as examples of broad cultural studies (McFarland and Guthrie, as well as the afterword by Rolf Goebel). Because we believe that this variety adds a richness often missing in disciplinary studies, we, the editors, have encouraged contributors to remain within the methodology with which they feel most comfortable. For this reason, while the volume promotes multidisciplinarity, individual essays are often highly disciplinary, except where the discipline itself, i.e. cultural studies, is implicitly interdisciplinary.

This diversity allows for both breadth and depth. The first section, "Groundwork," lays the foundation for readers perhaps unfamiliar with the developments and the discourse surrounding those developments. Geographer Heike Alberts provides the results of a survey concerning the reaction to preservation policies she conducted among residents of medieval homes in Quedlinburg. We open with her essay, "Preserving the Past Before and After the *Wende*: A Case Study of Quedlinburg" because it accomplishes two vital tasks for readers. First, it gives a detailed historical account of architectural and urban development over many centuries in a town that may act as a case study for similar preservation efforts around the former GDR and an ideal location by which to contrast cities with less preservation caché. Secondly, the results of Alberts's survey provide insight into the realities of these transformations for actual, rather than hypothetical, citizens, in contrast to the symbolic and ideal analyses of cultural studies. Whereas Alberts explains the historical and political ramifications of the transformations in question, Germanist Christopher Jones's reading of a crime fiction novel in "No

Man's Land: Fiction and Reality in Buddy Giovinazzo's *Potsdamer Platz*"
demonstrates how a literary analysis can lend insight into cultural, social, and political significance of real spaces, how literary studies can
contribute to urban studies. Several authors in this volume employ this
method (see below), and Jones's introduction with a familiar object of
study allows readers to become comfortable with the method before en-
countering it in unfamiliar territory.

In the second section, "Projections," the Germanist authors employ
traditional textual analysis to elucidate the cultural and historical significance of their urban sites as these are projected in literature or films.
Sebastian Heiduschke reveals in "Cinematic Reflections of Germany's
Postunification Woes: Architecture and Urban Space of Frankfurt
(Oder) in *Halbe Treppe, Lichter,* and *Kombat Sechzehn*" how the representation of architecture and urban design in three films that take place
in Frankfurt (Oder) promotes an understanding of this literal border city
as a figurative frontier line in the continuing negotiations of social delin-
eations such as East German/West German, eastern European/western
European, German/foreign, and privileged/unprivileged. With an interdisciplinary cultural studies approach that incorporates equally literary
analysis, spatial theory, and art history, Erika Nelson discovers a reinvention of a traditional German interest in Orphic poetics and dream
interpretation in the transformation of a spa town, Bad Sulza, into an all-
sensory meditative spiritual destination. She draws a line of commonal-
ity from the origins of the Orphic tradition in ancient Greece, through
the poetry of Rilke and the art and theories of Paul Scheerbart, to the
design of an operatic pool in rural Thuringia. In so doing, her essay,
"Reclaiming the Thuringian Tuscany: The Touristic Appeal of Bad Sulza
and its *Toskana Therme*," pulls at a red thread throughout a German
cultural history that is often marked by rupture rather than continuity.
Miller, Hosek, et al., investigate how well and with what degree of ease
and privilege characters of films from the *Achtung, Berlin!* festival navigate neighborhoods and public spaces in the capital. The spaces, most
particularly in the popular neighborhood of Prenzlauer Berg, examined
in "Berlin Through the Lens: Space and (National) Identity in the Postunification Capital," albeit in Berlin, are fundamentally localized and
diverge from the usual suspects of the Reichstag, Potsdamer Platz, and
the Schlossplatz. This chapter problematizes the conventionally agreed
upon trope of Berlin as the quintessential heterogeneous and socially
progressive utopia and conceives of the metropolis as *Dorf* (village) as
a counterpoint to Georg Simmel's interpretation of the metropolis and
the small town (*Kleinstadt*). Collectively authored by a group of German
Studies students and their advisor, Jennifer Ruth Hosek, this contribu-

tion lends the volume a chorus of voices representing the future of the discipline. Rounding out this section, Gwyneth Cliver's "The Amputated City: The Voids of Hoyerswerda," tests, by means of an interdisciplinary examination of urban shrinkage, Huyssen's famous theory that urban vacuums left by historical realities provide a unique opportunity for innovative and democratic approaches to historical narration alternative to the traditional memorial with its heavy-handed storytelling. Through both literary analysis and spatial theory, Cliver shows that the voids growing in Hoyerswerda provide a fertile field for the contemplation of civilization's inescapable transience through ruin gazing.

The third section, "Theories," includes three chapters that challenge commonly held notions regarding the significance of these transformed spaces. In "Sounding out Erfurt: Does the Song Remain the Same?" media historian Heiner Stahl studies the soundscape of the medieval Thuringian city and shows convincingly that despite great political drama, the common understanding of the *Wende* as the metaphorical turning point does not necessarily play out as such in the everyday lives of East Germans. By examining the public policy regarding the reduction of sound pollution in the GDR and in the FRG since unification, he reveals a historical continuity in urban life; whereas we conventionally consider this period as a moment that changed everything, Stahl demonstrates that aspects of everyday life, as lived by people on the ground, changed only very gradually. In "Restoration and Redemption: Defending *Kultur* and *Heimat* in Eisenach's Cityscape," anthropologist Jason James interprets extensive fieldwork to expose a sense of betrayal among activists regarding a perceived failure by bureaucrats to fulfill the preservationist promises of unification. For these activists, restoration and preservation constitute a means for historical redemption and relate to essential notions of Germanness and *Heimat* (homeland). Rhetoric in the debates concerning historical preservation becomes vehement, even vitriolic, because this preservation represents for many Germans a recovery from historical wounds while a circumvention of pureness in preservation represents a repetition of historical loss. The volume's final chapter, "The *Bauwerk* in the Age of its Technical Reproducibility: Historical Reconstruction, Pious Modernism, and Dresden's 'süße Krankheit'" by Germanists Rob McFarland and Elizabeth Guthrie, presents much of the historical-philosophical discourse at stake in discussing urbanism. McFarland and Guthrie reveal the manner in which the discourse takes on redemptive qualities, not only among the proponents of conservative reconstructionism but also among the self-proclaimed secular modernists who reject reconstruction efforts. Indeed, the authors demonstrate with theoretical boldness that these very modernists, in making claims to architectural authenticity, re-auratize architecture, and that it is actually the reconstructionists who accomplish a Benjaminian de-auratization. The volume concludes with an afterword by Rolf J. Goebel, who discovers among the chapters evidence that German Studies must broaden its analytical field by overcoming its staunch loyalty to textual interpretation, especially where urban studies is concerned. Instead, we should expand methods for analysis that incorporate the multisensory reality of urban experience.

Building on a broad scholarly interest in debates on the East German cityscape and their contemporary reframing for the future, *Bloom and Bust* pursues sites in the former East as case studies for understanding how the filling of previous absences and the absence of previous presence in the former East mark the variegated, evolving cultural landscape of a postsocialist and postindustrial, unified Germany. The chapters thus problematize the debate surrounding historical narration and preservation by diverting attention away from locations of broad rejuvenation to those where reconstruction remains localized to specific, celebrated sites, and to those left to decline.

Notes

1. "Durch eine gemeinsame Anstrengung wird es uns gelingen, Mecklenburg-Vorpommern und Sachsen-Anhalt, Brandenburg, Sachsen und Thüringen schon bald wieder in blühende Landschaften zu verwandeln, in denen es sich zu leben und zu arbeiten lohnt." All translations are our own unless otherwise indicated.
2. See also Fuchs 2012 and Rechtien 2010.
3. See Ladd (1997) and Huyssen (2003). For a very different look at memory, history, and built space, see the essays in Hell and Schönle (2010).
4. See, for instance, "Stadtschloss-Debatte" (2008) and "Hauptstadt" (2008).
5. See http://sbs-humboldtforum.de/Berliner-Schloss/Bau or http://www.city scope.de/bss, accessed 26 August 2013.
6. Jennifer Jordan clearly outlines how many of these fraught urban spaces persist in referencing national memory (2006). See also Strom (2001), Webber (2008), Verheyen (2008), Colomb (2007), Goebel (2003), and (2007).
7. Kerstin Barndt asks whether the evolution from an industrial past to a postindustrial present means a "loss of homeland or place" or whether it strengthens "local and regional identifications" (2010: 277).
8. These phenomena are not reserved for East Germany. For an interesting project on the changing face of East Germany, but also other cities around the world, that was influential in the discussions on the way in which people and spaces are in flux in the early years of the 2000s, see http://shrinkingci ties.com/.

9. Of course, the East does not monopolize such decline. Bernd and Hilla Becher's photography also documents industrial transformations across the former West, although these had occurred earlier (Lange 2000; Edensor 2005).

10. See Osman for an example based on Brooklyn, New York (2011).

11. This concern became central in the 1980s among preservationists, who questioned the fact that the vast majority of UNESCO protected sites lie in Europe. Japan challenged some of the regulations for UNESCO World Heritage Site status, because its wooden temples did not completely fulfill the requirement for original materials. Japan pointed out a centuries-long tradition of deconstructing and reconstructing the temples in order to replace deteriorating fabrics. Japan saw the preservation of this technique, as opposed to materials, as the maintenance of authenticity. Professional preservationist organizations were forced to reconsider the universality of their current notion of authenticity (Jerome 2008: 4).

12. Appropriately, in their collected volume on the discourse of remembering the GDR, Anna Saunders and Debbie Pinfold use the word authenticity in the plural (2013).

13. We use nostalgia here and not the popular neologism *Ostalgie* (nostalgia for East Germany), because the qualities discussed here are by no means only reserved for the built environment of the former GDR. See Huyssen for a discussion on the absolute interconnectedness of authenticity and nostalgia in the understanding of ruins (2010). Boym writes: "Nostalgia itself has a utopian dimension, only it is no longer directed toward the future" (2001: xiv).

References

Augé, Marc. 1995. *Non-Places. Introduction to an Anthropology of Supermodernity.* Translated by John Howe. London: Verso.

Barndt, Kerstin. 2010. "'Memory Traces of an Abandoned Set of Futures': Industrial Ruins in the Postindustrial Landscapes of Germany." In *Ruins of Modernity*, edited by Julia Hell and Andreas Schönle, 270–293. Durham, N.C.: Duke University Press.

Berlant, Lauren. 2011. *Cruel Optimism.* Durham, N.C.: Duke University Press.

Boym, Svetlana. 2001. *The Future of Nostalgia.* New York: Basic Books.

Colomb, Claire. 2007. "Requiem for a Lost Palast: 'Revanchist Urban Planning' and 'Burdened Landscapes' of the German Democratic Republic in the New Berlin." *Planning Perspectives* 22 (3): 283–323.

Costabile-Heming, Carol Anne. 2011. "Berlin's History in Context: The Foreign Ministry and the Spreebogen-Complex in the Context of the Architectural Debates." In *After the Wall: Germany and Beyond*, edited by Katharina Gerstenberger and Jana Evans Braziel, 231–248. New York: Palgrave Macmillan.

Der Himmel über Berlin. 1987. Dir. Wim Wenders. Road Movies Filmproduktion.

Doron, Gil M. 2000. "The Dead Zone and the Architecture of Transgression." *City* 4 (2): 247–263.

Edensor, Tim. 2005. *Industrial Ruins: Space, Aesthetics and Materiality.* Oxford: Berg.

Fisher, Jaimey, and Barbara Mennel, eds. 2010. *Spatial Turns: Space, Place, and Mobility in German Literary and Visual Culture.* Amsterdamer Beiträge zur neueren Germanistik 75. Amsterdam: Rodopi.

Frisby, David. 2001. *Cityscapes of Modernity.* Cambridge: Polity.

Fuchs, Anne. 2012. *After the Dresden Bombings: Pathways of Memory, 1945 to the Present.* Bastingstoke: Palgrave Macmillan.

Goebel, Rolf J. 2003. "Berlin's Architectural Citations: Reconstruction, Simulation, and the Problem of Historical Authenticity." *Publications of the Modern Language Association of America* 118 (5): 1268–1289.

———. 2007. "'Gesamtkunstwerk' Dresden: Official Urban Discourse and Durs Grünbein's Poetic Critique." *The German Quarterly* 80 (4): 492–510.

Habermas, Jürgen. 1991. "Yet Again: German Identity: A Unified Nation of Angry DM-Burghers?" *New German Critique* 52: 84–101.

"Hauptstadt: Die Palast-Revolte." 2008. *Spiegel Online,* 17 November. http://www.spiegel.de/spiegel/print/d-62127306.html, accessed 14 March 2012.

Hell, Julia, and Andreas Schönle, eds. 2010. *Ruins of Modernity.* Durham, N.C.: Duke University Press.

Highmore, Ben. 2010. "Bitter after Taste: Affect, Food, and Social Aesthetics." In *The Affect Theory Reader,* edited by Melissa Gregg and Gregory J. Seigworth, 118–137. Durham, N.C.: Duke University Press.

———. 2011. *Ordinary Lives: Studies in the Everyday.* London: Routledge.

Huyssen, Andreas. 2003. *Present Pasts: Urban Palimpsests and the Politics of Memory.* Stanford: Stanford University Press.

———. 2010. "Authentic Ruins: Products of Modernity." In *Ruins of Modernity,* edited by Julia Hell and Andreas Schönle, 17–28. Durham, N.C.: Duke University Press.

Jerome, Pamela. 2008. "An Introduction to Authenticity in Preservation." *APT Bulletin: Journal of Preservation Technology* 39 (2–3): 3–7.

Joel, Tony. 2012. "Reconstruction over Ruins: Rebuilding Dresden's Frauenkirche." In *The Heritage of War,* edited by Martin Gegner, Bart Ziino, and Tony Joel, 197–218. London: Routledge.

Jordan, Jennifer. 2006. *Structures of Memory: Understanding Urban Change in Berlin and Beyond.* Stanford: Stanford University Press.

Koepnick, Lutz. 2001. "Forget Berlin." *The German Quarterly* 74 (4): 343–354.

Kohl, Helmut. 1990. "Fernsehansprache von Bundeskanzler Kohl anlässlich des Inkrafttretens der Währungs-, Wirtschafts- und Sozialunion." http://helmut-kohl.kas.de/index.php?msg=555, accessed 14 March 2012.

Kulish, Nicholas, and Judy Dempsey. 2009. "Leaders in Berlin Retrace the Walk West." *The New York Times,* 9 November. http://www.nytimes.com/2009/11/10/world/europe/10germany.html, accessed 14 March 2012.

Ladd, Brian. 1997. *The Ghosts of Berlin*. Chicago: University of Chicago Press.

Lange, Susanne. 2000. *Bernd and Hille Becher: Life and Work*. Translated by Jeremy Gains. Cambridge: MIT Press.

"Merkel bei Mauerfall-Feiern: 'Was wir erlebt haben, sollte uns Mut machen.'" 2009. *Spiegel Online*, 8 November. http://www.spiegel.de/politik/deutsch land/0,1518,660077,00.html, accessed 14 March 2012.

Osman, Suleiman. 2011. *The Invention of Brownstone Brooklyn: Gentrification and the Search for Authenticity in Postwar New York*. Oxford: Oxford University Press.

Rechtien, Renate. 2010. "Cityscapes of the German Democratic Republic—An Interdisciplinary Approach: Introduction." *German Life & Letters* 63 (4): 369–374.

Ruge, Undine, and Daniel Morat. 2005. "*Deutschland denken*: Plädoyer für die reflektierte Republik." Introduction. In *Deutschland denken: Beiträge für die reflektierte Republik*, edited by Undine Ruge and Daniel Morat, 9–20. Wiesbaden: VS Verlag für Sozialwissenschaften.

Saunders, Anna, and Debbie Pinfold. 2013. *Remembering and Rethinking the GDR: Multiple Perspectives and Plural Authenticities*. Basingstoke: Palgrave Macmillan.

"Stadtschloss-Debatte: Und ewig mault die Berliner Schnauze." 2008. *Spiegel Online*, 28 November. http://www.spiegel.de/kultur/gesellschaft/0,1518,5 93263,00.html, accessed 14 March 2012.

Steinmetz, George. 2010. "Colonial Melancholy and Fordist Nostalgia: The Ruinscapes of Namibia and Detroit." In *Ruins of Modernity*, edited by Julia Hell and Andreas Schönle, 294–320. Durham, N.C.: Duke University Press.

Strom, Elizabeth. 2001. *Building the New Berlin: The Politics of Urban Development in Germany's Capital City*. Lanham, M.D.: Lexington Books.

Verheyen, Dirk. 2008. *United City, Divided Memories? Cold War Legacies in Contemporary Berlin*. Lanham, M.D.: Lexington Books.

Webber, Andrew. 2008. *Berlin in the Twentieth Century: A Cultural Topography*. Cambridge: Cambridge University Press.

Part I

❧ ◆ ❧

Groundwork

Chapter 1

Preserving the Past
Before and After the *Wende*
A Case Study of Quedlinburg

HEIKE ALBERTS

The *Wende* resulted in dramatic political, economic, and social changes in the former German Democratic Republic (GDR). These changes were also visible in the urban fabric, as some urban development projects from GDR times were stopped or modified and new projects started to promote the development of cities according to Western ideas and standards. For example, urban planning was now no longer aimed at producing "socialist cities"; instead, different planning priorities were set such as improving the quality of housing, implementing sustainable practices, and preserving valuable architectural heritage. Furthermore, money and construction materials were now available so that projects could be carried out that had been impossible before. Both of these factors instigated new developments in cities throughout the former GDR, but also played an important role in the implementation of historic preservation projects. The city of Quedlinburg provides a valuable case study of how approaches to historic preservation have changed after the *Wende* in response to these factors.

Quedlinburg is a small city of fewer than 30,000 inhabitants located north of the Harz Mountains in central Germany, not far from where the East German-West German border once was. It is well known for the important role it played in German history, its impressive Collegiate Church on Castle Hill, and the hundreds of half-timbered houses from over six centuries. While the importance of this legacy was recognized during the times when Quedlinburg was part of the GDR, and some projects to preserve the architectural heritage were carried out, it was only after the *Wende* that Quedlinburg could embark on the largest historic preservation project ever attempted in Germany. This chapter examines how and why preservation efforts differed before and after the *Wende* and how inhabitants evaluate the preservation measures.

Research Questions and Methods

I chose Quedlinburg as a case study for several reasons. The city played an important role in German history but is little known outside Germany. Most academic attention on urban development after the *Wende* has focused on Berlin and other major cities such as Dresden, but much less is known about smaller cities like Quedlinburg. Furthermore, most studies examine completely new developments (such as the government neighborhood in Berlin) or how cities are dealing with the socialist heritage (such as the demolition of the Palast der Republik in Berlin), but do not explore how approaches toward structures pre-dating the GDR have changed. The old city of Quedlinburg is the most extensive historic preservation project in Germany, so it is a particularly good case study of how cities are dealing with their architectural past.

Three main research questions guided this project. First, what was the GDR's approach to historic preservation and what factors determined how historic preservation projects were carried out? Second, how did approaches to historic preservation change after the *Wende* and how do the inhabitants of Quedlinburg evaluate the preservation efforts? Third, what influence did the UNESCO World Heritage designation that Quedlinburg received shortly after the *Wende* have on the preservation project and the inhabitants of the city?

In order to answer these research questions, I relied on a range of secondary sources (such as published works about preservation efforts in the GDR, publications by the city of Quedlinburg, and UNESCO reports) as well as fieldwork conducted in Quedlinburg. The fieldwork consisted of three components. I conducted a series of interviews with urban planners, architects, and other people professionally involved with the historic preservation process in order to get their perspective on the changing approaches and difficulties encountered with the preservation efforts. Additionally, I carried out a mail survey of people living in half-timbered houses to investigate their opinions concerning the preservation efforts and guidelines; as people living in the structures that have to be preserved, they are most immediately affected by any measures taken or guidelines imposed. The survey respondents represented a broad spectrum of people in Quedlinburg; the houses they own date to different centuries and were in different stages of disrepair when the *Wende* came, and the scope of the measures taken to preserve their houses varied from minor repairs taking a few weeks (e.g. installing new windows or painting the façade) to comprehensive and very costly multiple-year projects. Furthermore, the respondents had varying opinions about how preservation projects should be carried out, ranging from people who used only new materials in their projects and ignored historic preservation regulations to those who used authentic materials and techniques and went beyond what was required by the regulations despite the much higher cost. Finally, I conducted ten follow-up telephone interviews with survey participants to learn in more detail about the projects they had carried out and how they evaluated the overall preservation project in Quedlinburg.[1]

Even though Quedlinburg is in some ways unique, the insights gained from this case study are applicable to other cities, as historic preservation and the needs of the inhabitants are often at odds with one another. Before turning to the findings from this study, however, it is important to familiarize readers with the city of Quedlinburg and its significance to German history.

Quedlinburg—A Small City of Great Historical and Architectural Importance

Many Germans know Quedlinburg because of its impressive heritage of hundreds of half-timbered houses (see figure 1.1), but few are aware of the city's historical importance for Germany.

In 919, Henry I was elected to be the first German king and crowned in Quedlinburg, then called Villa Quitlingaburg. Henry I strengthened the castle and fortifications on one of the two sandstone hills (called Burgberg, or Castle Hill) overlooking the Harz valley and made Quedlinburg the capital of the East Franconian Empire from 919 to 1053. Under Henry and his successors (the Ottonians), numerous political assemblies and church festivals took place there, underlining the importance of the city.

Quedlinburg was not only noteworthy because it was the capital city of the Ottonians, but also because of the Collegiate Church dedicated to St. Servatius, built by Henry I's son and successor Otto I on Castle Hill. The Collegiate Church is considered an architectural masterpiece (see figure 1.2); it incorporates the crypt of an earlier basilica with cross vaults, mushroom-shaped decorations on the columns, paintings with scenes from the Old and New Testaments, and the tombs of the Ottonians. Furthermore, it held remarkable church treasures including several

Figure 1.1. Quedlinburg is known for its beautiful half-timbered houses. Photograph by Heike Alberts.

precious reliquaries, religious texts bound in beautiful covers, and the oldest remaining knotted carpet (UNESCO 2006).

In 944, Otto III granted the abbesses at the Collegiate Church the right to mint coins, an important medieval privilege. Merchants and craftsmen settled around the second sandstone hill known as Münzenberg

Figure 1.2. The Collegiate Church on Castle Hill. Photograph by Heike Alberts.

(Coin Hill). Eventually the small settlement around the two hills developed into a real city and was granted market rights in 994. These economic privileges, as well as the strategic location on the trade routes between Goslar and Magdeburg, stimulated the expansion of the city (Hoffmann 1994).

In the thirteenth century, a new city was founded on the eastern bank of the river Bode. The new city looked very different from the old city. The old city had developed organically from the merging of several small settlements over centuries and had a typical medieval street plan of winding streets. By contrast, the new city had a regular street plan. Furthermore, while many people living in the old city were merchants, most in the new city were farmers, resulting in a different style of houses with large entrance gates for farm equipment and protruding pulleys to lift agricultural products into storage areas. In 1330, the old and new cities merged and surrounded themselves with a joint city wall. The wall was four kilometers long and had twenty-eight towers, some of which are preserved to this day, as are the old parishes of St. Aegidius, St. Blasius, St. Benedictinus, and St. Nicolas inside the wall (UNESCO 1993).

The flourishing city became a member of the northern *Städtebund* (town alliance) for protection and in 1426 joined the Hanseatic League, the most important medieval trade alliance (Hoffmann 1994). The continuing prosperity of the city is still visible in the elaborate style of the half-timbered houses built in the sixteenth and seventeenth centuries. While many other cities were ravaged by the Thirty Years' War (1618–1648), architectural development reached its peak in Quedlinburg. During this time carved rosettes and suns were popular decorations on the façades; protruding ends of beams were shaped into rolls, and inscriptions in large letters were widespread. A special Quedlinburg style of half-timbering also emerged, where the ends of beams were carved in diamond form, and support beams were decorated with leaves (see Hoffmann 1994, Schauer 1999), further adding to the city's architectural importance. Fortunately, it sustained only minor damage in World War II, but the famous church treasures were taken to the United States and only returned to Quedlinburg in 1993 (Stadt Quedlinburg 2001).

In summary, the architectural importance of Quedlinburg rests on three main elements: the Collegiate Church of St. Servatius on Castle Hill, a masterpiece of Romanesque architecture, the almost perfect preservation of the medieval street plan, and the hundreds of high-quality half-timbered houses spanning six centuries (UNESCO 1993, UNESCO 2006). Preserving this impressive heritage is a major challenge that was handled quite differently under the GDR regime than in the united Germany.[2]

Deteriorating but Authentic—Quedlinburg in the GDR Era

In many ways, the approaches to historic preservation in the GDR era were contradictory. On the one hand, ideological convictions privileged new developments over the preservation of the past. On the other hand, the GDR realized the value of its architectural heritage and carried out some preservation measures, which were, however, hampered by a shortage of money and materials. These tensions are clearly visible in the case of Quedlinburg.

Cities and monuments in the GDR not only faced deterioration over time, but also an ideological threat (Hütter and Magirius 1990). Some historical buildings were purposefully destroyed because they were symbols of other religious and political belief systems that did not fit in with the self-image the GDR was trying to portray (see Marquart 1997). Furthermore, socialist ideologies dictated that socialist monuments had to eclipse historical monuments, leading to a neglect of historical structures. In some cases, prefabricated buildings and huge monuments replaced historic city centers.

Just as in many other GDR cities, a new socialist city center was envisioned for Quedlinburg, curiously at the same time as the city was declared a monument of national importance. This tension could be seen in the three different plans that were discussed in the 1960s. The first would have preserved most of the city's historic substance. The second was a compromise between historic preservation and a modern socialist city, and the third would have involved the demolition of large parts of the historic city and its replacement with modern prefabricated buildings (Schauer 1999). In the end the third plan was favored. It was most in line with the general policy that favored radical redevelopments and the preservation of only the most important historical monuments, such as the world-renowned palace, the Zwinger, in Dresden, or the National Theater in Weimar. The Collegiate Church in Quedlinburg was considered to be worthy of preservation as well as some of the half-timbered houses.

In the 1970s there was a sudden change in attitude toward historic preservation, and the GDR developed an exemplary historic preservation law in 1975. Probably triggered by the designation, "Year of Monument Conservation," it started a shift from the redevelopment of large areas to the preservation of the existing architectural heritage. However, the GDR simply did not have the means to implement these new policies. The Ministry of Culture decided which projects were funded, so historic cities that were not important to the government were left with no or minimal funding (Kiesow 1997, Marquart 1997). To make matters worse, most preservation efforts were concentrated on Berlin in preparation for the city's 750th anniversary in 1987. Craftsmen and artisans were ordered to Berlin and virtually all materials and funds were allocated to the capital city.

The scarcity of skilled workers, money, and construction materials had contradictory effects on Quedlinburg. On the one hand, the buildings that survived remained largely untouched from changes and therefore preserved a high degree of authenticity (see Kiesow 1997, UNESCO 2006).[3] The "planned neglect" protected cities in the GDR from the radical restructuring that many cities in the Federal Republic of Germany (FRG) underwent, so in hindsight, this may have been a blessing (Marquart 1997, Röhricht 1997). On the other hand, it was practically impossible to preserve the crumbling buildings under these circumstances. In addition to the lack of public money and materials, other factors made preservation projects difficult to carry out. During GDR times, rents were very low, thus little money was generated to be invested into the buildings. Furthermore, many people did not want to live in half-timbered houses due to the low standard of living; many of these houses only had coal ovens, no warm water, and toilets in the yards (even in the 1980s). As more people left the deteriorating half-timbered houses, even less money was available for their upkeep, so they crumbled even further (Herr Schmelz) (see figure 1.3).

Because of the serious deterioration of many of the historic houses, demolition and replacement by modern prefabricated buildings seemed like the only solution (Stadt Quedlinburg 1996). By the 1980s, some areas of the city had been torn down. Remarkably for GDR standards

Figure 1.3. In the late 1980s many of the half-timbered houses were in very bad condition. Photograph by Heike Alberts.

(and a reflection of the importance ascribed to Quedlinburg's heritage), a special construction technique was developed to fill the gaps left by demolished houses (see figure 1.4).

While this method was an industrial construction technique, it allowed for the individual design of façades. The new buildings therefore blended in with the urban fabric while being clearly distinct from the historic houses (Schauer 1999; Herr Schmelz). Frau Jerx, who worked for the planning office as an architect during GDR times, described the technique as follows:

> We developed this construction technique based on a concrete skeleton. So you have the concrete skeleton, the walls and ceilings. This way you can do whatever you want with the façades, as they have no structural function. This system was developed by the GDR to build houses that matched the manifold proportions, structures, and layouts of historic half-timbered houses. You never could have had this variety with prefabricated buildings. You could even have the upper floors protrude, have rounded buildings, or odd shapes. All of this was possible, and certainly quite exotic by GDR standards. We gave presentations throughout the GDR and foreign delegations came to visit us to see how it is done.

Figure 1.4. A special construction technique allowed modern houses to mimic half-timbered houses. Photograph by Heike Alberts.

The modern apartments in these buildings were very popular, as they had central heating, hot water, and indoor toilets. The plan in the 1980s was to extend this construction technique to a larger area to build a total of around 1,000 modern apartments. As Herr Plate put it, "many other cities would have been very proud of [the number of houses to be preserved], but for Quedlinburg this would have been a bitter loss."

The GDR made efforts to preserve Castle Hill as well as particularly valuable half-timbered houses (see figure 1.5). As Frau Jerx described, "Polish specialists were able to restore about one house per year, paid for with *valuta* (convertible currency). The houses selected were particularly important ones. For GDR standards this was amazing, and other cities were jealous that we had the *valuta* and the Polish specialists. The GDR had already realized that Quedlinburg was special, and that the locally available resources were not sufficient."

While the Polish craftsmen employed were skilled, they focused their efforts on only restoring the façades and used modern materials on the inside. There are even some examples of houses with restored façades that hide modern concrete buildings in the back. While this approach means that the façade is attractive and historically accurate, people advocating a pure preservationist approach see façadism as cheating, as so little of the original structure is preserved. So while preservation efforts

Figure 1.5. Some half-timbered houses were restored during GDR times with the help of skilled restoration workers from the Polish Pracownie Konserwacji Zabiytkow Torun (PKZ Torun). Photograph by Heike Alberts.

under the GDR preserved some outstanding structures, their authenticity was compromised and many other buildings were neglected.

In summary, Quedlinburg's development during the GDR era was marked by contradictions. The country had an exemplary historic preservation law since the mid-1970s but could not implement it due to the scarcity of funds, construction materials, and skilled craftsmen. As a result, preservation efforts in Quedlinburg were limited to the most prestigious areas, where a number of façades were restored. The lack of resources, however, also meant that the city was able to maintain a high degree of authenticity as many buildings remained virtually unchanged. Socialist ideologies had dictated the transformation of historic cities into socialist cities, but while such plans existed in Quedlinburg, some of the destruction of the urban fabric in Quedlinburg was ultimately driven by the deterioration of the buildings. The situation on the eve of the *Wende* was dire: More neighborhoods were meant to be demolished and replaced by prefabricated houses as the condition of many of the remaining buildings was deteriorating rapidly.

The *Wende*—A New Beginning for Historic Preservation

The *Wende* was indeed a turning point for Quedlinburg, as the demolition in the historic city and replacement of historic houses by prefabricated buildings was stopped immediately (Stadt Quedlinburg 2001). Furthermore, with German unification, the conditions for preserving Quedlinburg's heritage changed virtually overnight. Quedlinburg was now part of the FRG, so the preservation laws of this country applied. Even more importantly, however, money and construction materials were now more easily available.

Since the condition of many buildings in Quedlinburg was so dire, emergency measures to protect them from further damage were necessary, as was a long-term plan to coordinate preservation efforts. Partnerships with cities and states in the West were quickly established so that some measures such as repairing roofs could be carried out immediately. In 1991, three important steps toward implementing a long-term plan were accomplished. First, the 180-hectare *Sanierungsgebiet* (development area) was formally delineated. It is embedded in a larger (250 hectares) *Erhaltungsgebiet* (conservation area) (Röhricht 1997). Second, the *Gestaltungssatzung* (conservation charter) was developed to lay out guidelines for changes inside the *Sanierungsgebiet*. Third, an umbrella office, the BauBeCon, was created to coordinate the preservation measures, mediate between citizens and the state preservation office, distribute funds, and monitor adherence to regulations (Stadt Quedlinburg 2001).

With a general plan in place, the next major challenge was to come up with sufficient funds to carry out preservation measures. Some Westerners were able to claim ownership of houses or purchase buildings. They invested their private capital in them, so the preservation of these buildings made rapid progress (Röhricht 1997). These private efforts were stimulated by tax incentives; all expenses could be deducted on tax returns (Herr Plate). Few people who had lived in the GDR had sufficient private capital, so they were dependent on public funds to help pay for the preservation efforts. Public funds also allowed emergency measures to be carried out on houses without owners or where ownership was unclear (Röhricht 1997; Herr Schmelz).

Public funds came from a variety of sources. All German historic cities can receive funds from a program called Städtebauförderung (Urban Planning Support) with the tiered funding structure typical for the FRG. Under this system, the country of Germany pays one-third, one-third is contributed by the state in which the city is located, and the final third must be raised by the city. Since Quedlinburg suffers from a declining population and struggles economically, it is not able to contribute its share, so the Deutsche Stiftung Denkmalschutz (German Foundation for Monument Conservation) has paid the city's share since 1997 (Schauer 1999, UNESCO 2006). The second major source of public funding is the Städtebaulicher Denkmalschutz (Urban Heritage Conservation), a new program created specifically to help East German cities. Additional funding became available from a number of other foundations, some of which, like the Wüstenrotstiftung (Wüstenrot Foundation), paid for individual projects. While the sources for funding have increased substantially since the *Wende,* there is still not enough money for Quedlinburg, as so many structures are in need of preservation. For example, UNESCO reported that "although considerable funds have already been invested in Castle Hill with the Collegiate Church and in the Münzenberg with the remains of the Church of Our Lady, the desolate system of supporting walls of the two hills, including the building substance, requires comprehensive restoration" (2006).

In addition to the lack of funds, the second major problem during GDR times was the lack of building materials and the scarcity of skilled craftsmen. In 1998, the Deutsches Fachwerkzentrum (German Center for Half-Timbering) was created in Quedlinburg to facilitate the revival of traditional building techniques as well as the use of traditional materials. The Center offers advice and training for craftsmen, architects, and engineers; conducts research about half-timbering and building materials; and coordinates the recycling of old construction materials. Young people can now participate in the Jugendbauhütte (Youth Construction Hut), a program to learn about historic preservation, and volunteer to help with the preservation efforts (Stadt Quedlinburg 1999).

In united Germany, new construction materials were easily available. However, old materials should be used as much as possible to preserve the authenticity of the buildings. To facilitate the reuse of historical materials, the city has created an archive for construction materials. People carrying out preservation measures can pick up whatever they need, but have to pay for any repair or treatment of these materials that may be necessary (Herr Pellert). Herr Plate described the archive as follows:

> We have a storage facility for old construction materials. For exam-
> ple, we were able to save about two hundred historic doors. We also
> have other building materials, especially roof tiles. We also get mate-
> rials from neighboring settlements; for example when large barns are
> demolished we can get the wood. There are now a lot of people who
> specialize in the reuse of old materials, and they keep their eyes open
> when something becomes available. This works very well now. But it
> was not easy to convince people to use the old materials. So, as an
> incentive, we said that we would cover 80 percent of the costs for the
> materials and 65 percent of wages when people use old materials.

As becomes clear from this quotation, salvaging materials and making them available is one thing, but getting people to use the old materials was often only possible when incentives were provided. Some gave in to the temptations of the wide variety of new materials suddenly available. Herr Plate stated that it was crucial to step in quickly: "After the *Wende*, many people thought that they could do whatever they wanted. All of a sudden new construction materials were available. Before, a timber beam was as valuable as tooth gold, but now everything was available. Home improvement stores mushroomed, and you could buy plastic windows in all shapes, sizes, and colors. We had to counteract this right away and therefore had to come up with regulations very quickly."

The result was the conservation charter, which is applicable to the historic core of Quedlinburg, including Castle Hill and Münzenberg. The charter states that its goal is not to return Quedlinburg to its medieval condition, but to preserve the historical fabric and complement it with modern structures. To this end, it spells out the rules for roofs, façades, doors, etc. To cite just a few examples, the regulations specify that red clay tiles must be used for roofs (§4), façades must be preserved or reconstructed in their entirety including inscriptions, decorative carvings, etc. (§6), and windows must have dividers made from locals woods (§7). Modern additions such as balconies, antennas, or solar panels must be hidden from view (§6, 13) (Stadt Quedlinburg 2000).

Guidelines for what is allowed and what is forbidden can be controversial. Among my survey respondents, 72.7 percent did not have any objections to the guidelines or conflicts with the preservationists. Some specifically stated that they understood the importance of these guidelines. Herr Riede, for example, did not even consider modern plastic windows as "they simply don't fit here in Quedlinburg." Others sometimes found it difficult to implement the guidelines, but did their best to do so. Frau Mausser, for example, reported that they "have solar panels on the roof. That was a little difficult, as they could only be installed in places where they cannot be seen, because the historical roofscape is protected." Several respondents agreed that the overall beauty of the city trumps the restrictions imposed by the guidelines. For example, Frau Gutscher said that her family "had no problem following the guidelines. We agreed to all of them as they make Quedlinburg a much more beautiful city." Herr Maler, who carried out extensive preservation work on his house, reflected, "On the one hand, the guidelines are perceived as restrictive, but on the other hand, the beauty of the city justifies these guidelines." For some, the fact that funding is available only for measures that respect the guidelines was an incentive to following the rules. For example, the Runschkes, who carried out a decade-long preservation project on their house, said, "We did about 95 percent of the work the way the preservationists wanted. ... When you want to have financial support, you have to respect the guidelines. For example, we got money for the doors and the painting inside. When you apply for funding, someone will come and check that everything has been done correctly."

About 18.2 percent of those surveyed stated that they had some minor differences of opinion with the preservation authorities. However, many said that the disagreements could be resolved through dialogue with the preservationists. For example, Frau Scheil said that "the dialogue with the preservationists was very constructive and the interests of the owners and inhabitants were considered," so all issues surrounding the extensive restoration of her house were resolved satisfactorily. Frau Jerx, the architect who once worked for the GDR preservation office and now has her own architectural firm and therefore deals with preservation measures on a daily basis, also believed that differences of opinion can be resolved. She stated, "I do not understand why so many people complain about the historic preservationists—the things they had to do and what they were prevented from doing. I have not worked on a single project where we could not find an acceptable compromise in the end. You hear about cases where the preservationists demanded baby pink or an ugly blue, but most of the time these are misunderstandings."

Compromises have to be made in order to make the houses attractive for the inhabitants, but also to preserve the medieval street plan. Frau Jerx explained, "In a city like Quedlinburg it is especially important to preserve the structure and layout of the city as well as the houses. You cannot have a house deteriorate so much that it has to be demolished. Then we have a gap that has to be filled with a modern structure. When we do that the medieval urban structure disappears. It is therefore important that we make compromises to prevent gaps."

In the end, most people were satisfied with the compromises. However, 9.1 percent of the house owners surveyed reported serious conflicts with the preservation authorities. Conflicts most often centered on modern windows, whether in private homes or businesses. Some people did not like the traditional divided windows as they are expensive and difficult to clean. The BauBeCon was open to compromises and insisted on these windows only in the most precious buildings (Herr Plate). Furthermore, external funding sources, such as the Deutsche Stiftung Denkmalschutz, provided funds specifically to cover extra costs associated with these windows (Röhricht 1997). For some, the size of windows was controversial. For example, several people commented that larger show windows (or advertising signs) in shops were not permitted. This presents a "catch-22" situation, as retail use requires building modifications, but without retail functions, many preservation projects cannot be funded (Thoben 1997).

While some people had issues with specific regulations, other respondents focused more generally on preservation policies. For example, one house owner who carried out a multiple-year preservation project believed that "some of the guidelines prevent us from modernizing the interior. The preservationists sometimes forget that modern people live in these buildings." Another complained that "in some cases the citizen does not have any say." Obviously, some people perceived the regulations as more strict than others.

Finally, some respondents did not lump all preservationists together, but distinguished between the local authorities and those at the regional level. In general, the local BauBeCon received praise for their open-mindedness and willingness to find solutions that are acceptable to all involved, while the regional Office for the Conservation of Monuments was criticized for being out of touch with local realities. Herr Pellert formulated it best: "The BauBeCon is trying very hard and is open to compromises. The director, Herr Plate, lives in a half-timbered house himself and knows the problems well. By contrast, the state historic preservationist, Herr Schauer, only flies in every now and then and makes decisions without knowing the history or context."

It is not just private citizens but also some of the local professionals involved with the preservation efforts who have some conflicts with the regional preservation office and are unhappy about the lack of dialogue. For example Herr Mühle said: "The regional preservation officials define themselves as the executive—they make the decisions. In my opinion there should always be a dialogue with other people, and decisions should be made by all stakeholders together.... There is no dialogue; there are only orders. The rules of the *Gestaltungssatzung* in Quedlinburg are actually fairly moderate, but the preservationists think that they set the standards."

The regional preservation officials insist on a pure preservationist approach, one that does not allow adapting the city to modern uses and standards. Herr Mühle cited a number of examples of conflicts. Some of these involve modern standards for safety and accessibility. For example, the regional preservation office objected to the installation of wider doors in the tourist office to make it wheelchair accessible, and to the flattening of the sidewalks at intersections to make it easier for wheelchairs and people with strollers to cross the street. As Herr Mühle put it, "there are already a lot of rules in Germany, so one more about the color of the paint does not really make a difference. But there is an issue when these rules influence people's lives. ... Preservation measures only make sense when they are socially acceptable." The regional preservation office also insisted that the basements of the castle remain unchanged. As these rooms are used as exhibition spaces, and are therefore accessible to the general public, the fire code demands fire escapes. However, the preservationists did not allow them.

Too much emphasis on preserving the past can also lead to a freezing of a place in time, rather than admitting that change has always occurred and can be positive. A much-cited example involved the Mathildenbrunnenplatz, the market square in front of the town hall in the new city that was popular with tourists and young people. The regional preservation office determined that the square should be restored to how it was in 1800, when there were no trees on the square. Since the trees were removed, there is no longer any shade available and the square is deserted in summer.

Despite the regional office's purist preservation approach, some new developments are allowed that do not seem to fit with the policy. For example Herr Mühle believed that "something must have gone wrong in the regional preservation office," since a modern glass and steel design was approved for the Bergwerk, a mountaineering shop (see figure 1.6).

Discussions about this building were heated, as some people defended it as a modern interpretation of half-timbering, while others saw it as a completely unacceptable break with the historical surroundings. Trott lists additional examples of what he calls "inappropriate interventions," such as a concrete tower inserted into a half-timbered ensemble in Renaissance style (2008). Ironically it is Herr Schauer, the head preservationist of the regional preservation office, who is blamed for these "atrocities." His name lends itself to word plays, so locals now speak of the "schauerlicher Turm" ("atrocious tower") and comment that "a Schauer (shower) is worse than rain" (Trott 2008).

In summary, much changed for the better after the *Wende*. New sources of funding became available which allowed Quedlinburg to embark on an extensive preservation program. It was well designed, with moderate guidelines overseen by a local authority that is open to compromises between historic preservation and the demands of the inhabitants. While some inhabitants object to some of the guidelines, most serious conflicts are the result of decisions taken by the regional preservation office. From a preservationist point of view, the efforts in Quedlinburg must be seen as a success, which was confirmed by UNESCO by including the city on its World Heritage List.

Figure 1.6. Opinions about the Bergwerk are divided. Photograph by Heike Alberts.

Quedlinburg as a UNESCO World Heritage Site

In 1994, eighty hectares of the historic city of Quedlinburg were designated a UNESCO World Heritage Site. The GDR had already recognized
the value of Quedlinburg's architectural heritage and had submitted
an application to UNESCO in 1987 (Schauer 1999). At the time of the
Wende the application was pending, and the FRG decided to withdraw
Quedlinburg's nomination. It then submitted a revised application a few
years later, and in 1994 the "Collegiate Church, Castle, and Old Town of
Quedlinburg" received the coveted designation, becoming the first site
in the former GDR to receive this honor (UNESCO 2006).[4]

In order to be considered for inclusion in the World Heritage List, a
monument, group of buildings, or site has to meet the criteria of "universal value" and "authenticity" (§24 Operational Guidelines). Quedlinburg was judged to meet universal value "criterion iv," which states that
a site must "be an outstanding example of a type of building or architectural ensemble or landscape which illustrates (a) significant stage(s)
in human history" (UNESCO 2008). UNESCO recognized Quedlinburg
"as an outstanding example of a European town with medieval foundations which has preserved a high proportion of timber-framed buildings
of exceptional quality of the medieval and later periods." However, the
city's role as the capital of the Ottonian dynasty was seen as the primary
justification for the city's inscription (UNESCO 2006).

In addition to universal value, UNESCO demands that the sites inscribed on the World Heritage List "meet the test of authenticity in design, material, workmanship or setting" (§24b). UNESCO commented
on Quedlinburg's authenticity as follows:

> The authenticity of place in Quedlinburg is irrefutable. The town plan
> and urban fabric retain intact the essentially medieval townscape.
> Many of the buildings, especially the timber-framed residential struc-
> tures, have undergone little or no modification in the course of the
> centuries. The policy of the GDR which favored the use of industrially
> prefabricated structures to replace buildings that were demolished in
> the late 1980s has meant that there are elements within the town where
> all the authenticity of material and construction has been lost. How-
> ever, these represent a relatively small proportion of the total hous-
> ing stock and, moreover, in details such as scale and window lines, the
> overall townscape has been respected. (UNESCO 1993)

After their site visit in preparation for the inclusion of Quedlinburg
in the World Heritage List in 1994, ICOMOS (International Council

on Monuments and Sites, an advisory body of UNESCO) declared that "the restoration and conservation work now being carried out was to the highest international standards," thus legitimizing the work done in Quedlinburg since the *Wende*. In particular, it was emphasized that the conservation charter of the city "conforms in every particular with international standards, such as the Venice Charter of 1964, and with the principles enunciated in the Operational Guidelines" (UNESCO 1993). In 2006, UNESCO reported that "the authenticity and integrity of the site has been entirely preserved."

Even though interventions have to be carefully considered not to endanger the city's World Heritage status, in practice the UNESCO designation has changed little for Quedlinburg. For example, the city does not receive any extra funds for the preservation, but the title might make it easier to negotiate funding from other sources and increase tourism, which also helps to generate money. As Herr Gerhard put it, "the main advantage of the UNESCO designation is that the city's preservation is now the responsibility of all of Germany. The preservation is therefore not a burden but an honor."

Not everybody agrees, however, that the UNESCO designation does not present a burden. For example, some of the people I surveyed commented that "since the UNESCO title it takes a long time to negotiate with the authorities" and that the "UNESCO status helps incompetent administrators to become megalomaniacs." Some even indirectly blame UNESCO for making it more difficult to preserve the city; as Herr Tale explained, "A disadvantage (of the UNESCO designation) is that the strict guidelines freeze the city in medieval times. It is difficult to adjust the buildings to the demands of the twenty-first century, as even construction mistakes have to be reproduced. The restoration is extremely expensive, but the uses are limited due to the strict guidelines. As a result, many of the buildings are empty or not fully used."

This tension is common in cities embarking on historic preservation projects. For example, in his book about historic preservation, Norman Tyler asks why preservationists are committed to preserving the past when the challenge is the future (2000: 13). Preservation measures must not only aim at preserving architectural treasures, but must also consider the social and economic viability of historical cities. In fact, these two factors are closely linked; only a viable city can fund extensive preservation projects, and only carefully designed holistic preservation projects allow the development necessary to create a city in which the past and present coexist successfully (Ford 1985).

In the eyes of some Quedlinburg residents I surveyed, the city is failing to achieve these double goals. One complication is that Quedlinburg is located in an economically weak area, so it is experiencing high unemployment rates. As a result, many young people are leaving the city, and only the old are left behind (Trott 2008; UNESCO 2006). Furthermore, Quedlinburg has a shortage of attractive shopping opportunities. Herr Klausen reported that "there is not much good shopping. There is no department store, and few specialty stores. Both the retail and recreational offers are geared towards tourism; in particular, the high prices are a problem." Quedlinburg actually decided to restrict the development of new retail centers on the outskirts of the city to keep businesses in the core (Nutz 1998; Thoben 1997; Stadt Quedlinburg 1996), but does not seem to meet the demands of its inhabitants.

More generally, many Quedlinburg residents I talked to believe that the city has to be revitalized. For example, Herr Matzner liked how much the appearance of the city has improved. However, according to him "making the city beautiful is not enough. It also has to be revived." Like him, other residents believed that a more holistic approach would be preferable, as was carried out in other German cities. For example, Herr Klausen compared Quedlinburg's approach to nearby Wernigerode's: "Many things were done better in Wernigerode. They had a more holistic concept. For example, they made the city center a pedestrian zone. Younger people received lots of support for preservation. The city has a better transportation concept, more industry, and also more jobs. It may be less authentic, but it is more lively and successful."

It is precisely the pride in authenticity that has guided many of the preservation decisions in Quedlinburg, and a good number of Quedlinburg residents believe that the city avoided many of the mistakes of other cities that prioritized revitalization over authentic preservation. For example, Frau Jerx commented, "What is special about Quedlinburg is that people still live in these buildings. ... This is different from other half-timbered cities. For example in Celle and Hameln in the West you have these beautiful half-timbered houses, but they are all banks and shops, and nobody lives there anymore. Some big mistakes were made—for example the large shop windows in Celle. We try to avoid this here in Quedlinburg."

Like Frau Jerx, Herr Mühle also found that "a preserved ruin is more interesting than a Disneyland like Rothenburg." He believes that tourists are also attracted by this authenticity, "The fact that you almost get hit by a falling wooden beam here of course gives an impression of authenticity to the tourists."

These quotations make clear that Quedlinburg, like many historic cities, is struggling with finding the right balance between preserving a high degree of authenticity and making the city attractive to its inhabititants. Despite some interventions that compromised the authenticity of individual structures both during GDR times and since the *Wende*, the city's preservation program has overall been highly successful from a preservationist's point of view. However, it cannot be denied that this success comes at some cost for the city's residents.

Conclusion

The city of Quedlinburg provides an interesting example of how approaches to preserving the past and the conditions under which preservation measures are carried out changed dramatically with the *Wende*. During GDR times, there were both ideological and practical obstacles to preserving Quedlinburg's impressive architectural heritage. Socialist ideologies meant that there was a preference for radically restructuring historic cities into modern socialist cities, even though the GDR intended to preserve some of the most outstanding monuments, among them the Collegiate Church in Quedlinburg. From the 1970s on, the GDR showed more interest in preserving historic city cores, but the shortage of funds and construction materials limited public preservation efforts to twenty-six half-timbered houses in Quedlinburg. After the *Wende* it was clear that the goal was to preserve as much of the city as possible, and Germany's most extensive historic preservation project was begun. While in many ways a remarkable success, the project is not without problems.

Carrying out a historic preservation project of this scale is a major challenge. It appears that at least four conditions have to be met for a historic preservation project to succeed. First, there must be strong legal frameworks and concrete regulations to guide the preservation efforts. This condition is clearly met in the case of Quedlinburg, as the city— according to UNESCO—is doing an excellent job in respecting both national and international preservation guidelines. Its *Gestaltungssatzung* is detailed without being overly prescriptive. Second, funds must be available to carry out preservation measures for both publicly and privately owned buildings. Significant efforts have been undertaken by united Germany to secure funding for the preservation of Quedlinburg. In addition to already existing funding programs for historical cities, new programs were created after the *Wende* specifically to support cities in the East, and a number of foundations have also provided resources. Despite the large sums of money already invested in the city, funding shortages remain a problem, in particular because the city of Quedlinburg cannot raise its share of the funding and external funding sources have diminished over the years (UNESCO 2006). Third, authentic materials and skilled craftsmen must be available to carry out preservation projects. Quedlinburg successfully created an archive for authentic materials and has created facilities where people can learn traditional construction techniques, making it possible to preserve the overall authenticity of the buildings by using authentic materials and techniques. Finally, historic preservation plans have to be integrated with wider urban planning goals. It is in this area where Quedlinburg struggles the most, as the tension between revitalizing the city and preserving its authenticity seems difficult to resolve.

In many ways, Quedlinburg is certainly unique. Only a few historic cities had to experiment with two completely different approaches to dealing with the architectural past—the modernization of the city with the preservation of only the most significant historic buildings, and preservation of large parts of the old city—in the course of just a few decades. This succession makes it possible to compare the successes and the challenges associated with each one of these approaches in the same location. Insights gained from this comparison can hopefully guide preservation decisions in other cities in Germany and around the world.

Notes

This chapter is based in part on Heike Alberts and Mark Brinda, 2005, "Changing Approaches to Historic Preservation in Quedlinburg, Germany," *Urban Affairs Review* 40 (3): 390–401 (with permission).

1. While expert interviewees are listed with their real names, all names used for survey respondents and interviewees are pseudonyms. All translations are my own unless otherwise indicated.
2. In this chapter, the terms "preservation" (preferred in the United States) and "conservation" (preferred in Europe) are used interchangeably. The terms refer to the maintenance of a structure without significant alteration. The term "restoration" refers to returning a building to its original condition or its condition at a specific point in time, using original elements as much as possible. "Reconstruction" involves building a new structure based on historic designs to replace structures that have been lost. Adapting a historical structure to modern uses is often called "rehabilitation"; changes are usually more radical in the interior while an effort is made to preserve the exterior (Tyler 2000).
3. In the context of historic preservation, the term "authentic" refers to a building that is either largely unchanged, or a building that has been rebuilt based on historical plans and using historical materials and construction methods.
4. Since then, a number of other sites in the former GDR have been inscribed: the Bauhaus sites in Weimar and Dessau, the Luther memorials in Eisleben and Wittenberg, Classical Weimar, Berlin's Museum Island, Wartburg

Castle, the Garden Kingdom of Dessau-Wörlitz, the Historic Centers of Stralsund and Wismar, and Muskauer Park.

References

Alberts, Heike, and Mark Brinda. 2005. "Changing Approaches to Historic Preservation in Quedlinburg, Germany." *Urban Affairs Review* 40 (3): 390–401.

Ford, Larry. 1985. "Urban Morphology and Preservation in Spain." *The Geographical Review* 75: 265–299.

Hoffmann, Wolfgang. 1994. *Quedlinburg. Der Stadtführer.* Wernigerode: Schmidt-Buch Verlag.

Hütter, Elisabeth, and Henrich Magirius. 1990. "Zum Verständnis der Denkmalpflege in der DDR." *Zeitschrift für Kunstgeschichte* 53 (3): 397–407.

Kiesow, Gottfried. 1997. "Denkmalpflege im vereinigten Deutschland: Eine kritische Bilanz." In *Denkmalpflege im vereinigten Deutschland,* edited by Christian Marquart, 32–43. Stuttgart: Deutsche Verlags-Anstalt.

Marquart, Christian. 1997. "Inmitten des Ernstfalls: Denkmalpflege auf dem Weg zur erweiterten Praxis." In *Denkmalpflege im vereinigten Deutschland,* edited by Christian Marquart, 13–22. Stuttgart: Deutsche Verlags-Anstalt.

Nutz, Manfred. 1998. "Strukturveränderungen im Einzelhandel—die Städte im Harzvorland." In *Stadtentwicklung in Umbruchsituationen: Wiederaufbau und Wiedervereinigung als Stressfaktoren der Entwicklung ostdeutscher Mittelstädte, ein Raum-Zeit-Vergleich mit Westdeutschland,* 166–177. Stuttgart: Franz Steiner Verlag.

Röhricht, Rudolf. 1997. "Anmerkungen zur kommunalen Denkmalpflege." In *Denkmalpflege im vereinigten Deutschland,* edited by Christian Marquart, 54–62. Stuttgart: Deutsche Verlags-Anstalt.

Schauer, Hans-Hartmut. 1999. *Quedlinburg: Fachwerkstadt. Weltkulturerbe.* Berlin: Verlag Bauwesen.

Stadt Quedlinburg. 1996. *Stadtsanierung Quedlinburg.* Halberstadt: Koch-Druck.

———. 1999. *Das Fachwerkzentrum Quedlinburg.* Halberstadt: Koch-Druck.

———. 2000. *Gestaltungsfibel Quedlinburg.* Halberstadt: Koch-Druck.

———. 2001. *10 Jahre Stadtsanierung.* Quedlinburg: Quedlinburg Druck.

Thoben, Claudia. 1997. "Wirtschaft, Stadterneuerung und Denkmalpflege—ein Ausblick." In *Denkmalpflege im vereinigten Deutschland,* edited by Christian Marquart, 69–76. Stuttgart: Deutsche Verlags-Anstalt.

Trott, Christopher. 2008. "Managing Change in the Urban World Heritage Context: Probable Impacts on Site Management of the New Urban Landscape Category. Case Study Quedlinburg." Master's thesis: Brandenburg University of Technology Cottbus. http://www-docs.tu-cottbus.de/alumniplus/public/files/master_theses/Chris_Trott.pdf, accessed December 2010.

Tyler, Norman. 2000. *Historic Preservation: An Introduction to Its History, Principles, and Practice.* New York and London: W.W. Norton and Company.

UNESCO. 1993. *Quedlinburg.* http://whc.unesco.org/archive/advisory_body_ evaluation/535rev.pdf, accessed December 2010.

———. 2006. *State of Conservation of World Heritage Properties in Europe: Collegiate Church, Castle and Old Town of Quedlinburg.* http://whc.unesco .org/archive/periodicreporting/EUR/cycle01/section2/535-summary.pdf, accessed December 2010.

———. 2008. *Operational Guidelines for the Implementation of the World Heritage Convention.* http://whc.unesco.org/archive/opguide08-en.pdf, accessed December 2010.

⊰· Chapter 2 ·⊱

No Man's Land

Fiction and Reality in
Buddy Giovinazzo's Potsdamer Platz

CHRISTOPHER JONES

Potsdamer Platz ... even today how many myths do we
connect to this former center of Berlin! The legend is simply
a jigsaw puzzle, consisting of great names such as "Haus
Vaterland" or "Pschorr-Bräu." In the "Hotel Esplanade" and
the "Café Josty"[1] the important people of the world sat down
to eat, and influential politicians, writers, and artists would
meet ... These are all lost worlds. It cannot be our task to
restore them, but we must be aware that we are building on
historic ground.
— Former Berlin Mayor, Eberhard Diepgen[2]

Times of great social upheaval have frequently created fertile ground
for crime fiction, as authors and readers join forces in the attempt to understand the transformations and also to seek comfort in the hope that
all will turn out for the best. Arthur Conan Doyle's Sherlock Holmes,
for example, appears just in time to reassure the population of late-
nineteenth-century London that this rapidly expanding and changing
city is not to be feared at all; keen observation and clear logic can still
provide the keys to understanding the city. Some hundred years later,
Buddy Giovinazzo's *Potsdamer Platz*[3] sends its first-person narrator, the
mob hitman Tony, into the Berlin of 1995, in particular to the former
no-man's land of Potsdamer Platz, the largest building site he has ever
seen. Here, too, we see a vast metropolis undergoing rapid change. If
Holmes's London was a cause for worry because of growing crime, previously unseen technological innovations, and new urban rhythms, then
the Berlin of the 1990s presents different but equally powerful sources
of concern. What is being lost from the former German Democratic Re-

public (GDR) as the new Germany drives relentlessly forward? If the GDR has to change, who will have the power to influence those changes? What will this new Berlin, this new Germany, be like?

These changes are at the heart of Giovinazzo's novel thanks to the multifaceted microcosm of a building site, which becomes the location for the struggle among the contesting forces seeking to preserve, change, and not infrequently profit from urban and social renewal. Blending great irony and shocking displays of violence, the novel pits key stakeholders against each other in the arena of Potsdamer Platz, including German-Turkish gang members and a rival gang composed of former GDR Stasi officers and Russians locked in physical and commercial combat. The novel projects its narrator into the heart of this melting pot, suggesting a detached, stable gaze from outside, which soon crumbles to be replaced by one of personal and emotional involvement. Inevitably, Tony's rejection of the agenda set by his American paymasters marks him as a traitor and places him in a position of mortal jeopardy: the price required for having any chance of redemption from his previous crimes.

Tony's function in the novel, then, undergoes a radical change, which allows the novel to present—in a single narrator—multiple views of the same location and historical situation. At the beginning there is a detached point of view, which seeks to emulate the gaze of the fascinated tourist, a gaze with which Berlin became very familiar in the 1990s. Indeed, the opening scene of the novel is Tony's arrival at Tegel Airport where he tells the officer at passport control that his reason for visiting is "vacation" (2004: 10). His later status as a fugitive, however, sends him on a quest for urban knowledge, forcing him to attempt a far deeper understanding of Berlin. Driven by fear and a growing emotional attachment to Monica, a local, Tony must look through the shadow of the past that haunts Potsdamer Platz, in order to understand that his own life is on the brink of transformation; having betrayed the mob, his old life becomes meaningless and his future dependent on eluding the lethal punishment for his act of betrayal. In this way, *Potsdamer Platz* shares much with other crime fictions that react to, and try to dismantle, social fears. Its bleak ending, however, rejects any possibility of easy closure, and is a fitting response to a period of change in Germany that is still marked by many doubts.

The Attractions of the City for Crime Novelists

From the beginnings of the genre there has been a close association between crime fiction and the city, ranging from the streets of nineteenth-century Paris where Edgar Allan Poe's Dupin tracked down the killer in "The Murders in the Rue Morgue" to the fog-enshrouded London of Sherlock Holmes. In the twentieth century, the large American cities supplied the mean streets for a new generation of hardboiled detectives, such as Raymond Chandler's Philip Marlowe. Now, in the early years of the twenty-first century, the reunified city of Berlin has drawn the attention of many crime fiction writers, such as Pieke Biermann or Thea Dorn. Additionally, many recent studies on crime fiction and the city have come from fields not usually associated with literary studies. Of particular interest in this respect is the fascination that radical geographers have shown with crime fiction. Radical geography is characterized by its critical view of urban development, arguing that social problems such as poverty and crime are increased within the city. David Schmid's 1995 essay "Imagining Safe Urban Space: The Contribution of Detective Fiction to Radical Geography" and Philip Howell's 1998 response "Crime and the City Solution: Crime Fiction, Urban Knowledge, and Radical Geography" present approaches to urban crime fictions that focus on the process of decoding the cityscape. As such, they will be of use in understanding Giovinazzo's aim in *Potsdamer Platz* to weave the critical responses to the reconstruction plans into a work of fiction.

Early in his essay, David Schmid states: "Whether it is Victorian London or 1950s Harlem, detective fiction sees urban space as chaotic and in need of order. Detectives have widely varying degrees of success in systematizing the chaotic city, but in the process, detective fiction exposes its readers to a fund of images of violent and disordered urban spaces" (1995: 243). This establishes the dynamics of the genre very clearly, as it highlights the disorder and impenetrable complexity of the modern city and locates the detective in that chaos as the reader's guide in search of understanding. Since crime fiction foregrounds the search for a solution to a mystery, it lends itself well to other forms of investigation; for Giovinazzo, this becomes a dissection of the conflicting forces behind the reconstruction work on Potsdamer Platz. Schmid is at pains to emphasize that the cities in crime fiction are never merely backdrops, but integral to the desire to force "the detective to engage with the setting she / he inhabits in order to understand and therefore solve the crime" (1995: 244). It is this notion of engaging with the city that sets the detective apart from the otherwise superficially similar figure of the flâneur who reads, but does not write, the text of the city. Moreover, the reader is similarly engaged, allowing Giovinazzo's novel to become a lens through which the opposing factions in the real debate surrounding the development of Potsdamer Platz can be seen more vividly.

If we contrast the classical Great Detective of the British tradition, such as Agatha Christie's Hercule Poirot, with his hardboiled American counterpart, the private investigator, such as Raymond Chandler's Philip Marlowe, we come across a very significant difference. The former "knows the spaces of the city intimately and thus assures his readers that the city, contrary to appearances, can be mastered" (Schmid 1995: 248–249). The hardboiled PI certainly cannot make that claim. And here, in this distinction, resides the reason why radical geographers have found this type of fiction so interesting. The Great Detective novels of the Golden Age of the 1920s and 1930s can be easily interpreted as a hegemonic tool for dissipating the fears that the modern city creates through both its supercomplexity and its potential to harbor violence. As Philip Howell comments, "The force of the anxieties raised by the modern city is absorbed and repelled by the reassurance that the city can through description be known and by knowledge be controlled" (1998: 360). The figure of the Great Detective, someone whose life is defined by the successful pursuit of knowledge, can be read as a desire to demonstrate that the city is not beyond our potential to comprehend.

For radical geographers such as Howell, the contemporary descendants of the Great Detectives, private investigators, present a more accurate reading of the city. Howell feels that "some forms of crime fiction develop what can be called 'urban knowledges' that are as critical and counterhegemonic, if not more so, than much of what passes for radical urban geography" (1998: 358). The key thing is to realize that these "urban knowledges" are at best partial and limited, for in Howell's conclusion the city can never "be fully understood and known" (1998: 373). As discussed below, postunification Berlin can be seen as a quintessential example of such a city, because its complex histories, multicultural population, and contested plans for future development hamper all attempts at full description and comprehension.

Buddy Giovinazzo's Novel *Potsdamer Platz*

Giovinazzo had good reasons for choosing the Berlin of the mid-1990s as a location for a crime novel. The opportunities for corruption generated by the real-life construction boom map effortlessly onto the needs of a crime fiction text, providing it with contemporary relevance as well as verisimilitude: "Once the Wall came down, the center of Berlin quickly became known (or at least advertised) as Europe's largest construction site. New government buildings, corporate headquarters, and miles of underground tunnels for subways, trains, and roads were built.

Whole new city quarters were constructed, and block after block of nineteenth-century tenements was converted into high-end apartments" (Jordan 2006: 92). Renovation on such an enormous scale can provide opportunities for criminal activities to go unnoticed, but for Buddy Giovinazzo there may also be a personal reason. In an interview, he makes his love of Berlin clear:

> I've been to East Berlin a few times, and I've gotten to spend some time there. To me, it's like this wild city that had been repressed for many, many years and now they are free, with art and film and books ... and nightclubs, and I just want to try and capture that. It's almost like a child giddiness, of having this freedom, being able to travel wherever you want, into the west. East Berlin is like the lower East side without crime. It's one of the most beautiful cities I've ever been to.[4]

Following a tradition of American noir fiction, which has its roots in German cinema of the 1920s and 1930s, Giovinazzo's interests lie more in the criminal than in the investigator. But it is certainly not just the detective who needs to know the city. For the criminal, knowledge of the city can be the very key to survival. Tony, the first-person narrator of *Potsdamer Platz,* experiences first-hand this kind of struggle to survive. At the opening of the story he is forced to relocate to a city wholly unknown to him. In addition, the locations in Berlin in which he is obliged to operate are in flux. Urban knowledge, so important to the investigator, has a different but possibly even greater, life-or-death significance for the criminal. Once Tony is on the run from his erstwhile employers, he needs to draw on his familiarity with the streets of Berlin if he is to elude his pursuers and a brutal killing.

The plot of *Potsdamer Platz* is quickly related: first-person narrator Tony has been sent by his boss, Riccardo Montefiore, to Berlin to carry out some killings in a gang war that has erupted between rival gangs mentioned above. The enormous sums of money that stand to be made in the construction work on Potsdamer Platz provide the reason for this power struggle. Tony's boss Riccardo is married to a relative of the German-Turkish gang leader and sees an opportunity to exploit a pretense of family matters to gain access to profits. Caught in the middle of these battles and double-crosses is Tony. The narrative becomes split between his reminiscences and his present day activities in, and observations of, mid-1990s Berlin. His recollections are drawn from his childhood and from his activities as a violent criminal. The reader is invited to seek some understanding of Tony's actions in a childhood characterized by the growing insanity of his father, but in light of Tony's extremely brutal behavior such understanding does not come easily. Similarly, Giovinazzo assigns Tony an even more violent companion, Hardy, whose function in the novel seems to be that of doppelganger, presenting a distorted image of what Tony may become. By the end of the novel Tony has killed Hardy—his other self—in a symbolic act that marks a final break from his violent past, before heading off into an uncertain future. The battle for the building contracts goes on, but it is clear that the Americans will not be involved in any of the decisions.

From a certain point of view, then, it is very tempting to read the novel as a black comedy that satirizes the American desire to return to the days of the immediate post–World War II period and the early years of the Cold War, with the Americans fighting the Russians in and over Berlin. This has its basis in reality, as Karen E. Till observes, "Above ground, the nascent cityscape proclaims an American occupation of a different sort" (2005: 26), referring to the numerous signs of American investment in the area. The fact that Riccardo intends to ignore the German-Turks and secure as many of the spoils as possible for himself only serves to strengthen this view. Indeed, one of the characters says, "The Americans want again to be an occupying force" (158). Superimposed onto this is Tony's feeling that the years of the Cold War have given the Russians an advantage in East Berlin the Americans could never match: "The Russians have been here since World War II, this is their back yard, they know every inch of the place and they are completely entrenched" (80). Knowing "every inch" of a place is a very simple example of the importance of "urban knowledge," since it can bestow a strategic superiority on those who possess it. But the novel also illuminates inner-German conflicts that marked the public debate about the future development of many of Berlin's construction opportunities.[5] In particular, the common complaint from former East Germans about the too-rapid pace of change finds expression through the character of Monica, Tony's German girlfriend who functions as a catalyst in his transformation, forcing him to revisit his past and consider his present actions in Berlin, before propelling him along a path that will see him betray the mob as the crucial step toward redemption. Her unhappy views regarding the transformation of her home concur with the critical studies of Berlin discussed below: "The contrast of old and new was not a harmonious one. Monica told me it was all happening too fast, that every week some familiar, cherished place from her childhood was replaced by something new and strange. It was unsettling to her. Building by building the whole neighborhood was being lobotomized" (184). As I shall show later, this anthropomorphization of Berlin, in the final striking image of the lobotomy, is a recurring element in the public discussions over the reconstruction plans for Potsdamer Platz.

Tony interacts with Berlin in multiple ways throughout the novel. His original task of providing brutal support to the criminal activities of his bosses gradually becomes abhorrent to him after his discussions with Monica, who forces him to turn away from physical violence to intellectual enquiry. Unthinking action gives way to reflection, or to borrow David Schmid's turn of phrase, Tony is forced to engage with the city. This begins, somewhat disconcertingly, with Tony's conviction that although he has only just got off the plane at Berlin Tegel, he already knows this city. Sitting in the back of a car he notices that "all the buildings and shops and abandoned lots and crooked narrow alleys made of cobblestone cubes and soft beige dirt—even the names of the streets which I could barely read or pronounce—somehow looked familiar to me, as if I'd been here before; as impossible as I knew that to be" (15–16). This sense of familiarity, which is the reader's first major insight into the narrator's thoughts, turns out to be a false sense of security designed to unsettle both the main character as well as the reader, as both are dragged into an unknown and unstable world over the four hundred pages that follow. This sense of unease also manifests itself in the intrusion of extremely violent acts into the narrative and into Berlin. The accidental killing of a young girl during an early mission by Tony and Hardy prompts Yossario, their main contact in Berlin, to remind them that such violence is unacceptable here. In particular, "public acts of retribution" are seen as typical of American gangsters, whereas in Berlin one must be "more discreet" (23). This is the start of a thread running through the novel in which the American gangsters are reminded of the differences between America and Berlin. For Tony, in particular, this exposure to different points of view facilitates and encourages his personal transformation.

In the course of the narrative, the city responds by affecting both Tony and his partner, Hardy, in such a way that their innate tendencies increase, so that Hardy becomes ever more violent, and Tony more contemplative. Giovinazzo treats the city of Berlin as an organism, choosing two German characters, Heinrich and Monica, to act as agents of the city, standing out in significance in a novel which is otherwise populated almost entirely by Americans, Russians, and Turks.[6] Under the malign influence of Heinrich, Hardy goes to ever further extremes in his violent perversions; under the spell of Monica, Tony starts to rediscover his human side until he finds that he can no longer carry out the brutality that his profession demands. Obviously, this is a very positive development in his personality, as one of the characters points out to him: "You seem different somehow ... You look better. Europe has had a good effect on you" (253). Heinrich and Monica therefore function as antibodies in the living system of the city, seeking and locating the intruders before attaching themselves to them. By amplifying aspects of Tony's and Hardy's characters in such a way as to hinder their ability to function properly, Heinrich and Monica prevent their assault on the health of the city.

As the novel progresses and Tony becomes ever more unfit for duty, his early sense of familiarity with Berlin also deserts him. This reaches its point of crisis when he exclaims that, "these people were as foreign to me as aliens from a distant planet" (99). Clearly, Tony's inability to recognize his external surroundings is a mirror to his growing inability to recognize his newly emerging self. The primary concrete reason for his dwindling sense of familiarity is that his own experiences of Berlin are centered around Potsdamer Platz. As a former part of no-man's land between the two German states, Potsdamer Platz had been without an identity for fifty years by the 1995 of the novel, which makes it a very difficult place to acquire urban knowledge. It is also a part of Berlin that has not yet settled into a fixed and definite form; in Tony's own words, it is the largest building site that he has ever seen, measuring the equivalent of about twenty blocks in New York. This condition as a building site means that it has yet to acquire the features and contours that would allow it to be known. The fact that Tony's crisis of identity is triggered by his arrival at a building site is certainly no accident. Brian Ladd sees a similar link: "German architecture and urban design cannot escape the crisis of German national identity" (1997: 234). What for Ladd is a strictly German concern, becomes for Giovinazzo a more general exploration of the connections between the mind of an individual and the city he inhabits.

The distinction Michel de Certeau makes in "Walking in the City" between voyeurs and walkers is also illuminating in this respect. The former are characterized by the desire to achieve an objective, detached view often from a high vantage point, such as a high-level apartment, but at the expense of being a part of the city. For de Certeau, the walkers are people at ground level who experience and indeed write the "urban 'text'" without being able to understand it as fully (1993: 153). Tony finds himself able to interact with the city neither as observer nor as participant. This is because, just like Tony, Potsdamer Platz is in a state of transition, in its case awaiting the people and the buildings that will give it a lasting shape. This lack of buildings also means a lack of high-level vantage points for any observer wanting to know the city from a height. Yet at the same time it also lacks the layout that would allow the walker to come to know this part of the city through traversing and inscribing its streets. For Tony, as outsider, this is not a city that he will help to fashion, nor—it seems to be the message of the novel—will other American outsiders. Giovinazzo thereby creates a fictional ending for Berlin contrary to the reality; ignoring actual West German and foreign intervention in the shaping of this city, he hands over control to the former GDR Stasi officers and the German-Turks, who will give this part of the city its form.

Giovinazzo has brought a set of expectations derived from the U.S. crime fiction tradition that are then overlaid onto Potsdamer Platz, resulting in a seamless fit for some elements and a jarring mismatch for others. It is this lack of complete congruence that creates an original, alienated view that forces the reader to reconsider and re-evaluate the reconstruction work and plans for the future of this significant part of Berlin. Giovinazzo's alignment of this rebuilding project with various gangster factions highlights an unresolved tension between the commercial needs of international investors and more idealistic visions. This outsider's gaze establishes a detached view that is too cynical to be wholly objective but that is nevertheless effective in directing attention to real-life controversies in a newly emerging Berlin. In the pages that follow I shall demonstrate how the *fiction* that Giovinazzo has created allows us to understand the *reality* behind the public discourse surrounding this major reconstruction project in the heart of Berlin.

Berlin: The New Capital

One advantage of setting a novel in Berlin is that it can be seen as "a kind of microcosm of Germany" (Smail and Ross 2007: 183). However, this does not necessarily address the more particular question of why to set a *crime* novel in Berlin, although there is evidence that it has become a hugely popular location.[7] In its current incarnation Berlin is certainly one of the world's newest cities, and in the late 1980s and throughout the 1990s it was frequently the subject of world attention on account of the dramatic changes that were going on in a country experiencing an unprecedented process of unification. This high public profile, as well as the end of the Cold War, have certainly been contributing factors to Berlin's increasing attractiveness for crime fiction authors. Berlin has become the capital once more and for this reason has achieved a greater national significance. These changes in Berlin's status have made it easier to compete with the many Anglo-American cultural products that have permeated nearly every type of popular culture in Germany. In her survey of German crime fiction on the radio, Elisabeth Weber remarks about German crime novels and radio plays of the 1950s and 1960s, "A murder on the Lüneburg Heath is simply not as interesting for people as a murder in London or New York" (Cornell 1997: 95–96). With regard to Giovinazzo's *Potsdamer Platz*, I would like to focus on three particular reasons for choosing Berlin as a crime fiction setting: the quest for urban knowledge, which radical geography regards as so essential to the modern crime fiction genre; the competing histories vying for attention and commemoration in post-1989 Berlin; and the real-life public debates that hoped to influence the shaping of Berlin into a capital city fit for a new Germany and a new millennium.

Consider the emphasis that Schmid and Howell place on urban knowledge. Because Berlin has been in a state of transition for such an extended period of time, it functions very well as an example of a city that is almost impossible to know. After all, how can one claim knowledge of a city where the street names and layouts are changing and where old buildings are disappearing while new ones are appearing? As Andreas Huyssen observes, "Eight years after the fall of the Wall, seven years after the unification of East and West Germany, and just a couple of years before the final transfer of the national government from Bonn to the city on the Spree, Berlin is a city text frantically being written and rewritten" (2003: 49). This image of Berlin's constant reinvention has gained widespread acceptance and has been further adapted, with some commentators even going so far as to reject the idea of the city of Berlin as a text, or indeed any sort of product, and favoring instead the concept of process, where the final result is unsure or unimportant. Ulrike Zitzlsperger suggests that this is symptomatic not just of the Berlin of the 1990s, but of Berlin in general: "'Remake Berlin' is not a result of reunification, but a process that repeats itself, each time illuminating intersections among politics, culture, and public life" (2007a: 9). This backdrop of uncertainty provides an effective setting for a type of crime fiction that seeks to deny easy access to the comfort and closure offered by the cozy detective novels of the British Golden Age. For writers in the more brutal, hardboiled school, Berlin feeds the doubts and paranoia of their criminal protagonists.

Many commentators, not just Huyssen but also Ladd and Till, have explicitly linked the ruins of contemporary Berlin to specific eras in the city's past, establishing a bond between space (architecture) and time (historical events). This is clearly a model that can be applied equally well to the understanding of any city and its projects for urban renewal. But Berlin's history, unsurprisingly, sets it apart from most cities. Huyssen, for example, concludes that "there is perhaps no other major Western city that bears the marks of twentieth-century history as intensely and self-consciously as Berlin" (2003: 51). This notion of Berlin, and indeed its citizens, as highly self-conscious of the dark legacies of National Socialism and Stalinism is significant, in that it has colored public discussions surrounding the conflicting needs of urban rebuilding projects, where some factions would see buildings, ruins, and plots of land preserved as testimonies to a past which should never be forgotten, while other factions plead in favor of laying the foundations for a new future. For Ladd (1997: 11), the city is alive, responding to these irreconcilable demands like a suffering human: "In Berlin, Germany's wounds still lie open everywhere," and the "buildings, ruins, and voids groan under the burden of painful memories" (1997: 3). Ladd's anthropomorphization of Berlin effectively highlights the very personal nature of many of the desires and arguments that have dominated the public debate about Berlin's architectural heritage and future. These personal responses were facilitated, or even encouraged, by the construction of viewing sites for members of the public to observe ongoing work at the major building projects.

Within this context, much recent scholarship of Berlin has employed the image of the ghost, a metaphor that creates a powerful emotional link between Berlin's past and its troubled, uncertain present. "The specters of the past are felt in the contemporary city when groups or individuals intentionally or unexpectedly evoke ghosts," notes Till (2005: 6). Ladd goes one step further by entitling his study *The Ghosts of Berlin* and opening with "Berlin is a haunted city" (1997: 1). In these discussions, the metaphor of the ghost serves many functions. Its polyvalency encompasses the multiple, frequently traumatic pasts linked to Berlin's cityscape; the victims of National Socialism; and the limbo of no-man's land where enforced stagnation over the many decades of the Cold War meant that the physical ruins remained as reminders of World War II. This last point is especially persuasive, as no-man's land was not just an imaginative symbol but instead a concrete visual presence in the middle of Berlin. For Ladd, this visual presence was able to gain power on account of the differences between pre–World War II Berlin and postwar Berlin: "What was striking about Potsdamer Platz by the 1960s, then, was the contrast between the memories (or, if you needed them, the pictures) of bustle and the utter desolation that had replaced it" (Ladd 1997: 118). Ladd is evoking here the concept of the palimpsest, a text that permits echoes of an earlier text to persist in the present. This is an attractive way of reading the city, particularly one like Berlin, as it can draw attention to the multiple layers of meaning in a given urban space, such as Potsdamer Platz.[8] Of course, ghosts do not just serve as neutral metaphors for a past that cannot be forgotten; they also have the potential to evoke emotional responses, in particular the "fears of returning to traumatic national pasts" (Till 2005: 6). In light of such concerns it is easy to understand why architectural planning in Berlin attained such a high degree of public involvement and why that involvement was so emotionally charged.

Public engagement, then, became a key factor in establishing parameters for many of the building projects of Berlin in the 1990s. As Ladd points out, "Planners and developers at work in the new Berlin come to grief again and again when they try to treat the city's streets and buildings and lots as mere real estate" (1997: 3). As discussed earlier, the reasons for this lie in the connections among the real buildings, ruins, and empty lots and their abilities to summon up for the public various memories of the past. For Ladd, "Architecture has always been deeply invested in the shaping of political and national identities, and the rebuilding of Berlin as capital of Germany gives us significant clues to the state of the German nation after the fall of the Wall and about the ways it projects its future" (1997: 49). He is certainly not alone in this view. Godela Weiss-Sussex and Ulrike Zitzlsperger also highlight the interconnectedness of architectural display and the new German identity: "The practical and symbolic aspects of this reconstruction task are inextricably linked with each other, and are of central importance in the symbolism of the new Germany" (2007: 183). Giovinazzo is able to employ this predisposition to link architecture and symbolic meaning within Berlin's cityscape in a productive manner; when the Potsdamer Platz building site starts to mirror the reconstruction of Tony's identity, this literary conceit appears wholly natural to the reader.

Significantly, this new Germany does not just face the task of reconciling the past with the present, but must also reconcile a capitalist West with a previously socialist East, a problem to which I shall return later. Additionally and perhaps more importantly for a crime novel set against a backdrop of corruption in the construction industry, it is vital to remember the vast sums of money at stake here: "In October 1990, less than a year after the fall of the Wall, the *Frankfurter Allgemeine Zeitung* reported that Berlin had 'become the leading metropolis for real estate investment in all of Europe'" (Jordan 2006: 59). These opportunities for financial profits can lend authenticity to any work of fiction seeking to explore the murky underworld of building commissions and contracts. Giovinazzo also exploits the potential for contrast afforded by this situation, using all the money associated with the Potsdamer Platz (bribes, investments, profits) as the backdrop against which the human problems of love, fear, and remorse that Tony has to deal with stand out in sharper relief.

Potsdamer Platz: Fiction and Reality

The real-life planning decisions made in the Berlin of the 1990s, particularly those concerning Potsdamer Platz, delivered a process of such conflict and complexity that any knowledgeable reader of Giovinazzo's novel is immediately willing to believe in any amount of corruption. However, it must be recalled that there was also great energy and enthusiasm for the projected work. As Ladd states: "It offered a symbolic as well as a practical reconciliation of East and West. And it built on the myth of bustling Potsdamer Platz—an image much in favor among the promoters of the new German capital. Leaders of government and business advertised Potsdamer Platz as a prestigious address that bespoke centrality and visibility as well as tradition" (1997: 120). Indeed, the involvement of so many disparate interest groups in these discussions created a forum for public interest in architecture that has been rarely seen elsewhere:

> Since the start of the 1990s, architectural criticism benefited in particular from the rebuilding of Potsdamer Platz, which touched on all aspects of current Berlin topics and which took on civilisatory scope: the controversy between historical duty and the necessity for a new beginning; the building works themselves, which in their technical execution allowed the creation of numerous metaphors and connections; the architectural debate, at times polemical, taking place in the media on account of the plans for the inner city; the link between architecture and culture to create 'Architainment' and numerous events, increasingly subjected to a critical gaze; and finally the question about the future for a utopia in the city and in public space. (Zitzlsperger 2007b: 89)

Whether these widespread discussions served to dissipate public anxiety over planning decisions or merely infected a broader section of the population than normal with such anxieties is difficult to answer. Certainly, Ladd suspects that Berlin suffered more than most cities from such worries, and with good reason: "Amid the city's fragile and contested urban traditions, the prospect of so much that is new raises fears of losing whatever historical identity remains" (1997: 226). Nevertheless a recurrent ideal in many of the endeavors to win over the skeptics and to dispel further any anxieties was the attempt to create a genuine sense of transparency in the planning and construction work. Till quotes former Berlin mayor, Eberhard Diepgen, who proclaimed that "Berliners and their guests have an unusual chance to participate in this exciting process of planning and construction. In front of the eyes of the public, a capital city that was once divided for decades grows freely together, the worksite of unification" (2005: 33). This was definitely not just empty rhetoric but alluded to the proliferation of viewing sites where interested members of the public could observe the work in progress. Indeed, it was not just the Berliners themselves who chose this as a leisure-time activity: "The empty plain in the heart of the city, leveled by wartime bombing and postwar demolition, filled with massive construction sites that became tourist destinations in their own right" (Jordan 2006: 92). Huyssen also remembers "the many *Schaustellen* (viewing and spectacle sites), which the city mounted in the summer of 1996 at its major *Baustellen* (construction sites). Berlin as a whole advertised itself as *Schaustelle* with the slogan '*Bühnen, Bauten, Boulevards*' (stages, buildings, boulevards) and mounted a cultural program including over two hundred guided tours of construction sites, eight hundred hours of music, acrobatics, and pantomime on nine open-air stages throughout the summer" (2003: 64).

As well as drawing attention to the plans for Berlin's future, such a variety in entertainment would also have served to draw attention away from the grim past that had been uncovered, quite literally, at these sites. In spite of such efforts, it cannot be overlooked that the practical task of rebuilding became loaded, or maybe even overloaded, with public interest, concern, and suspicion, "making Berlin's landscape uniquely politicized" (Ladd 1997: 3). Hanns-Uve Schwedler points out the "numerous conflicts with investors, with concerned experts and citizens, and also among differing city and district departments" (2001: 33). These multiple types of conflict in the real developmental history of Berlin make it easier to believe that other conflicts of a hidden and criminal nature could also be taking place.

For an author such as Giovinazzo, the attractions and advantages of the Berlin setting will now be clear: a background to his work that is rooted in reality and, in return, an opportunity to employ the crime novel format as a vehicle to comment on that real-life situation. If Berlin has been seen as a microcosm of Germany, then perhaps it is possible to go one step further and regard Potsdamer Platz as an emblem of Berlin, as a location that embodies the shared traumas of the past and the competing hopes and fears for the future. Till describes this in a very personal way: "It is then, standing partially below ground and partially above on the exit steps of the Potsdamer Platz metro station, that I realize I am in the city's Roman mundus, a site connecting the fertility and hopes of a New Berlin with the buried traumas, tragedies, and social imaginaries of new Berlins from the past" (2005: 28). Potsdamer Platz itself embodies a vast number of dichotomies, such as past/present, West

German/East German, German/non-German, and Till's reference to the metro station in this description is powerful, summoning up an image of a railway map of interconnections with the potential to assist literal and metaphorical navigation.

Diepgen, in his speech at the dedication ceremony for the new Sony buildings on 11 October 1996, focuses not just on the links between the past and present, but also on the Cold War–era division between West and East: "The wasteland in front of us is an ugly scar left over from the cold war, a tragic display of the division of Germany. This segment of the death strip was once Europe's most heavily trafficked square. Before Potsdamer Platz, the dead heart of our city, fell into its dormant existence in the shadow of history, it had been an interface between east and west" (Jordan 2006: 126). This reference to Potsdamer Platz as an interface between East and West is telling, not just as evidence of the Potsdamer Platz as a heterotopia, but also in the context of Giovinazzo's novel, in which it becomes the setting for the two former Cold War opponents, the United States and Russia, to clash violently by proxy of their representatives: the mob thugs and gangsters.[9]

Inevitably, the planning process was seen as further evidence of interference by the West in East German matters. Permeating Giovinazzo's novel is a powerful sense of external meddling rooted in the reality of the time; indeed, the first description of Potsdamer Platz in the novel positions "the future Sony headquarters across from Daimler-Benz" (44) as two iconic titans of non–East German investment, reminding the reader of Japan and West Germany respectively. The removal of the Berlin Wall, as Schwedler observes, had an impact on the layout of Berlin, "a shifting of the city's entire spatial structure, and unattractive vacant lots, such as the empty fields in East Berlin, suddenly found themselves in central locations, and quickly became desirable areas for development for investors and architects" (2001: 27). A redevelopment project on this scale required practical coordination, and it was the "Planwerk Innenstadt" (Comprehensive Plan: City Center) that took on this role, as well as the responsibility of balancing the needs and wishes of the many interested parties. Wolfgang Süchting and Patrick Weiss, both members of the "Planwerk Innenstadt" team, acknowledge the significance of this task: "For the creation of a common identity, the city centre takes on a decisive importance as an area that connects and brings together citizens of the East and West halves of Berlin" (2001: 57).[10] It is their hope that the "Planwerk Innenstadt" would "re-create and strengthen relationships between these two city centres, re-expose a common history and future, and assist the further development of these city centre identities" (2001: 57). However, it must also be remembered that the "Planwerk Innenstadt" was itself not immune to criticism and charges of Western bias.

Simone Hain's (2001) provocatively titled essay, "Struggle for the Inner City—a Plan Becomes a Declaration of War," articulates the dissatisfaction that many East Berliners felt at the prospect of having their cityscape rewritten by outsiders in the above-described manner. As her starting point, Hain takes "the expectations of several million East Germans who believe that they have a right to find in the future some reminders of their former capital city. This means not only to continue using the Palast der Republik (Palace of the Republic), but also to be able to trace in the former city centre the history of the state which was their starting point as they set out into the new and reunited republic" (2001: 72). However, the planning team did not include adequate representation of East German interests. In fact, "not one single East Berlin architect or town planner was involved in Planwerk Innenstadt. On the contrary, there were two planning teams from the West" (2001: 77–78). It is hardly surprising, then, that the outcomes might be regarded with much mistrust: "It can be predicted that a process which was not conducted in good faith with democratic public participation and enlightened urban planning practices will now turn around into obstruction, depression or even violent altercations" (2001: 81). Hain's commentary on the processes of architectural planning may express a particularly East German dissatisfaction with the biased composition of the planning team, but the stress she places on the close links between public space and public participation has wider relevance. The prospect of "violent altercations," which she fears in her conclusion, finds its fictional counterpart in the tale of corruption and opposing factions seen in Giovinazzo's novel.

Conclusion

Although a fictional treatment of the real-world issues surrounding the plans for the reconstruction of Potsdamer Platz, Giovinazzo's novel nonetheless draws on constellations of opposing interests to fuel much of its internal conflict. For example, the suspicion and unease that former East Berliners feel at the speed of some of the redevelopments is reflected clearly in the character of Monica and her growing inability to recognize her home city. The intense arguments surrounding the "Planwerk Innenstadt" and its failure to satisfy the demands for equal representation of all interest groups is mirrored in the novel by the more violent conflict between the two main factions composed of, on the one side, German-Turks and U.S. gangsters and, on the other side, East Germans and Russians. Additionally, a strong sense of unwelcomeness with regard to outside influence permeates the story. The novel's narrator, Tony, is especially sensitive to this. On the one hand, he has to experience the anti-American sentiments of many of the local characters, while on the other hand, the reader observes his growing feeling that he does not belong. His outburst, "This could be our Vietnam" summarizes the notion of the undesirability of American interference in Berlin (80). As shown above, the novel also revives the Cold War antagonism, in which the United States and the USSR stood on opposite sides of no-man's-land. That they should now be fighting in that former no-man's land, and vying for commercial superiority, casts an ironic light on the new post-socialist Europe. In its conclusion, the novel denies the American gangsters any hope of contributing to the shaping of Potsdamer Platz, and therefore by extension to Berlin and the new Germany. In the final analysis, the novel is not only concerned with the politics of the reconstruction processes in Berlin, but it also seeks to employ them as a realistic background to chart the main character's transformative journey from violence to redemption. The sheer scale of the Potsdamer Platz project, with its constantly mutating layout, forms an ideal background for the main character's inability to establish any sense of understanding or familiarity with his new temporary home; he can neither read nor write this "urban text." Much like Berlin, Tony discovers that there can be no plans for the future that do not depend on the past, and that the powerful will always have a greater say in that future than the weak. In *Potsdamer Platz*, the novel, Giovinazzo has created a fiction that employs personal change as the vehicle to explore the reality of urban transformation.

Notes

1. Café Josty on Potsdamer Platz appears in Erich Kästner's most famous book, *Emil und die Detektive,* thereby securing its place in the hearts and minds of many Germans.
2. As quoted in Zitzlsperger. (2007a: 16). This translation and all others are my own unless otherwise noted.
3. First published in 2003 in a German-language translation, followed in 2004 by the original English-language version. The publishing history of this novel is somewhat unusual. Buddy Giovinazzo is an American author and filmmaker who wrote the novel *Potsdamer Platz* in English. However, American publishers rejected that version of the novel on account of its extremely violent content. A German translation by Ango Laina and Angelika Müller was published by MAAS Verlag in 2003 in their "pulp master" series. An English-language version appeared in 2004 after the German

translation from No Exit Press, a UK publishing house. All quotations are from the English-language version with page numbers in parentheses.
4. From http://www.noexit.co.uk/features/buddy_giovinazzo_2002_interview _with_sex_and_guts_magazine_73.php, accessed 1 February 2011.
5. As seen, for example, in the study by Simone Hain discussed below (2001).
6. See Mazzoleni for a discussion of the city as body (1990).
7. Authors and publishers have been making frequent use of the word "Berlin" in their titles. Examples include Thea Dorn's *Berliner Aufklärung*, Pieke Biermann's *Berlin Kabbala*, or Bernd Udo Schwenzfeier's *Kälter als Eis: Authentischer Berlin-Krimi*. The publishing house Emons Verlag even has a series called "Berlin Krimi" (Berlin Crime).
8. Note that Andreas Huyssen titles his collection of essays on Berlin and other cities *Present Pasts: Urban Palimpsests and the Politics of Memory*.
9. Godela Weiss-Sussex comments, "If in the Weimar Republic, the Kufürstendamm was seen as a symbol of the city's mutability and of its capacity for re-invention—a topos famously evoked in texts by cultural commentators and feuilleton writers such as Joseph Roth and Siegfried Kracauer— the same symbolism was attributed to Potsdamer Platz in the 1990s. This square came to be regarded as a space containing several—mythical and real—spaces, a heterotopia in Foucault's sense, namely a space 'in which all the other real sites that can be found within [a given] culture, are simultaneously represented, contested, and invented'" (2007: 55).
10. "Wolfgang Süchting, town planner and architect, is a civil servant in the Berlin Ministry of Urban Development, where he heads the project group dealing with 'Planwerk Innenstadt'" and "Patrick Weiss, town planner, works as a civil servant in the Berlin Ministry of Urban Development. He coordinates the section dealing with the historical city centre 'Historisches Zentrum' in the 'Planwerk Innenstadt' project group" (Neill and Schwedler 2001: xv).

References

Cornell, Alan. 1997. "The 'Fernsehkrimi': Traditions and Developments." *German Life and Letters* 50 (1): 82–102.
de Certeau, Michel. 1993. "Walking in the City." In *The Cultural Studies Reader*, edited by Simon During, 151–160. London: Routledge.
Giovinazzo, Buddy. 2003. *Potsdamer Platz*. Translated by Ango Laina and Angelika Müller. Berlin: MAAS.
———. *Potsdamer Platz*. 2004. Harpenden, UK: No Exit Press.
Hain, Simone. 2001. "Struggle for the Inner City—a Plan Becomes a Declaration of War." In *Urban Planning and Cultural Inclusion: Lessons from Belfast and Berlin*, edited by William J.V. Neill and Hanns-Uve Schwedler, 69–84. Basingstoke and New York: Palgrave.
Howell, Philip. 1998. "Crime and the City Solution: Crime Fiction, Urban Knowledge, and Radical Geography." *Antipode* 30 (4): 357–378.

Huyssen, Andreas. 2003. *Present Pasts: Urban Palimpsests and the Politics of Memory.* Stanford: Stanford University Press.

Jordan, Jennifer A. 2006. *Structures of Memory: Understanding Urban Change in Berlin and Beyond.* Stanford: Stanford University Press.

Ladd, Brian. 1997. *The Ghosts of Berlin.* Chicago: University of Chicago Press.

Mazzoleni, Donatella. 1990. "The City and the Imaginary." *New Formations* 11: 91–104.

Schmid, David. 1995. "Imagining Safe Urban Space: The Contribution of Detective Fiction to Radical Geography." *Antipode* 27 (3): 242–269.

Schwedler, Hanns-Uve. 2001. "The Urban Planning Context in Berlin: A City Twice Unique." In *Urban Planning and Cultural Inclusion: Lessons from Belfast and Berlin,* edited by William J.V. Neill and Hanns-Uve Schwedler, 24–41. Basingstoke and New York: Palgrave.

Smail, Deborah, and Corey Ross. 2007. "New Berlins and New Germanies: History, Myth and the German Capital in the 1920s and 1990s." In *Berlin: Kultur und Metropole in den zwanziger und seit den neunziger Jahren,* edited by Godela Weiss-Sussex and Ulrike Zitzlsperger, 183–194. Munich: Iudicium.

Süchting, Wolfgang, and Patrick Weiss. 2001. "A New Plan for Berlin's Inner City: Planwerk Innenstadt." In *Urban Planning and Cultural Inclusion: Lessons from Belfast and Berlin,* edited by William J.V. Neill and Hanns-Uve Schwedler, 57–68. Basingstoke and New York: Palgrave.

Till, Karen E. 2005. *The New Berlin: Memory, Politics, Place.* Minneapolis: University of Minnesota Press.

Weiss-Sussex, Godela. 2007. "'Ich gehe und gehe […] und gehe und sehe.' Female Experience of the City." In *Berlin: Kultur und Metropole in den zwanziger und seit den neunziger Jahren,* edited by Godela Weiss-Sussex and Ulrike Zitzlsperger, 46–61. Munich: Iudicium.

Zitzlsperger, Ulrike. 2007. "Einführung." In *Berlin: Kultur und Metropole in den zwanziger und seit den neunziger Jahren,* edited by Godela Weiss-Sussex and Ulrike Zitzlsperger, 9–27. Munich: Iudicium.

———. 2007. "Die Bebilderung der Stadt: Berliner Feuilletons, Kolumnen und Reportagen." In *Berlin: Kultur und Metropole in den zwanziger und seit den neunziger Jahren,* edited by Godela Weiss-Sussex and Ulrike Zitzlsperger, 78–96. Munich: Iudicium.

Part II

♦

Projections

Chapter 3

Cinematic Reflections of Germany's Postunification Woes

Architecture and Urban Space of Frankfurt (Oder) in Halbe Treppe, Lichter, *and* Kombat Sechzehn

SEBASTIAN HEIDUSCHKE

In brief succession, three German films about the eastern German bordertown Frankfurt (Oder) were released during the early years of the twenty-first century. At first glance, the films *Halbe Treppe* (Grill Point; Andreas Dresen, 2002), *Lichter* (Distant Lights; Hans-Christian Schmid, 2003), and *Kombat Sechzehn* (Kombat Sechzehn; Mirko Borscht, 2005) appear to have little in common other than their primary location at the easternmost fringe of the Federal Republic of Germany (FRG), divided from its Polish twin city Słubice only by the river Oder. I propose, however, that the choice of setting is far from coincidence. The directors use Frankfurt as a magnifying glass to examine a selection of societal woes following German unification, such as high unemployment, the rise of rightwing extremism, and problems with smuggling and trafficking. More specifically, all three directors employ architecture and urban space to represent those contemporary issues during the new millennium, a time when German society was still struggling with the fallout of unification.

Andreas Dresen examines distinctions between eastern and western Germans in a way much different from other films such as *Sonnenallee* (Sun Alley; Leander Haußmann, 1999) before or *Good Bye Lenin!* (Wolfgang Becker, 2003) after. Dresen takes a stand against a stereotypical reduction of Germans to their birthplace and socialization as he presents the picture of an at-first-glance unified German society. Layer by layer, he unveils how western Germans dictate the German way of life after unification by juxtaposing a makeshift grill joint run by the somewhat hapless but blithe eastern German Uwe with the Frankfurt landmark Oderturm (Oder Tower) occupied by the western German radio host Chris. The film becomes a statement of the lingering internal problems in the confluence of two countries, a process that still is not concluded. Hans Christian Schmid, on the other hand, identifies border issues as Frankfurt's central problem and associates a variety of these issues with the city skyline. The longing for a better life marked by peace and personal wealth are the unifying aspects of the film's otherwise detached vignettes, strung together by Frankfurt's skyline. The viewer can clearly identify how Schmid deploys the distant lights throughout the film by means of panoramic shots in order to reinforce the tensions and simultaneously the reciprocal relationship between Germany and Poland. Frankfurt serves as gateway to the promised land of Germany and as model of change for postcommunist societies. Upon critical observation of the film's case studies, *Lichter* reveals omnipresent problems of unemployment in the former eastern Germany, failure of the social network, and German colonial attitudes. Finally, Mirko Borscht visualizes the xenophobia and nationalistic movements that changed the character of many cities of the former German Democratic Republic (GDR) in the 1990s with a blunt set design and cinematography that leverages buildings as mirrors of emotional constitution. The film appears to be a modern take on expressionism in that the urban environment replicates the emotional state of protagonist Georg. Corresponding to his mental transformation from cosmopolitan teenager dating a woman of color into skinhead spewing racial hatred slogans, the urban space of Frankfurt perverts into a neofascist location. The camera selects buildings to follow Georg's change in psychological state, from idyllic panoramic shots of the cityscape to the concrete maze of slab buildings imitating fascist iconography. Taken together, the three films deliver snapshots of Frankfurt in the first one and a half decades following unification that serve as matrix of other cities in eastern Germany with similar problems.

While Frankfurt is close to Berlin, barely 100 kilometers from center to center, it is far enough to possess a radically different social landscape. The problems of Berlin are not the problems of the rest of the former GDR, and the capital by no means represents postunification eastern German cities. A neverending stream of tourists and the relocation of the German capital from Bonn in 1990, concentrating the majority of federal offices once again in Berlin, have restored the city to its prewar glory, reminiscent of its status in the Golden Age of the Weimar Republic. While Berlin has mostly overcome the problems of unification and become a European metropolis again, one can still perceive the consequences of unification in the architecture and spaces of other cities in the east (and will for some time). Nevertheless, looking at Berlin proves helpful in the study of any German city, as it is the focus of vast theoretical scholarship on German urbanity. For instance, Philip Broadbent and Sabine Hake recently highlighted the centrality and model character of Berlin by emphasizing that "architecture has assumed the function of a master discourse allowing scholars both to read urban topographies as special manifestations of German history and identity and to probe the politics of urban space through alternately archeological, allegorical, and critical materialist readings" (2010: 3). Berlin, thus, proves to be a useful example for someone interested in uncovering the treasures situated beneath the groundcover of Germany because unification has caused the capital to overflow with historic significance. Indeed, as Rolf J. Goebel rightly points out, "Berlin's architectural cityscape ... is saturated with concrete historical references," an observation Lutz Koepnick shares by locating architectural memory in Berlin (Goebel 2002: 198). When Koepnick proceeds to claim that "in itself, built space signifies nothing" as "given groups of people at given moments in time perceive and make use of [buildings]" (2001: 346–347), he strips Berlin of its significance as sole urban space for the representation of German history and urges a shift of attention to other places. The concentration of at least three German films set in Frankfurt within only three years hints at the significance of this city as paradigm for the transformation and new significance of eastern Germany within the Berlin Republic.

The recent, usually overlooked history of Frankfurt (Oder) indicates that it shares, with Berlin, the fate of being a divided city, although it experienced a different outcome after German unification. Before 1945, Słubice belonged to Frankfurt; the retreating German army destroyed the bridge connecting the district Dammvorstadt on the eastern shore from the rest of Frankfurt, and after the Potsdam conference regulating the occupation of Germany, Poland received the lands east of the Oder (Reiß 2003). The GDR already recognized the Oder as forming the border between Poland and East Germany in the 1950 Treaty of Görlitz, but only in 1970 did the FRG sign the Treaty of Warsaw, guaranteeing the nonviolation of the border. In the German-Polish Border Treaty of 1990, the borders were fixed, and while Berlin as a city was rejoined by German unification, Frankfurt's division became permanent as a consequence of this treaty. Some residents of Frankfurt may have hoped for a restitution of the pre-1945 borders, yet the city remained divided.

Buildings as Space of East-West Tension: *Halbe Treppe*

This and other "historic re-imagining[s] of community" in eastern Germany may be the reason that Dresen set his films in Frankfurt (Halle 2007: 77). He integrates the neighboring Poland casually in the German-German conflict embedded into the *Alltagsgeschichte* (everyday history) of western Germans Chris and Karin Düring and their eastern German friends Uwe and Ellen Kukowski, all of whom struggle to navigate through life in *Halbe Treppe.* Both couples have grown accustomed to their way of life, all having lost the attraction to their respective partners. Things change when Chris and Ellen engage in a relationship and it is discovered. Both try to make their marriages work again, with different outcomes; Chris returns to his wife, but Ellen leaves Uwe for good.

Throughout the film, a multiplicity of contrasts abound that mimic the love-hate relationship between eastern and western Germans at the time the film was made, although Dresen never states them explicitly. Instead, he implies a viewer's background knowledge of Germany's political developments since unification when he refuses to set clear visual markers that define Uwe as Eastern and Chris as Western. In fact, he seems to be taking no notice of Germany's issues of the day at the time of filming, when the relationship between eastern and western Germans was mostly captured in the terms *Jammer-Ossi* (whiny Easterner) and *Besser-Wessi* (know-it-all Westerner); eastern Germans were believed to lament and complain constantly about rising prices, high unemployment, and having had a better life under socialism overall, whereas western Germans were thought to have had quick answers to any problem and were said to have enforced their ideas without consideration for alternatives put forth by eastern Germans. Dresen does not mention the heated discussions about the despised solidarity tax levied to bring the new states of the former East Germany slowly up to West German standards or the slogan "Baut die Mauer wieder auf" (put the Berlin Wall up again) Germans repeated all over the country to express their discontent with the economic strain caused by unification. There are no traces of *Ostalgie,* eastern German nostalgia for the socialist past that was omnipresent at the time of filming, the mood captured by *Good Bye Lenin!,* therefore suggesting Dresen was looking elsewhere to point out the tensions between Germans. These tensions are reflected in his look at Frankfurt's edifices. He uses the interplay of horizontal and vertical axes to contrast the Oderturm with the snack bar Halbe Treppe, housed in a temporary tent structure, to point out some of the discontents of German unification. Altogether, the dense symbolism of these two buildings warrants closer unraveling through a comparison of the structures as extensions of Uwe's and Chris's personalities to reveal how Dresen realizes the lingering aversion for Easterners and Westerners alike, by setting up the buildings as representations of regional character traits.

The Oderturm represents the dominance of the new, western German influence in the city (see figure 3.1). The almost ninety-meter-tall building houses offices and shopping areas for more than 1,400 people on twenty-five floors, and its sheer size compared to the surrounding buildings evokes power. Chris works in this tower on the top floor, symbolizing that he rules the land below from his remote, access-controlled space that can only be reached by elevator. He hosts the daily morning radio show "Die Power Hour mit Chris vom Tower" and is able to influence the lives of a significant number of people, with, for instance, his daily horoscope. Chris is inconspicuously marked with Western characteristics: his name is a shortened and Americanized variation of Christian or Christoph(er) that flows well with the name of his radio show, and Chris's speech has no dialect that would tag him eastern German. As radio station host, Chris plays mostly American pop tunes, branding him in the tradition of a German culture that has adopted U.S. pop culture to a large extent since the end of World War II. He thus references the influx of the Western way of life.

In contrast, the snack bar Halbe Treppe, run by eastern German Uwe, is the stark opposite of the Oderturm (see figure 3.2). Uwe, whose name is genuinely German, converses with his customers in a thick eastern

Figure 3.1. The Oderturm dominating the frame, compared to the snack bar in the lower left corner. Screen capture, DVD, *Halbe Treppe*.

Figure 3.2. The snack bar *Halbe Treppe.* Screen capture, DVD, *Halbe Treppe.*

German accent, again clearly setting Uwe apart from his friend Chris. The name of Uwe's workplace, which translates to Stair Landing, harkens back to the days when bathrooms in many East German apartment buildings were located in between floors, halfway up or down the staircase, and were shared by two or more families. The snack bar symbolizes the continuity of this East German abode in a society now dominated by western German structures, and it is no coincidence that it is named somewhat self-deprecatingly and with a touch of irony, suggesting that it may be hosting Germany's equivalent of trailer trash. It is striking that the title of the film places the small tent and its one-story horizontal arrangement in contrast to the visually dominating twenty-five-story vertical tower. If Chris's workplace is the pedestal western Germans stand on, Uwe's snack bar represents the down-to-earth mentality and camaraderie that helped preunification eastern Germans deal with their everyday struggles in society. In the flimsy tent structure, most of his customers are fixtures, congregating there every day for *Bier und Bu-letten* (beer and burgers) while keeping each other company on plastic furniture. Chris, on the other hand, is removed from the people as he sits in his studio on the twenty-fifth floor, behind glass windows, and only engages in one-way communication through his microphone without listening to his conversation partners. Essentially, he fails to engage in meaningful dialogue and remains anonymous. Uwe, on the other hand, is not only in the middle of the conversation, but can also regulate and react immediately, symbolizing certain advantages of eastern German close ties over western German competition and personal gain.

Even though we never receive confirmation that Uwe and Chris are indeed eastern and western German, respectively, Dresen juxtaposes the two concepts, East and West, almost as mirror images of each other in the figures of Uwe and Chris and their workplaces on the ground and in the sky. In fact, Dresen presents a Lacanian account of Germany in the "mirror stage," as if he intended to compare the unification woes and Germany's internal struggle to infantile behavior and the inability to separate the self from the other (Lacan 1994). Similar to the infant attempting to understand her or his movements in the mirror while struggling to control these movements, Dresen shows the two Germans appearing to be in synchronicity, having mastered the divided past. The Imaginary—the successful completion of German unity symbolized by the harmonious friendship between Uwe and Chris—however, appears to be elusive, as the Real—everyday life—reveals rather stark differences set up in opposites such as their workplaces, their faithfulness to their partners, their engagement with the environment, etc. In the end, there is no cathartic moment, and both eastern and western Germans continue with their lives, suggesting that reconciliation will take time. Until the child Germany has realized that forming the Ego (German unity) requires mastery of one, not two bodies, only illusion persists. But while the enlightened child is able to overcome the mirror stage, Dresen shows that real unity has not yet been accomplished and Germany is not cognizant that it still remains trapped in its old dichotomies.

Dresen's idea of a diverse Germany with coexisting experiences, Eastern and Western, has only been further confirmed in the years following the film's release. Since its completion, a shift has taken place, made evident by the emergence of a post-Wall generation that is reconsidering regional differences. Even though they are unaware of or at least indifferent to holdovers from the Cold War, this group of eastern Germans reframes the notion of a "wall in the head" that would "take longer [to tear down] than any attempt to pull down the visible wall", affirmed by a rallying cry "Wir sind der Osten" (We are the East) (Schneider 1982: 102).[1] In contemporary eastern Germany, the population has emancipated, finding pride in their regional identities and displaying them proudly. Frankfurt's buildings reflect the underlying tensions in the Germany of 2002: although social strata intermingle and Germans attempt to arrive at equality, the historical burden of the wall in the heads makes it difficult to overcome the differences that appear to remain among older generations. In their eyes, Halbe Treppe and Oderturm, or the film's architectural representations of eastern and western Germans, will never be equal, and the question remains whether they ought to be. Clearly, Halbe Treppe addresses a more down-to-earth, autochthonous part of society, sympathetic to the plights of the neighbor with an open ear—all traits that were once representative for life in the GDR.[2] The Oderturm, in contrast, introduces the cultural realities of a unified Germany, with the cultural legacy and the historic burden of western Germany towering over Frankfurt. Both have their unique raison d'être and both have to arrange themselves in the new Germany, Dresen seems to propose, as he weighs assets and drawbacks of each regional part of the country in the equal and objective treatment of two buildings that at first appear unbalanced.

The Skyline as the 'Other': *Lichter*

Social issues are at the center of Schmid's film *Lichter*, as well, only this time they are presented through a different dichotomy. Frankfurt represents the possibilities of the new unified and larger Germany now that Poland no longer borders the GDR but the FRG instead. Schmid's feature frames Frankfurt's skyline from the vantage point of the Polish city Słubice across the river as a manifestation of Europe's changing borders and of Germany's shifting position as golden gateway to the West for eastern Europeans. The film constantly plays with the discrepancy between illusion and reality that the buildings embody for the observers congregating on the Polish side, raising issues similar to those Brian Ladd observes in *Ghosts of Berlin* (1997). From the distance, he cautions, buildings "give form to a city's history and identity," but they "might be seen as history with the people left out" (1–2). When the camera zooms in onto Frankfurt and begins to depict life behind the façades, it uncovers the realities of life in the former GDR, warning movie audiences that things are often not what they appear to be.

Through a series of vignettes taking place in and around the sister cities Frankfurt and Słubice, Schmid's film juxtaposes everyday life in the border region of Germany with events on the Polish side but leaves the sketches unlinked in the plot of the film. The title *Lichter* and two brief panoramic shots reveal Frankfurt as common denominator of the various sketches. Frankfurt's skyline promises a better life not only for a number of refugees from Ukraine trying to enter Germany illegally in one sketch, but also for a Polish taxi driver hoping to make extra money by helping two of the refugees cross the river in a second. In a third scenario, Frankfurt's memorable skyline stands in contrast to that of Słubice when a group of German architects presents plans to build a shopping center on the Polish side of the Oder. While Frankfurt is densely built along the shoreline and distinguishable by newly renovated buildings and a number of highrises in the distance, Słubice is the opposite: sparsely developed with dilapidated and aging buildings set back from the water. The planned shopping mall would begin to fill the void of buildings using Frankfurt as a model, suggesting that juxtaposition of the empty Polish skyline with the new construction in Frankfurt since unification serves as symbol of economic disparity between Germany and Eastern Europe.

Once the film zooms in on Frankfurt, the city's contemporary façade of prosperity begins to crumble, and the lights and tall, modern buildings visible from the Polish shore of the Oder, objects that created desire from a distance, are now testimonies to problems in society. In essence, the film is a snapshot of the borderland that "presents the border as an apparatus of abjection with disastrous effects on the people who cross it," foregrounding immigration and illegal border crossings as primary problems of postunification Germany (Halle 2007: 88). Many of the quandaries the film presents—for instance high unemployment figures, cigarette smuggling, prostitution, and bribery—are not necessarily limited to the states of the former East Germany. However, because the economic and political border still existed at the time Schmid shot the film, as Poland did not join the European Union until 2004, this suggests a cause-and-effect impression that Germany's eastern neighbor is responsible for many of Frankfurt's problems. Simultaneously, the film weaves a layer of domestic affairs and internal struggles stemming from German unification—for example, high unemployment, dysfunctional family relationships, and psychological depression—into its thrust. Considering the strong allure of Frankfurt's skyline on observers on the Polish bank of the Oder in contrast to the rough reality visible to those positioned within the city itself, the buildings become the film's unifying leitmotif.

Regardless of the human actions and interactions on both sides of the border that leave audiences with more questions than answers by the end of the film, the way buildings are embedded in the film illustrates Frankfurt's recent transformation. Before 1990, the East German town shared a political system of socialism with adjacent Poland, and citizens of both Frankfurt and Słubice were equally unable to enter the FRG because of the Iron Curtain. When German unification made Frankfurt a part of the FRG, the city became a frontier city and the first point of entry not only into Germany but into the European Union, as well. Frankfurt thus no longer acts as a familiar East German city but turns into a romanticized image of the economic power of the West. By contrasting it with Słubice, Schmid shows that Frankfurt symbolizes the completed remapping

of Europe (see figure 3.3). Pictures of Frankfurt's skyline constantly interrupt the flow of the film, both breaking up and structuring the narrative by repeatedly repositioning viewers in the different scenarios. The
lights of Frankfurt seem to shine brighter, symbolizing paradise—or at
least better economic conditions—but they remain only a façade.

The presentation of Frankfurt's skyline resembles a cinematic depiction of the famous skyline of New York City. Read on a macro-level,
the distant lights in their entirety function as monumental space with a
"supercoding," an expression Henri Lefebvre used to describe the overwhelming and all-embracing impression monumental space creates
(1997). It is precisely the interplay of the buildings and the associations
ascribed to them by the viewers from the other shore of the Oder that
help fabricate an illusion. Yet the micro-level, invisible from Słubice,
reveals the problems of Frankfurt—and Germany; once the camera
traverses the river, the filmic vignettes set in Germany reveal high unemployment, crime, and other problems invisible from across the Oder.

Schmid shifts the gaze on Frankfurt as he ventures beyond the skyline, and looks underneath the façade of an attractive, longed-for place
in order to investigate everyday life. The vignettes set in the German city
reveal the ugliness behind a superficial attraction. Parts of the film take
place in the middle of highrises populated by masses of unemployed eastern Germans, walking around aimlessly (or so it appears) or spending
their days on their balconies. For instance, we see a few people walking

Figure 3.3. The skyline of Frankfurt an der Oder dominated by high rises.
Screen capture, DVD, *Lichter.*

around with mattresses tied around their bodies like sandwich boards. As the scenario develops, we learn that Ingo, the owner of a mattress store, has unsuccessfully attempted to build a business. In the course of his entrepreneurship, he loses his driver's license, forcing him to rely on temporary workers to drive his car pulling a trailer full of mattresses. Instead of selling his goods from the unsuccessful store, he sets out to take them directly to the people like a traveling salesperson. Eventually, Ingo loses his mattress inventory for lack of payment, and we discover that he is homeless, bunking in an office space in the back of his store.

In this case, Schmid makes use of the anonymity of *Plattenbauten* (East German highrises) that are home to a population indifferent to its environment to visualize and reinforce Ingo's ill success in both his professional and private life. In contrast to the oft-cited utopian visions for "socialist new towns" in the GDR, originally intended to create networks combining the private and the public spheres, the changes to society after unification upended the living complexes and turned them from utopian to dystopian social clusters (Fulbrook 2005: 57). Evoking ghettos inhabited by unemployed and disillusioned eastern Germans, the concrete complexes mirror the new anonymity accompanying the cultural changes since 1990. Ingo's fate is even worse, as he no longer can afford to live in one of these apartments, but has to manage even his personal life from the back of his now-empty store. The barren space Ingo has appropriated as shelter signals how capitalism has transformed life on all levels for eastern Germans, who must now find new ways to earn a living. Thus, the sleek, modern skyline of Frankfurt turns out to be a palimpsest of Germany, reinscribed with postunification problems of high unemployment and difficulty adjusting to a new social system.

Rising unemployment is not the only problem the East faces. *Lichter* also addresses the issues of youth crime. Once more, space amplifies the disillusioning reality of life in contemporary Germany in the story of Marko and Katharina. Although they share a tiny room with Marko's brother in a cabin erected in a junkyard on the outskirts of Frankfurt and make a living by smuggling untaxed cigarettes across the border from Słubice into Frankfurt, they are not branded as drug abusers or participants in prostitution. In this instance, Schmid breaks with the illusion of Frankfurt as a "perfect" city as he directs the gaze of the viewer to a fringe group of German society. Not coincidentally, the teenagers do not live in Frankfurt proper but in an industrially zoned suburb. Their residence in a junkyard develops the image of negligence even further, dispelling the notion of a city willing to accommodate social outcasts in its center. The living conditions resemble those of squatters, and residing in the middle of a junkyard implies that they, too, are rejected by society. Moreover, their contact with the city proper is only visual. Marko always has the Frankfurt skyline in view when he returns by train from his trips to Poland to smuggle in untaxed cigarettes, and Katharina takes advantage of the "lawless" space of a border region when she retrieves the smuggled cigarettes Marko hurls out the open train windows. The order of the urban space is absent from the countryside, suggesting that survival of the fittest may be a rule that applies in the border region of Germany. At the same time, the film implies that a new socioeconomic divide in addition to the political divide facilitates this type of crime.

This antagonism surfaces in another episode, which follows young German architect Philipp. His model of a modern shopping mall on the fringes of Słubice has won a competition. It is not until he arrives in Poland with senior members of his company that he realizes that his success was based largely on the company's bribing and entertaining Polish officials with liqueur and prostitutes. Philipp's former girlfriend, a Polish native, now works as an interpreter during the day and an escort at night. By insinuating that Germany uses its resources to gain an advantage in Poland, the film raises the question of a modern form of colonialism. Schmid links both countries through a criticism of transnational cooperation, which often took advantage of the new economic situation after German unification. He sets the images of a Frankfurt, modernized within a decade with money from Germany's domestic solidarity tax and funds granted by the European Union, against the empty space in Słubice to allude to Poland's attempt to duplicate former East Germany's comparatively quick economic success. The lacuna on the barren land refers therefore to more than an empty space waiting to be developed; aspiring to bring the Polish border town in line with its German counterpart across the river is spuriously kindled by Frankfurt's distant lights and its skyline. Eventually, the original plans fall through, as the ambitious center turns out to be too expensive, and the scaled-down version of the complex, as the film suggests, is no more than a generic building that will no longer resemble the sleek, modern appearance of Frankfurt's shopping centers. In essence, the failure of the project reaffirms the status quo of power within Europe and depicts the forces at play in the creation or appropriation of monumental space as "collective mirror" of not one, but two societies (Levebvre 1997). Whereas in the case of *Halbe Treppe*, Frankfurt is situated within a Lacanian mirror stage and struggling to make sense of its domestic problems, *Lichter* uses an external stimulus to reflect on Frankfurt as a driving force in a larger Central and Eastern European region; the shopping mall, the film shows, will not benefit Słubice but the wallets of German entrepreneurs and architects receiving compensation regardless of the project's outcome. Eventually, the failure of the project symbolizes how the empty space to be filled with only a lone and unimpressive building will symbolize Słubice's inferiority, whereas Frankfurt's lights will remain a place of desire.

Dystopian Frankfurt: *Kombat Sechzehn*

A third film, Mirko Borscht's *Kombat Sechzehn*, addresses the origins of racial hatred and reasons for the upsurge of neo-Nazis since unification, especially in the former East Germany, through an iconography of concrete structures and visual signifiers of a dystopian city. As in the excerpt of Schmid's film discussed above, it also mobilizes the topic of creating a shopping center, this time in Frankfurt, to discuss the urgent matter of most neo-Nazis appearing in the East. The planned building, however, is only a pretext in order to explain the relocation of the main character Georg from Frankfurt (Main) to Frankfurt (Oder) with his father, the architect in charge. Sociologist Georg Simmel claimed an emotional link between the metropolis and the mental life of its residents, an idea *Kombat Sechzehn* reiterates in the manner in which Frankfurt's architecture symbolizes Georg's mental condition. The more he drifts into neo-Nazi circles, the less appealing Frankfurt becomes, supported by the camera slowly narrowing the view as it increasingly centers on the ugly parts of the city. The initial impression of a modern town resembling the familiar Frankfurt (Main) with a city center dominated by highrises now yields to fascist iconography prying open the newly renovated Frankfurt (Oder). Aged and anonymous gray concrete slab buildings do not show signs of life and eventually, colorful buildings such as the suburban row house Georg lives in disappear from the film completely, while Georg drifts into radical circles. The living conditions change in conjunction with Georg's mental state. In the end, Frankfurt turns into what Fredric Jameson calls "political space," linking Georg's human condition with Frankfurt's architecture in an "allegorical relationship" (1997: 256).

At the outset, Georg's background in martial arts puts him into opposition with many of his new classmates at school in Frankfurt (Oder). When he learns that he will not be allowed to compete in the Tae-Kwon-Do championship of the Western state Hesse because of his relocation to the state Brandenburg and is further faced with his girlfriend's infidelity, he expresses his frustration by cutting his hair with pieces of a broken mirror. He eventually shaves his head completely and later joins a group of neo-Nazis, convening with them at an outdoor gathering, taking up binge drinking, terrorizing Frankfurt by putting up flyers with nationalist content, and becoming violent. His conversion is accompanied visually by a transformation of buildings in the film. As the film progresses, the camera no longer captures places of nature and colorful houses in the city, but Frankfurt appears threatening as it becomes monochromatic and limited to anonymous highrises. Slowly, fascist iconography begins to take on a dominating role. The former modern and scenic Frankfurt now shows its Janus face of both beauty and ugliness, while the film's cinematography unveils layer by layer a historical legacy of fascism. For example, a set of newly renovated buildings is altered by a monument (see figure 3.4), whose architectural style references the so-called "marathon gate" of Berlin's Olympic Stadium built for the 1936 Olympic Games in Nazi Germany.

Neither is attached to neighboring buildings, and both monuments reference the Third Reich but do not reflect critically on the legacy or even perform *Erinnerungsarbeit* (memory work). A third pillar in the Frankfurt monument suggests an even stronger structure than the bi-pillar tower of Berlin. Crowned by an eagle that is eerily reminiscent of the National Socialist bird of prey (the latter holds a wreath adorned with a swastika in his claws), the monument mocks this psychological approach of coming to terms with the Nazi past. It is somewhat fitting that, in the film, Frankfurt's neo-Nazis take ownership of the monument by gathering underneath. Instead of appearing as "memory landscape … reduced to ruins—from gruesome World War I battlefields to the bombed-out cities of World War II" that served as permanent markers

Figure 3.4. Fascist iconography in Frankfurt an der Oder, resembling the Olympic Stadium in Berlin. Screen capture, DVD, *Kombat Sechzehn.*

of the destruction caused by fascism, the intact monument symmetrically divides the two apartment buildings to form a circular shape and evokes the impression of a neofascist symbol (Koshar 2000: 11).

The further Georg's transformation progresses, the more colors disappear gradually from the city, and the bleakly represented neo-Nazi movement begins to control public spaces (see figure 3.5). Soon, the city turns into a sea of gray, devoid of much life, with fascist graffiti symbols as lone specks of color. With the city taken over by neo-Nazis, its inhabitants seem to withdraw into the private sphere, as the streets and public places appear empty and hostile.

Within this changed landscape, the film looks at one of the East's most pressing problems: rising hostility toward foreigners following unification. Although by no means restricted to the East, at least four events that took place—in Hoyerswerda in 1991, Rostock in 1992, Magdeburg in 1994, and Guben in 1999—illustrated the presence of rightwing extremists and their support by local citizens. First, neo-Nazis attacked Vietnamese street vendors, followed by six days of assaults on foreign guest workers in Hoyerswerda, which injured more than thirty-two people. Many bystanders applauded, while others ignored the events. Similar scenes took place in Rostock, when several hundred extremists attacked an apartment building housing 120 asylum seekers for five days, while up to two thousand people watched. In Magdeburg, police forces did not intervene when more than eighty neo-Nazis chased a

Figure 3.5. "Liberated" urban space. Screen capture, DVD, *Kombat Sechzehn.*

group of Africans through downtown, and in Guben, a group of juvenile
neo-Nazis killed an Algerian asylum seeker. The film thus tackles a per-
petual problem in German society with rightwing extremism that is not
only tolerated but also sometimes endorsed by a substantial part of the
population. The lack of presence and involvement, let alone resistance,
of Frankfurt's population to condemn the neo-Nazi presence finds expression in the film's presentation of the city. The formerly livable place
offered up as an alternative to its western German namesake Frankfurt
(Main) turns into a nightmare.

At its culmination, *Kombat Sechzehn* employs a number of high-
angle shots of the buildings that have become the combat space for the
neo-Nazis and the locus of the final battle between Georg and gang
leader Thomas (see figure 3.6). This removal allows a better understanding of the city's composition by leaving the actual city and its human
interaction behind. Michel de Certeau describes a similar experience in
his observation of New York City. "To be lifted to the summit ... is to be
lifted out of the city's grasp," he states, emphasizing how the city turns
into geometric structures devoid of human life (1974: 91). Whereas the
viewer has participated in the narrative by way of the camera following the action at eye-level, the new perspective keeps the audience from
identifying with the violent fight. The final fight between Georg and
Thomas puts them, both severely injured, in the middle of the concrete
structures. The most prominent aspects of this fight are the graphic

Figure 3.6. Abstraction of Frankfurt's buildings and Georg's body through
high-angle shots. Screen capture, DVD, *Kombat Sechzehn.*

violence and the rendering of this violence in new perspectives of the buildings depicted earlier. The audience can barely spot Georg's lifeless body in the middle of trash and concrete, allowing Borscht to expose spectators to the coping mechanisms of actual citizens in cities like Frankfurt. The rightwing violence that keeps cities like Frankfurt under the control of neo-Nazis, as the film claims, becomes possible because bystanders remove themselves mentally from their responsibility. The conflict remains unresolved and the ending open to speculation about the future of rightwing extremism in Frankfurt.

A Frankfurt railroad shunt yard also serves as "historical" space in *Kombat Sechzehn,* not because of visual signifiers of history existent in the mise-en-scène dominated by storage buildings and train tracks, but because of the film's textual references to the Nazi past and the link to the present. Georg joins a martial arts club that practices in a converted shed in the shunt yard. Only in this building in the middle of industrial zoning is he able to continue his Tae-Kwon-Do away from the urban space of Frankfurt's residential and commercial districts that are controlled by neo-Nazis. While the railyard and the shed initially function as refuge, marked by the Korean flag symbolizing the peaceful character of martial arts in the shed, the advent of Thomas at the club marks the appropriation of the space by neo-Nazis. Once the war ensign of the First German Empire is placed on the wall next to the Korean flag, the deserted railyard evokes another marginalized space: the concentration camp. The empty railcars, the shed as a location on the fringes of society, and the railroad tracks which appear to be seldom used act as signifiers, reminding viewers of the camps that were also located outside the cities and used by the National Socialists for forced labor and for the extermination of Jews, homosexuals, political prisoners, and other people deemed unacceptable for German society. The human transports took place via rail, using boxcars without adequate air, food, or sanitary facilities. The takeover of the shed by neo-Nazis in *Kombat Sechzehn* perverts the facility into a place for training in violence, counteracting the ideal of mutual understanding martial arts traditionally promote. With the conversion of the railyard into a concentration camp, Frankfurt turns into a town controlled completely by neo-Nazis.

Frankfurt (Oder)—Frankfurt (Main)—Słubice—Berlin

Common to all three films is the explicit choice of Frankfurt (Oder) to place the urban space of the town in Brandenburg in opposition to other cities: its namesake in the West, Frankfurt (Main), in *Kombat Sechzehn;*

its Polish twin city Słubice in *Lichter;* and its implied countermodel Berlin as the locus of discourses about the direct confrontation of eastern and western Germans in *Halbe Treppe.* As different as these three films appear, a number of factors provide them with a common theme. The fact that three directors within brief succession selected Frankfurt as location for their films singles this city out over others in similar situations. Schwedt, Eisenhüttenstadt, Cottbus, and Görlitz would have lent themselves equally well by means of their location on the eastern fringe of Germany adjacent to the Polish border. These cities share similar problems as those of Frankfurt: a dwindling and rapidly aging population, along with cultural, political, and economic changes as a result of unification, as well as high unemployment and finally a neo-Nazi presence in reaction to the lack of jobs and future prospects. Hence, reasons for Frankfurt as location ought to be sought elsewhere than in geography and demographics. Two possibilities lend themselves to speculation: the city name and the fact that Frankfurt (Oder) was divided after 1945.

Its larger and better known western German namesake Frankfurt (Main) is the city that comes to mind first when the name Frankfurt is mentioned. "Mainhattan" boasts one of the largest European airport hubs and is the center of the European Central Bank as well as of many global companies. Dominated by twelve skyscrapers, its skyline can be seen from afar, and it is home to an ever-growing population of over two million residents, of which almost 700,000 live in the city proper and 26 percent are foreigners. Connected to its western German counterpart only in name, Frankfurt (Oder) does not nearly rival Frankfurt (Main)'s global significance, yet the eastern German town acquires national significance as it exemplifies a number of Germany's problems concentrated mainly in the East. The expectation of progress, wealth, and globalism evoked by the name Frankfurt turns into confusion and even repulsion similar to Georg's feelings in *Kombat Sechzehn* when issues such as narrowmindedness, xenophobia, and provincialism become signifiers of an "urban turn" that describes changes to the livability of a city (Webber 2008: 1). Frankfurt (Oder) is inscribed with negative connotations as the counterpart to a progressive Frankfurt (Main).

Interestingly, the concept of a negative counterimage to Frankfurt (Oder) is also developed in these films in the form of Słubice. The areas of Germany with a higher concentration of societal problems are located in the eastern border region, where the cosmopolitanism of the metropolis Berlin yields to the mundane realities of everyday life on the fringes of the FRG. Yet it is the Polish city that turns into a hotbed of prostitution, illegal immigration, and petty crime such as cigarette trafficking or pocket theft in *Lichter,* and into a departure point for extramarital sex in *Halbe Treppe.* In *Kombat Sechzehn,* the visual absence of "foreign" (non-German) elements make Frankfurt appear *ausländerfrei* (free of foreigners) and eerily reminiscent of *judenfrei* (free of Jews) cities in Nazi Germany. Frankfurt represents a Germany struggling with both its past and recent history. Matters of illegal immigration are prevalent at the eastern border with Poland. Until 2007, Poland was not a member of the Schengen Area, the treaty ratifying free travel among member states, making German border towns such as Frankfurt the initial point of entry into the European Union; from there, people can travel without passport control.

Frankfurt claims a somewhat unique position among eastern border towns. It is largely unrecognized for its international character despite being at least as diverse as Berlin and the home of the Europe University Viadrina, which also operates one branch of its campus, Collegium Polonicum, in Słubice. At the university's main institution in Frankfurt, about 20 percent of the students enrolled are of Polish or Eastern European nationality, and the German university has the largest percentage of foreign students—over 30 percent (Europa Universität 2010)—in the country. After the fall of the Iron Curtain, the university and therefore the city served as gateways to Eastern Europe, yet it appears that the mentality of a country divided into East and West has not disappeared from the films almost two decades later. The old attitudes toward Poland still remain; for instance, when Chris shows Ellen the view from his radio studio on top of the Oderturm, he makes a claim reminiscent of the style of a German general: "All of Poland is at my feet." Frankfurt becomes not only *judenfrei* and ostensibly dominated by neo-Nazis in *Kombat Sechzehn,* but the prevalent mood in all three films also suggests that Słubice may have taken on the role of a ghetto, one conveniently located outside of Germany.

The identity problem of former East Germany permeated by western German influences is preeminent in locations that have struggled since unification, although eastern German border cities are less likely to have experienced a west-to-east migration than perhaps Dresden or Leipzig. Cases of west-to-east migration, such as Georg's in *Kombat Sechzehn,* are less common than relocation to the West, and Georg's difficulty in "assimilating" reminds viewers of culture shock experienced upon leaving one's home country for an extended period of time. Thus, the population of these towns has remained much more homogenously Eastern, allowing for the development of a unique identity along the preunification division of East Germans and West Germans. Although this conflict remains unmarked on the surface structure of the films, the love quadrangle in *Halbe Treppe* works out this dichotomy in a number of ways throughout the plot, and it climaxes when the Oderturm and the snack bar Halbe Treppe become inscribed with Eastern and Western identities. Essentially, the dominance of the western German Chris over the eastern German Uwe in a city lacking a western German population influx encapsulates perhaps the strongest criticism voiced by opponents of German unification. In their opinion, little remained from the former East Germany and most positions of power were held by western Germans exhibiting the mentality of a colonial power (Cooke 2005).

Frankfurt has changed much since the time the three films were shot, and the woes of unification that plagued the city are no longer referred to as consequences rooted in unification. Since the brief period in the 2000s when Frankfurt became a metonymy for the long-term political and economic problems caused by the changes in Germany, interest in the city as backdrop for visual stories has waned. A quarter of a century after the fall of the Wall, new generations no longer feel the impact of German division on their lives the same way. From a historical perspective, however, the three films remain important as documents of a time when Germany was struggling with its recent past, trying to grow together into one new entity. The concentration of three films within a relatively brief time period makes clear the urgency of this struggle, and suggests that Germany still had work to do before the population would accept and internalize the changed reality. What was important then is elusive for someone in the present. As snapshots in time, the three films about Frankfurt remain documents to illustrate the impact of unification on smaller urban environments other than Berlin.

Notes

1. See, for example, the interview with eastern German politician Andrea Wicklein (2010). Note that all translations are my own unless otherwise indicated.
2. See, for example, Mühlberg 2000.

References

"Bevölkerungsstand Brandenburg Dezember 2009." 2009. Amt für Statistik Berlin Brandenburg. http://www.statistik-berlin-brandenburg.de//Publikationen/OTab/2010/OT_A01-04-00_124_200912_BB.pdf, accessed 7 December 2010.

Broadbent, Philip, and Sabine Hake, eds. 2010. *Berlin Divided City, 1945–1989.* New York: Berghahn Books.

Cooke, Paul. 2005. *Representing East Germany Since Unification: From Colonization to Nostalgia.* New York: Berg.

de Certeau, Michel. 1974. *The Practice of Everyday Life.* Berkeley: University of California Press.

"Europa-Universität Viadrina: Die Viadrina—Eine multikulturelle Versuchung." 2010. Europa-Universität Viadrina Frankfurt (Oder). http://www .euv-frankfurt-o.de/de/ueber_uns/portrait/viadrina/index.html, accessed 7 December 2010.

Fulbrook, Mary. 2005. *The People's State: East German Society from Hitler to Honecker.* New Haven, C.T.: Yale University Press.

"German Court Upholds Upholds Hotelier's Refusal to Accomodate Far-Right Leader." 2010. *Deutsche Welle,* 22 June. http://www.dw-world.de/dw/arti cle/0,5720991,00.html, accessed 8 December 2010.

Goebel, Rolf J. 2002. "Forget Hermeneutics? A Response to Lutz Koepnick." *German Quarterly* 75 (2): 197–200.

Good Bye Lenin! 2003. Dir. Wolfgang Becker. [DVD]. Culver City, C.A.

Halbe Treppe. 2002. Dir. Andreas Dresen. [DVD]. Hollywood, C.A.

Halle, Randall. 2007. "Views from the German-Polish Border: The Exploration of Inter-National Space in *Halbe Treppe* and *Lichter.*" *German Quarterly* 80 (1): 77–96.

Jameson, Fredric. 1997. "Is Space Political?" In *Rethinking Architecture,* edited by Neil Leach, 255–269. New York: Routledge.

Koepnick, Lutz. 2001. "Forget Berlin." *German Quarterly* 74 (4): 343–354.

Kombat Sechzehn. 2005. Dir. Mirko Borscht. [DVD]. Berlin.

Koshar, Rudy. 2000. *From Monuments to Traces: Artifacts of German Memory, 1870–1990.* Berkeley: University of California Press.

Lacan, Jacques. 1994. "The Mirror-phase as Formative of the Function of the I." In *Mapping Ideology,* edited by Slavoj Žižek, 93–99. London: Verso.

Ladd, Brian. 1997. *The Ghosts of Berlin.* Chicago: University of Chicago Press.

Lefebvre, Henri. 1997. "The Production of Space." In *Rethinking Architecture,* edited by Neil Leach, 139–147. New York: Routledge.

Lichter. 2003. Dir. Hans-Christian Schmid. [DVD]. Hollywood, C.A.

Mühlberg, Dietrich. 2000. "Leben in der DDR—warum untersuchen und wie darstellen?" In *Befremdlich anders: Leben in der DDR,* edited by Evemarie Badstübner, 8–39. Berlin: Dietz.

Reiß, Eckhard. 2003. "Das Ende der Frankfurter Dammvorstadt und das Entstehen von Słubice." *Historischer Verein zu Frankfurt (Oder) e.V.–Mitteilungen* 2: 26–40.

Schneider, Peter. 1982. *Der Mauerspringer.* Darmstadt, Germany: Luchterhand.

Simmel, Georg. 1997. "Die Großstädte und das Geistesleben." In *Rethinking Architecture,* edited by Neil Leach, 69–79. New York: Routledge.

Sonnenallee. 1999. Dir. Leander Haußmann. [DVD]. Germany.

Webber, Andrew. 2008. "Introduction: Moving Images of Cities." In *Cities in Transition: The Moving Image and the Modern Metropolis,* edited by Andrew Webber and Emma Wilson, 1–13. London: Wallflower.

Wicklein, Andrea. 2010. "Das Selbstverständnis der Ostdeutschen." Interview in *The European Circle,* 10 November.

Chapter 4

Reclaiming the Thuringian Tuscany

The Touristic Appeal of Bad Sulza
and its Toskana Therme

ERIKA M. NELSON

With its focus on the less known, little town of Bad Sulza—a federally recognized brine spa and wine town of three thousand inhabitants tucked away in the idyllic Thuringian landscape at the foothills of the Finne mountains—this case study goes where few have gone before. As Tim Coles has pointed out, in spite of the German Federal Government's constitutional guarantees of convergence, its drive, and considerable progress to develop tourism, the so-called "under-developed and under-exploited sector" in the former German Democratic Republic (GDR), the new German *Bundesländer* (federal states) have "been practically invisible in discourses on tourism in post-socialist states," especially in comparison to the considerable scholarly attention that has focused on the restructuring of the tourist industries in Poland, the Czech and Slovak Republics, Hungary, Rumania, and Bulgaria (Coles 2003: 217; Hall 1998; Williams and Balaz 2000). The scholarship that does exist primarily investigates urban, business, and heritage tourism, the key markets and most dominant forms of consumption in the East, thereby neglecting rural forms of emerging tourism in these states (Coles 2003: 222).

Bad Sulza lies off the beaten path, not only of academic investigation, but also of Thuringian tourist destinations. Inbound and international tourists rarely venture into the rural landscapes of Thuringia, preferring to follow the more trodden paths of urban tourism to the better known cities of Erfurt, Jena, Weimar, and Eisenach, renowned for their historical and cultural significance. During the systematic post-*Wende* restructuring of political, economic, and social legislations, which identified growth opportunities primarily in the area of tourism as a means to eliminate disparities in production and consumption between the former GDR and the Federal Republic of Germany (FRG), these cities offered inherent advantages. As Coles explains, "Personalities and periods that were viewed with great nostalgia, relentlessly marketed, and voraciously consumed in western products and experiences had resonances with and, hence, were relatively straightforward to transcribe in the east. Eastern towns played pivotal roles in the 'golden ages' of German history, not least the Reformation, Enlightenment, and fin-de-Siècle modernity" (223).

These cities naturally attracted more visitors from the West German states and also from abroad. Visitors to the less-traveled areas of Thuringia, both before and after the *Wende*, were typically limited to domestic hikers, nature lovers, and the health-conscious who sought to explore the diverse countryside of mountains, lakes, valleys, and nature reserves; trek the Rennsteig, the longest and oldest hiking trail in Germany; view the breathtaking beauty of the region's natural parks and the Thuringian Forest; or benefit from the healing springs and mineral sources at its recognized spa towns, including Heilbad Heiligenstadt in Eichsfeld and Bad Liebenstein, the oldest spa town in Thuringia.[1] Even on these lists of rural Thuringian destinations, Bad Sulza has traditionally remained absent.

Nevertheless, since the *Wende*, this former GDR *Kurort* (spa town) has experienced unparalleled development and change culturally, historically, and artistically, making it a popular, yet unexpected, tourist destination for domestic and international visitors alike.[2] Through strategic reframing of its natural resources and landscape within the context of key elements of German literary, musical, historical, and spa culture injected into Western-style narratives of consumption, Bad Sulza has created a marketable allure enhancing its touristic appeal, and thus presents an important example of emergent rural tourism in eastern Germany.

This case study of Bad Sulza, though not intended to be a representative or comprehensive study of the totality of emerging tourism endeavors in the new German states, nevertheless introduces a less known example of budding international touristic appeal, in order to explore some of the major trends and challenges in transitioning former GDR locations into attractive and sustainable destinations.[3]

Rewriting Thuringia's Routes and Roots

The public presentation of Bad Sulza and its spa is founded on the historical evolution of Germany's *Kur* (cure) and *Kurhäuser* (cure resorts and treatment centers) with their iconic tradition of "taking the waters," a practice that originally served the aristocracy and the bourgeoisie for both medical and recreational purposes (Maretzki 1989: 25). Germany remains the largest spa-going nation in Europe, with its well-documented "recreational" spa history dating back to the seventeenth century and its "medical" histories of the early nineteenth century, which sought to legitimate water cures (Maretzki 1989: 26). *Badeärzte* (spa physicians) and "spa medicine" played a far more significant role than in the Anglo-American world. Even today, when the efficacy of water cures has become dubious, spa therapies based on balneology and hydrotherapy are still accepted as part of orthodox medical practice in Germany, which sets rules and standards for mineral waters and professional organizations dealing with balneology, thalassotherapy, and hydrotherapy, and clearly differentiates three key terms relating to the German spa: *Bad* (bath), *Therme* (a hot mineral water source or pool), and *Kur* (cure, or the spa regimen, incorporating hydrotherapy and physiotherapy) (Maretzki 1989: 25–27).

In both the former GDR and FRG, *Kur* treatments were made accessible to the general population. In the 1950s, the FRG's social welfare legislation recognized the *Kur* as a prominent form of rehabilitation therapy with costs covered by the national health insurance system, leading to the transformation of many communities into *Kurorte* (spa destinations), offering medical services, hotel accommodations, and park-like atmospheres (Maretzki 1989: 25 and 26).[4] By 1981, 848,000 patients had been treated with average stays lasting between 15.5 and 19.9 days with the possibility of additional two-week extensions (Statistisches Bundesamt 1983). A year later, *Kur* treatments were offered to insured workers, as a legislative incentive to restore and maintain workers' health. The national healthcare system covered a *Kururlaub* (*Kur* vacation) once every three years, with personal contributions kept to 10 percent of the overall cost. The state socialism of the former GDR also supported economical therapies with a dual purpose: as a reward for hard work and an economic rationale of extending the productive life of the worker.

This democratization of spa practices prior to the *Wende* meant that the general populations of both countries were familiar with a plurality of therapeutic modalities, including spa and alternative treatment therapies, available to patients and typically covered by government and private health insurance (Maretzki 1989: 24). Unlike the general populace in the United States and United Kingdom, who often cannot afford a lavish stay at a costly retreat, Germans came to accept spa visits as part of their cultural background. Harish Naraindas summarizes key differences between the German and Anglo-American regard for spas with the following facts: There are nearly three hundred spa towns in Germany with 273,000 annual visits, 50 percent of which are covered by insurance, employing 350,000 people, and comprising 30 percent of overnight stays; these have seen nine million visitors over the past forty years (2010: 69). Between 1995 and 2008, due to escalating healthcare costs related to demographic shifts, the German system introduced a number of reforms and new restrictions that had vast implications for the German health and wellness tourism industry, in particular for the role that spas played in Germany. These restrictions posed great challenges, but also brought new opportunities. Modern German, post-*Wende* spas needed to adopt new practices in order to compete in an aggressive global market, continue to attract German tourists, lure new clients from competition abroad, and cater to this completely different clientele, all while remaining both sustainable and profitable. This has typically translated into a demedicalization of facilities and a strong movement toward "wellness" and pluralism, i.e. variety, innovation, and entertainment.

The rebranding of Bad Sulza as a modern place of attraction, leisure, and consumption exemplifies this type of change. As a modern spa, it has not necessarily replaced the old spa model; rather, it has reinvented it to better suit consumers' desires and needs, which have changed with globalization. The essence of the old spa tradition survives, while projecting its image as a transformed, up-to-date retreat, able to cater to a variety of leisure, cultural, heritage, and "wellness" tourism demands.

As Dean MacCannell asserts in his work on tourism, modern tourists seek to "take a voyage of discovery" on which they attempt "to discover or reconstruct a cultural heritage or a social identity," regardless of whether this heritage or identity is their own (1989: 13–14). This search for what Tim Coles and Dallen J. Timothy call "routes and roots" aims to reaffirm their own sense of identity (2004: xi). Central to their quest is the search for artificially constructed opportunities for "authentic" experiences, i.e., those marked as real and different from everyday life, even though, as MacCannell points out, their search is often frustrated by the usually prepackaged way tourist experiences are constructed and "staged" by the tourist industry (1989: 91–107).

Increasingly, modern tourism emphasizes the enhancement of lived experience, rather than simply providing a lens through which visitors gaze on foreign communities. Moreover, spa vacations have become increasingly popular in recent years within the middle class, as a way to augment individual and collective identities that accent physical health and emotional wellbeing. Spas have become today's pilgrimage sites, not only for authentic experiences in terms of vacation, tourism, and consumption, but also for personal development, health, and spiritual insight. The billion-dollar international spa industry thrives on an image of modern leisure destinations as "places of metamorphosis," where visitors escape the daily stresses of life, explore a change from the ordinary, and find deeper meaning in their lives (Baranowski and Furlough 2001: 5). Spa goers, like tourists, actively seek meaningful experiences of self-discovery. As seekers and self-help consumers, they embark on a modernized and secularized traditional "spiritual journey."

The modern love affair with spas is deeply steeped in the desire to be swept away from our mundane existences. As Sara Firman-Pitt suggests, "our longing for the soulful life," which is connected to water, the heart of all spa experience, "links physical, emotional and mysterious worlds" and functions as a "metaphor and more for all existence" (2001). Modern spa goers, desirous of both relaxation and productivity for their limited leisure time, have high expectations. In response, spas worldwide have developed a proliferation of new commercial forms of entertainment, including time-efficient rituals of bathing and massage services aimed at creating maximum benefits. Spas today are amalgams of many different experiences, forming all-inclusive worlds of their own that offer a type of "one-stop shopping" (Baldwin 2004).

Bad Sulza has capitalized on this trend. Heralded as the center of the "Tuscany of the East," which comprises the neighboring towns of Auerstedt and Apolda, this small futuristic and historic spa town features the internationally acclaimed Toskana Therme with its crowned architectural jewel, the Liquid Sound Temple.[5] Developed by Micky Remann, this modern multimedia, holistic underwater concert hall/opera house blends tradition and innovation and offers visitors the experience of "bathing in light and sound."[6] Though visually unique, the new artistic music/spa venue nonetheless fits into the heritage and geography of the region. The Orphic dimensions of Liquid Sound invoke the imaginative cultural and architectural inheritance of the German artistic tradition, harkening back to the works of Paul Scheerbart, Bruno Taut, and Rainer Maria Rilke, while the complex itself, housed in a large, amorphous building on a hilltop above the underground Trias Sea, resembles a UFO or a whale with its "tail" lining up against the ridges of the Finne mountains. It is indeed, as Firman-Pitt suggests, as if "on the rural landscape of Bad Sulza a spaceship has landed … and it is not out of place" (2008). Spa visitors are lured aboard, given a central position, and invited not only to choose from a vast array of offerings, but also to actively participate in the "dream-making" process.

Transforming Thuringia into Tuscany

The primary motivation for this spa's transformation—from what originally began as a small clinic in the nineteenth century that first operated
on a minimal scale, then later on a larger scale in GDR times, to become
finally a multi-million dollar resort—was to offer a uniquely holistic vision of healing, reinvigorating the tradition of an artistic retreat.[7] This
newly built, postsocialist environment capitalizes on features prominent
in cultural and heritage tourism; it echoes a German humanist past as
well as an Expressionist vision, and as such evokes both performative
and ritualized aspects of life and culture. As a project of renewal in this
once-impoverished area, Bad Sulza represents a specifically targeted case
of how creative manipulation of tourist attractions, coupled with artistic
vision, have productively transformed the construction into an economically and ecologically sustainable project, where the interrelationship
of architecture, business, and the popular wellness industry prospers.
The area's evolution is as much an event as an environmental shift. Bad
Sulza's tremendous growth into a dynamic place of significance for modern seekers and their longed-for experience of metamorphosis has been
achieved through a thorough process of cultural reframing, aimed at attracting the widest audience possible. Amid the therapy and recreational
fun is a unique blend of culture and history—a bit of Bauhaus with a
touch of Ancient Greece, a little Goethe and some techno pop.

For Bad Sulza, the idea of metamorphosis takes on significance in
every aspect of its influence: cultural, social, and economical. Bad Sulza's transformation from a sleepy brine town into a unique cultural center was inspired by the married couple Klaus Dieter Böhm and Marion
Schneider, the founders, initiators, investors, and post-*Wende* developers of the Klinikzentrum Bad Sulza (KBS) Medical Spa and the Toskana
Therme, as well as by Micky Remann, a self-proclaimed *Globaltrottel*
(literally: global dork, a word play on the term globe trotter) and dreamer
captivated by "silly ideas" (Krutsch 2003). Taking up Goethe's original
recommendations that the salt extracted from the underground saline
reservoirs in the area be used for healing purposes for thermal baths—
much like the ones in Karlsbad and Marienbad in Bohemia—Böhm,
Schneider, and Remann realized a collective dream, achieved through
holistic orchestration of various units.[8] The new space offers color, style,
character, personality, and uniqueness, purposively put together to
embody a utopian vision of a world made right by the natural blend of
lights, colors, glass, and sound. Remann had closely studied the works of
Paul Scheerbart (1863–1915), known for his sound poetry and belief in
the transformative potential of colored glass architecture. Scheerbart's

vision, realized momentarily in architectural form as the *Glashaus* of the Werkbund Exhibition of 1914 with the help of his friend Bruno Taut, did not survive the horrors of World War I. Had it not been for curious poetry lovers, including Remann, Scheerbart's vision might have been forever lost to future generations. Remann, a trained Germanist and avowed freethinker, followed in Goethe's footsteps from Frankfurt to Weimar, taking with him Scheerbart's vision, which he crystallized again in architectural form: this time in the shape of the modern Liquid Sound Temple, housed in Bad Sulza.

Thus, the unique case of Bad Sulza is one rich in both historical and imaginative culture, and the mining of these cultural origins comprises the task of this chapter. Its appeal capitalizes on its constructed experience of otherworldliness and moves beyond a subtle orientation of asymmetrical power dynamics of values the West might imbue on the East. Here, any perceived sensuality, innocence, and backwardness relates most significantly to the constructed artistic dreamscape created in the spa landscape. Bad Sulza remains after all, much like Disney World, a space apart from reality, an exoticized other world where "silly ideas" and inspirations from the cultural past find moments of continuity.

Reinventing Bad Sulza's Relevance

Until recently, new spas were a rarity in Germany, and old spas that had reinvented themselves were almost as rare. Bad Sulza's post-*Wende* development thus reads like a modern fairytale; out of the eradication of its Eastern economic structures and the erasure of viable meaning in the post-*Wende* landscape, this region offered its developers from the West an existing slate on which to rediscover treasures while simultaneously inscribing new narratives of cultural significance.

The unification of the two Germanies in 1990 comprised a watershed moment for the tourist and leisure industry in the former GDR. Thuringia was incorporated into the FRG on 3 October 1990. The imposition of a radically different system resulted in noticeable contradictions in this new capitalism. Unification did not simply translate into an expansion of the old FRG but also meant that states had to "undergo a rapid and fundamental metamorphosis" (Cooke 2005: 13). Often this change was perceived as a takeover of the East by the West, as Western entrepreneurs typically looked eastward with resources available for investment.

For Bad Sulza, the *Wende* meant the surrender of the SDAG Wismut mining and its medical clinics. The medical establishment that had existed in Bad Sulza as a miners' sanatorium could not continue as before; the period immediately following the *Wende* was marked by a dramatic stagnation in the spa and tourism industries and by prolonged privatization of health facilities. In 1992, the former miners' sanatorium was surrendered, modified, and extended into the TOMESA Hospital. Bad Sulza began its downtown redevelopment by seeking out concepts for infrastructure. Outside investors Böhm and Schneider identified a need for innovation while capitalizing on the town's strength—its water—and recognizing the need to reinvent the spa industry by building relationships to other businesses within a new commercial configuration that integrated the spa into the wider community.

Böhm and Schneider benefited greatly from the generous subsidies offered by the federal government and the state of Thuringia for reconstruction.[9] They also benefited from the timing of events. The opening of the KBS Medical Spa in 1993 marked the founding of one of the most modern rehabilitation clinics in the new German states. Born out of the previous Wismut-Sanatorium and the TOMESA Hospital, the KBS Medical Spa is an interdisciplinary center, specializing in the treatment of chronic skin, joint, and respiratory ailments, orthopedics, and psychosomatic illnesses. Böhm and Schneider transformed one of the buildings of the medical clinic into a hotel—to attract tourists and not necessarily patients—and expanded the complex to include the Toskana Therme, opened in 1999, which features the Liquid Sound Temple.

This opening also heralded a fundamental shift in the function of the German bath culture.[10] The Toskana Therme began a strategic rethinking of bathing in terms of its international marketing campaign, beckoning guests to "dive into a different world" (*Eintauchen in eine andere Welt*). This "new experience" was the "Liquid Sound" concept, marketed as "Bathing in Light and Music" (*Baden im Licht und Musik*). In 1992/93, the KBS Medical Spa first incorporated an early Liquid Sound pool into its existing facilities and then into its newly constructed thermal baths, in conjunction with the celebration of Weimar's designation as European Capital of Culture. The concept was then introduced as an external project, entitled "Liquid Sound in the Tuscany of the East," at the World EXPO 2000 in Hannover. The clinic found the integration of body temperature, saltwater, color, light, and music to be particularly beneficial to patients' recuperation. This innovation, moreover, proved lifesaving to Bad Sulza's spa industry.

In 1996, German spas were dealt a blow when the German government severely cut back national health insurance funding for the traditional water cures, the centerpiece of most German spas. As many as three hundred specialized clinics closed. Surviving spas had to redefine and market themselves in more attractive ways, especially since many Germans had changed their health, wellness, and spa-going expectations. With its innovations, the Toskana Therme was able to redirect its trajectory more easily than others.

As the number of national health patients drastically sank, demand for new offerings for private patients and health-conscious individuals rose. The KBS Medical Spa quickly mobilized to respond to these new structural changes, introducing initiatives alongside its conventional medical approaches—a decision that proved crucial for its sustained development. Böhm and Remann were particularly interested in putting Bad Sulza on the map. For Böhm, this translated into underscoring Bad Sulza's central geographic location, situated close to the Hermsdorfer-Kreuz, one of the largest thoroughfares in the former East. Remann emphasized its cultural significance; the East was simultaneously home to the great German humanist tradition and what he calls "foreign" territory. The lure of Bad Sulza's beautiful forests, called *Wunderwald*, reminded him of Thomas Mann's *Zauberberg*. The founders consciously worked to re-create a sense of communal and cultural identity for Bad Sulza in and around Thuringia.

The founders sought to win over the citizens of the area, gaining trust in their intentions for greater prosperity, not only of their business, but of the region as well. Through concerted networking of a variety of initiatives, including the Apolda Avantgarde Art Gallery, the European Capital of Culture in Weimar, the global cultural village in Auerstedt ("Auerworld is Auerstedt"), and numerous other national and international contacts, including involvement on the local tourist board, the Weimar Bauhaus Institut, and the Jena Observatory, and in the founding of the regional television station, Salve TV, they contributed to making Bad Sulza an attractive place for tourists.[11] Promising *Glück und Gesundheit* (health and happiness), as their company Toskanaworld's slogan boasts, the KBS Medical Spa has had marked success; it emerged as a nationally recognized modern brine spa and has attracted over three million visitors from around the world. The spa has been covered by the international press, and the founders' efforts in contributing to this region's sense of pride were captured in an award-winning short film, *Thüringen: Wo der Weltgeist spazieren geht* (Thuringia: Where the World's Spirit Goes for a Stroll, 2009).[12] The Toskana Therme underwent an expansion in 2008 with the introduction of a new innovative sauna landscape, heralded as the "Sauna of the Future," featuring new attractions, such as a space devoted to public readings of literature, called a *Lektarium*, and a sweat lodge. Toskanaworld has also opened two complexes featuring Liquid Sound in Bad Schandau, Saxony, and Bad Orb,

Hesse. Future plans for the Toskana Therme include a far-reaching collaboration between the KBS Medical Spa and the University Skin Clinic in Jena, which has had considerable success in treating patients with acute symptoms using the spa's rehabilitation facilities.

Spascape as Dreamscape with Orpheus as Guide

In the years following the *Wende,* the KBS Medical Spa courted the international industry leaders and clientele with slow but steady success. The prioritization of opening up the offerings to an international market led to the creation of a collaborative common culture, steeped in both "low" and "high," the popular and classic, history and vision for the future, enabling Bad Sulza to address financial challenges with relatively greater success than other rural areas in former East.

A key component of Bad Sulza's allure is the experience of deep listening in the Liquid Sound Temple, marketed as part of this spa's particular brand of mystique and otherworldliness. In spite of multimedia technological equipment and a sci-fi appearance, the Liquid Sound Temple harkens back to ancient Greek spa traditions—those of *aesclepieia,* or dream temples, as found in Epidaurus in northeastern Peloponnese and Delphi. Lectures offered at the Toskana Therme and as video presentations on its various websites introduce guests to this historical reference. Jonathan de Vierville, a regular speaker at Bad Sulza and a specialist in dream therapy who offers workshops on dreams and rituals in bathing waters, suggests that the modern spa temple at Bad Sulza functions as a re-envisioned replica of the Asclepieion of Epidaurus.[13] Such temples were dedicated to the Greek god Asclepius, who represents the healing of medicine, and were thought to have been ancient pilgrimage sites that served as carefully controlled centers of medical prognosis, counsel, and purported healing.[14] The Asclepieion of Epidaurus, for instance, still houses marble boards dating back to 350 B.C.E. that preserve the names, case histories, complaints, and methods for curing of about seventy visitors.

The temples, built near healing springs, were important pilgrimage sites, where the practice of receptivity, i.e. "inner hearing," was used to facilitate the process of dream incubation, or *incubatio,* derived from the Latin words *in,* meaning "upon," and *cubare,* meaning "to lie down." Visitors were instructed to watch for signs in their dreams that signaled the correct time to visit the temple. Once the omens were right, the seeker would enter the main temple, lie down on its large open floor in one of the many of the little dream-rooms, and ponder the question at hand in a dream-like state of induced sleep, known as *enkoimesis.* Then she or he would dream, hoping to gain guidance from a deity in the form of insight, salvation, purification, solace, and healing in a vision or direct visit, metaphorically or symbolically. The belief in being able to be cured by one's dreams was so firm that the sites were considered to be sacred temples of healing and constituted the roots of modern medicine (de Vierville 2000).

Male temple attendants were present as priests, offering dream interpretations and prescriptions, counseling the seekers, and guiding them on their journey to receive answers. Part physician and part metaphysician, they were skilled in the art of healing through herbs, incantations, and the rituals of the temple, and well versed in all aspects of dreaming. They also consulted the priestess, the *pythia,* who would sit on her tripod in a trance and speak as the medium of the oracle.[15] The male priests would interpret her words and review the visitation from the gods, helping to make sense of the dream and secure the insights appropriate to the seeker's stage of development. Through dream incubation, seekers were thought to awaken to a more authentic sense of self, which could assist them in regenerating themselves physically, mentally, and spiritually. By 700 to 500 B.C.E. the interpretations were exploited to increase the political power of Delphi, and by 500 B.C.E., the oracle had fallen into disrepute, charged with being ambiguous and not fitting with the rational spirit of Greece.[16]

Interest in dream incubation and interpretation is fostered at Bad Sulza's spa through workshops, lectures, and promotional materials that re-engage with the early twentieth century's interest in dreams by Sigmund Freud and Carl Jung, as well as by visionary poets like Rainer Maria Rilke and Expressionist poets like Paul Scheerbart, who sought to gauge the deeper, unknown aspects of the self. Rilke, perhaps the best-known German-language poet among English-speaking New Agers and spiritual seekers, is a comfortable and well-chosen guide for the Liquid Sound experience. Although Rilke is not a natural fit in this former GDR landscape, he is, especially for many international spa visitors to Bad Sulza, "German" enough to fit into the experience of a self-stylized German spa experience without further explanation and rationale. Rilke's work on the importance of sound and attuning to one's inner self through listening, and in particular, his insights into the Orpheus myth also tie in nicely with Bad Sulza's overall objectives of luring one into a sensual world of inner-focused experience that bridges life and death, dream and reality, and the known and unknown worlds.

Rilke's evolving engagement with the Orpheus myth throughout his life redefined a modern understanding of the Orphic tradition in lyric poetry in such a way as to establish the visionary poet as the mediating shamanic figure upon and through which expressions of human emotion are expressed. Rilke's poetry also instructs modernity in the lost art of deep listening, intuitive insight, and lucid dreaming. Especially in his *Sonnets to Orpheus* (1922), Rilke emphasizes the exploration of the inner self through the power of sound as the key aim of Orphic poetry. Rilke's understanding of the Orphic experience provides a map with which to expound Liquid Sound's dreaming in sound.

The early animating presence and dreaming companion in Rilke's work, introduced in the poem from 1914, "Wendung" (Turning Point), is an "inner woman," or girl (*Mädchen*), who enables the poet to turn away from visual representations and undertake the assignment of transforming himself through inner "heart-work" (*Herz-Werk*):

> For there is a boundary to looking.
> And the world that is looked at so deeply
> wants to flourish in love.
>
> Work of the eyes is done, now
> go and do heart-work
> on all the images imprisoned within you; for you
> overpowered them: but even now you don't know them.
> Learn, inner man, to look on our inner woman,
> the one attained from a thousand
> natures, the merely attained by
> not yet beloved form. (Rilke 1989: 133)

Rilke's avowed move from the work of the eyes, and a patriarchal sense of focus, to the subtler, i.e. "feminine," tasks of the heart is simultaneously a shift from the visual to the aural, from externalized focus to inner vision, as mirrored in Rilke's move away from the preferred form of his *Dinggedichte* (thing poems) of his *New Poems*, inspired by Rodin, to the celebratory expression of praise in his *Sonnets to Orpheus*. In his sonnets, Rilke realizes the transformative and jubilant potential of the "tragic" Orpheus myth. Here, human participation in the great mysteries of the world is celebrated through identification with the figure of Orpheus, who transforms pain into praise and silence into song. This transfiguration overcomes opposites: male/female, Orpheus/Eurydice, sight/sound, and reality/dream. Rilke's second sonnet reintroduces the girl-like figure (*ein Mädchen fast*) of Rilke's "inner woman" after the invocation of Orpheus, as a figure reminiscent of Orpheus's beloved companion, Eurydice. In this image of reunion, the feminine presence makes herself a bed in the poet's, i.e. Orpheus's, ear:

And slept there. And her sleep was everything:
the awesome trees, the distance I had felt
so deeply that I could touch them, meadows in spring:
all the wonders that had ever seized my heart. (Rilke 1998: I, ii, 229)

The animating feminine figure not only inspires the poet through her dreaming, but also imaginatively brings into being every desire (and all wonders) in his heart. This Orphic dimension in Rilke's work emerges through what Elizabeth Sewell describes as an "exploration of the labyrinth of body-and-mind, a field between living and dead with the poetic self as the instrument of investigation" (1971: 326). Orpheus, known from classical sources as the greatest poet-singer, half-man, half-god, who can charm and tame the hearts of wild beasts, thereby transforming reality into vibrating resonance, is first and foremost a great lover who seeks to be reunified with his beloved wife Eurydice. In Rilke's later work, Orpheus also emerges as the poet's crowning achievement "in sound married to image" in the form of the dismembered god, dispersed into nature, and resurrected as oracle and song (Masson 1951: 419).[17] Rilke sums up the eschatological dimension of the Orphic in his *Sonnet to Orpheus* I,V: "Once and for all/ it is Orpheus, when there is song" (*Ein für alle Male / ists Orpheus, wenn es singt*) (Rilke 1989: 233). Here, the Orphic is understood as underlying all forms of musical expression, analogous to the impersonal shaman's song and the essence of Orphic music, which is not mimetic in nature, but rather the "inner song of creation" (McGahey 1994: 31). It is the point when the "poet-as-instrument" expresses him- or herself through the body, such that the body itself becomes the "mouthpiece" for larger forces (McGahey 1994: 31). Like the Romantics' image of the Aeolian harp, the Orphic poet serves as an instrument that is passively sounded by the divine winds passing through it. The Orphic song created is said not to be audible as normal sound by the physical ear, as it lies beyond the reaches of the normal senses. Rather, as inner music, it shatters its own confinement in the body that produces it. It is the experience—much like that experienced in Liquid Sound—of being submerged in sound, listening with one's whole being.

Rilke's late Orpheus thus has an audible presence as well as an imaginary presence within the interior landscape of the body, one closely linked to ideas of inner health and healing. In the *Sonnets to Orpheus*, Rilke achieves not merely supreme poetic craftsmanship in terms of his use of expressive devices, he also undoes habitual expressions of reality, achieving what H.W. Belmore describes as the "goal of poetry," which strives to recreate the primitive connection between sound and meaning on a higher plane: "Speech ... when it is used poetically ... heals itself, so that denotation and expression, which are normally treated as separate in our culture, come together and regain their original unity, and denotation becomes a form of expression, while expression itself names" (Belmore 1954: 191). As Belmore suggests, poetic speech enacts a reunion of fundamentals.

Rilke's poetry, like the experience of Liquid Sound, harmonizes and interweaves the senses, drawing the attention away from the dominating influence of the eye, into a synaesthetically unified world inhabited and embodied by Orpheus—an idea closely aligned with the Pythagorean ideal of *harmonia mundi* and the belief that musical resolution can affect human wellbeing by bringing the human body back into sympathetic vibration with the cosmic order and rhythm of the harmony of the spheres. For Pythagoras and Rilke's modern Orpheus, such musical resolution is achieved through the experience of hearing, particularly the actualization of inner hearing. In his essay, "Ur-Geräusch" (Primal Sound, first published in 1919), Rilke praises the much-undervalued aspect of hearing and discusses the possibilities for creating multisensory poetry similar to Arabic poems, "which seem to owe their existence to the simultaneous and equal contributions from all five senses" (Rilke 1978: 54).

Ontologically, the desire to hear takes one back not only to a "collective" beginning of time, as expressed by Pythagoras, but also to one's own beginnings and sense of being alive, as the ear is one of the first human sense organs to develop in the womb. Early in fetal development, an infant can hear the sound of the mother's voice, as filtered through bone, flesh, and amniotic fluid. As the infant's hearing is extremely sensitive and perceives only high frequency sounds at this stage, it adapts the ability to hear not only through its ears but through its whole body, so that it functions as what Alfred Tomatis describes as a "full-body sound resonator," able to perceive the "whole universe of relationship [that is] established *in utero*" (1991: 212). The ears thus prepare the path for the development of speech, as well as for the adaptation to self and environment. Music therapist and composer Kay Gardner explains that this neurological pathway can nonetheless become developmentally blocked by emotional and physical traumas (1990: 63). Gardner maintains that a countermeasure for such trauma is to reestablish the sonic atmosphere experienced in the womb, in order to retrain one's ability to listen from the formative stages, so that "gradually two tiny but important ear muscles are reconditioned to respond to a broader frequency spectrum" (1990: 63). According to Gardner, the individual's auditory faculty is then "drawn toward previously unexplored areas" and experienced as learning to "hear" with one's whole body (1990: 63).

Poetry's selected speech and rhythmic patterns elicit similar imaginative responses that foreground previously unnoticed patterns or sound clusters and as such are thought to have particular therapeutic value. For instance, the patterning or sustained repetition of certain sounds that function as meditative mantras can stimulate the memory to remember long-forgotten emotions and associations and act as a means of discharging suppressed emotions. Mantras, revered in Hinduism for their power to connect with and even control the gods, are believed to bring about remarkable transformation if intoned with the proper sound and rhythm. The ancient belief that the sound of words is invested with magical power also connects to Orphism and the "primitive theory that human words could make things happen in the supernatural realm, which in turn influenced the natural one" (Walker 1983: 579). Poetry, particularly as it was understood in the Orphic tradition, constitutes a form of therapeutic power over the external world.

Rilke understands Orpheus as the very embodiment of poetry: where the poetic voice, experienced as the body-as-instrument, becomes the mediator that travels between the worlds of actualities and possibilities, the living and the dead, the past and the present, and is capable of transforming the self *and* the world through the experience of hearing Orphic song. In the first of his *Sonnets to Orpheus*, Rilke evokes the presence of Orphic song in the image of a tree. The tree, however, is firmly planted not in the ground, but in the ear as a means to foreground the ontological importance of hearing. Rilke's sonnet also introduces the idea of a "temple of hearing" (*Tempel im Gehör*) created by the evocation of Orpheus's song:

> And where there had been
> at most a makeshift hut to receive the music,
>
> a shelter nailed up out of their darkest longing,
> with an entryway that shuddered in the wind—
> you built a temple deep inside their hearing. (Rilke 1998: I, I, 227)

This "temple of hearing" is said to heal nature of its difference, acting as a sanctuary of hearing that brings harmony to the wild noise of the uncivilized world. The poem's message is articulated on two levels: first, thematically in its imagery and story, and second, in its structural and architectural sound-patterning that merges and melds different sound clusters within the poem, such that the sounds appear to create their "own world" (Belmore 1954: 53). This emphasis on sound and hearing within the poem, both thematically and aurally, sets the example for this possible embodied change of perception through hearing, a precondition for the experience of Orphic song.

Musicologist Joachim-Ernst Berendt similarly introduces architectural imagery to communicate the experience of hearing in the form of a sound temple or "cathedral," erected in a specific, for him tangible, time and space. As part of an evolution of a new sound ideal, these sound cathedrals stand apart from the collective classical sound ideal as the more individualistic ideal sound of modernism. For Berendt, this difference between "old World" and "new World" sounds are experienced corporeally as gendered differences, which work along the same lines as Rilke's understanding of the poet and his inner woman, where femininity is equated with both receptivity and inclusion:

> Old-world sound seems to be more male-oriented, it grows, rises, searches you out, penetrates you.... New-world sound, on the other hand, has more female traits. The sound of a rock group, for instance, is a body that incorporates a musical process and in which the listener himself is incorporated. There are sounds in rock that can be said to be "as large as a cathedral." When hearing them, the listener "stands inside them." ... Like the "cathedral" of rock sound, [the female sound] provides a space in which the mediator lives and that he carries with him wherever he may go. (Berendt 1987: 129)

The reception of sound, understood here as feminine in nature, within Berendt's analogy of the "cathedral" of sound echoes Rilke's aims in his first sonnet: to create a "cathedral-temple" of sound that voices a modern structuring of "new World" sound, incorporating both the speaker and listener.

In Bad Sulza, this musical, poetic idea has been realized in the architecture of its Liquid Sound Temple as a womb-like space. The new sound temple embodies such an immersive sound experience, which acts as an entryway into the landscape of consciousness and a place for dream incubation. It consists of a showpiece swimming pool in a free-standing, windowless building called the *Tempel*, kept dark so the colored lights appear to dance on the water's surface. Here Orphic poetry and the ancient tradition of the healing dream temples merge. The result is a modernized, revised, and secularized, even democratized, version of these traditionally male, classical traditions with the modern, multimedia world of spa culture and tradition, without high culture pretensions. Such pretensions are quite literally stripped away, as one enters the temple in one's bathing suit. As one floats on one's back in warm thermal saltwater, which carries the body effortlessly, the body relaxes. Embraced by luring underwater sounds, one's own body becomes part of the instrument in the Orphic sound experience, so that one begins to hear and resonate with one's whole being the "water melodies," underwater concerts, lectures, and readings made with the liquid-sound system. Remann insists that this temple is best understood as an "underwater opera-house" with an "aquatic stage," not merely as a swimming pool. Indeed, swimming is virtually impossible in the pool and only floating is allowed. Bad Sulza's modern "temple" is a cross between a multimedia stage and a meditation center—a place where each visitor simultaneously becomes participant, director, actor, and instrument in their own inner story. The question of one's own agency and participation is a key component in the process of this spa experience. As in the ancient temples, seekers lie down in the water, "sleep," and dream.

This whole-body listening allows the body to become instrument, receptor, and participant in a way that the staging of traditional theater, and traditional spa practices for that matter, have not made possible. Such bathing in thermal water, coupled with active listening, relaxes the body and engages all of the senses, while also inciting a lucid dream-like meditative state of heightened inner awareness. The warm saltwater further underscores the maternal womb-like environment in which one is taken back to a primal state of one's being. Renate Maerten, clinical psychologist at the Klinikzentrum Bad Sulza, has found in her investigation of Liquid Sound and relaxation studies that the experience of floating in Liquid Sound evokes deep transpersonal experiences, memories from the childhood, the sense of being in the womb again (2001: 66), and echoes what Sigmund Freud described as the "oceanic feeling" that is the sensation of weightlessness and a feeling of experiencing "eternity" as something limitless and unbounded (Freud [1930] 2010: 72). The participant begins to "dream" and become part of the dream, echoing Rilke's famous exhortation from his 1908 poem "Archaischer Torso Apollos" (Archaic Torso of Apollo), prompted by a sense of not only witnessing art, but conversely being witnessed by art: "You must change your life" (Rilke 1989: 61).

Dreams of Glass Architecture

Although Rilke's Orphic exploration clearly explains the dynamics of the Liquid Sound experience, it is another, less known bohemian poet of German modernism who is its true inspiration: Paul Scheerbart. Scheerbart was heralded by *Der Sturm* (The Storm)'s founder Herwarth

Walden as "the first Expressionist" and even the "high-priest of Expressionism" (Haag Bletter 1975: 83; Curl 2000: 684). Scheerbart is known for writing the first published examples of sound poetry and science fiction in German. His experimentations with nonverbal communication and abstract rhythms of nonsense verse predate Dada poetry. His love poem "Kikakok!ú Ekoralábs!," for instance, written in 1897, has no literal meaning, but rather consists of purely fantastical words and sounds that do not belong to any language. Relying on sound to create coherence, it expresses emotional content and creates new "sense" beyond natural language.

In 1914, Scheerbart composed a full-fledged treatise on a world set right by colored glass. The book entitled *Glasarchitektur* (Glass Architecture) imagines a complete change in the architecture and cultural vision of the time, outlining Scheerbart's beliefs in the transformative power of glass architecture:

> We live for the most part in closed rooms. These form the environment from which our culture grows. Our culture is to a certain extent the product of our architecture. If we want our culture to rise to a higher level, we are obliged, for better or for worse, to change our architecture. And this only becomes possible if we take away the closed character from the rooms in which we live. We can only do that by introducing glass architecture, which lets in the light of the sun, the moon, and the stars, not merely through a few windows, but through every possible wall, which will be made entirely out of glass—of colored glass. The new environment, which we thus create, must bring us a new culture. (Scheerbart 1972: 41)[18]

Scheerbart envisions a spiritual opening of society, created when the light and sun of the moon move freely through the colored glass panes. His color symphony resembles artistically Berendt's "cathedral" of sound.

Scheerbart's treatise places great emphasis on the architecture of the future. As Rosmarie Haag Bletter suggests, Scheerbart was "inspired by such disparate things as light mysticism, the Gothic cathedral, and nineteenth century glass structures" and "foresaw the building of opulent and colorful glass constructions symbolic of extra-dimensional space and of a modern spiritual world" (1975: 83). In *Glasarchitektur,* Scheerbart expresses a glorious utopian vision of the "beauty of the world, when glass architecture is everywhere," supplanting masonry: "The surface of the Earth would change greatly if brick architecture were everywhere displaced by glass architecture. It would be as though the Earth clad itself in jewelry of gems and enamel. The splendor is absolutely unimaginable. And we should then have more exquisite things than the gardens of the Arabian Nights. Then we should have a paradise on Earth and would not need to gaze longingly at the paradise in the sky" (Scheerbart 1972: 46).

Scheerbart's writing reveals what Haag Bletter describes as "a compelling architectural vision," which grew out of his friendship and correspondence with the visionary yet practical architect Bruno Taut, to whom Scheerbart dedicated the book (1975: 83). Taut enjoyed a "pivotal and commanding" position throughout the period of architectural Expressionism in Germany, and Scheerbart's work fundamentally influenced Taut's architecture (Haag Bletter 1975: 83). The political upheaval during the establishment of the Weimar Republic in November 1918 was accompanied by the beginnings of an artistic and architectural revolution in the founding of the Arbeitsrat für Kunst (Workers' Council for Art), led by Taut. The Arbeitsrat, composed of architects such as Walter Gropius and Eric Mendelsohn, artists, art historians, writers, and journalists, sought to use architecture and art to improve society and shared its ideas in public exhibitions, programs, and manifestoes. In 1919/20, Taut supervised an exchange of correspondence among a loosely associated group called the Gläserne Kette (Glass Chain) in an effort to challenge the imagination of its participants, which included Scheerbart.

Inspired by Scheerbart's work, Taut simultaneously opened a *Glashaus* pavilion at the May 1914 German Werkbund Exhibition in Cologne, which is credited with combining function, form, and fantasy. Sponsored by the German glass industries, the *Glashaus* explored the possibilities of combining colored glass and concrete in architecture. Taut's structure comprised a fourteen-sided prismatic dome of colored glass with glass-block stairs, decorated with a mosaic and cascading waterfall. Taut, in turn, dedicated his *Glashaus* to Scheerbart. Both saw the construction of shimmering glass monuments not merely as a symbolic act, but also as a means of encouraging social cohesion and spiritual renewal through spiritual transformation (Haag Bletter 1975: 90). Shortly before the *Glashaus* was completed, Taut invited Scheerbart to write sixteen poems and aphorisms celebrating glass architecture, six of which were inscribed on the walls of the pavilion. These included clever turns of phrases or childlike rhymes that verged on nonsense and were emblematic of Scheerbart's writing style, characterized by brief epigrams of descriptive clarity: "Ohne einen Glaspalast ist das Leben eine Last" (Without a glass palace, life is a burden) or: "Das Glas bringt uns die neue Zeit; Backsteinkultur tut uns nur leid" (Glass brings us the new era, brick architecture only does us harm) and "Das Ungeziefer ist nicht fein, ins Glashaus kommt es niemals rein" (Vermin is not nice, it'll never be allowed into the glass house).[19]

Although the sides of Remann's Liquid Sound Temple are not made of glass, they retain the shape of the original *Glashaus* building and have inscribed onto them verses of Scheerbart's glass architecture poetry. The hint of lights projected onto the walls evokes an effect of multi-colored transparency, as does the colored glass mandala through which one looks out into the sky and through which light of the sun and moon pours into the building. Remann, much like Taut before him, has appropriated Scheerbart's words, which describe the hope for a qualitatively different lived experience of modernity and its environment, and has turned them into an architectural phenomenon that preserves the sacredness of color, sound, and space. The experience of Remann's temple translates, and thus preserves in contemporary terms, Scheerbart's hope that this modern architecture of luminosity and color will improve people and society.

Capturing Interspecies Communication

A further inspiration for the Liquid Sound Temple grew out of a ten-day boat excursion off the Pacific northwestern coast of Canada, led by Jim Nollman in 1985, in which Remann participated. Remann hoped the experience would guarantee him breakthrough recognition in his freelance writing career with an article in *GEO*, a popular geographical magazine. Nollman is a composer of music for theater, an internationally distinguished conceptual artist, and an environmental activist with the desire to communicate with whales through music. Nollman is also the founder of Interspecies Inc, which sponsors research in human communication with animals through music and art—a gift Orpheus was said to have had. Nollman's life-long exploration involves discovering whether music is truly a universal language and hence a form of cross-species communication. His work has led him to record interspecies music with wolves, desert rats, deer, elk, whales, and dolphins. However, Nollman's best-known field project is a twenty-five-year communication study using live music to interact with wild orcas that inhabit the waters off the west coast of Canada.

Nollman does not force communication with the whales, but rather beckons them, enticing them with individual or group music, which is then amplified under water. The orcas choose whether to approach the boat. During such expeditions, nearby orcas often do. However, in the case of Remann's expedition, the whales did not approach.[20] Days passed without any sign of whales and most of the expedition's grandiose ideas about making music with whales were shattered one by one until all participants finally realized that they would most likely face disappointed expectations. At that point, a group of whales suddenly encircled their boat. Their movement around the boat illuminated the bioluminescent fish and plankton so that the water sparkled in colors. The orcas joined in their music-making, and musicians and non-musicians alike participated as best they could. The concert lasted a mere thirty minutes. Yet this musical celebration of light and sound forever changed Remann, leaving him with a sense that simply writing a magazine article would not do the experience justice.

Instead, the larger dream of Liquid Sound was born. Remann imagined what it would be like to hear music in the water as whales do. Remann jokes that he was "perfectly qualified" to create such a multimedia swimming center with an underwater speaker system, as he knew nothing about the technological aspects involved with a project of this magnitude. However, having studied German literature, he knew what poetic vision was. As he approached experts about his idea, he was repeatedly told that technically, it was simply not possible. Nonetheless, Remann finally developed an underwater light and sound experience that mirrored his visions, and he, like Scheerbart, witnessed his poetic ideas realized in architecture.

Remann's quest to preserve not only Scheerbart's vision, but also his epiphany on his expedition, is founded upon the modern tradition of erecting monuments as a means of memorialization. Remann's temple is a modern sanctuary of the sacred, meant to be experienced with the same reverence as cathedrals and houses of worship. The interiority of sacred experience is established with the effects of modern lights and sounds. One enters in silence, submerges oneself in the experience of being cocooned by luring underwater sounds under the skylights of the mandala, and soaks up the secular, yet sacred silence under the stars of his vision. As spa critic Judy Lazarus keenly observes: "What's ... cutting edge in spas is really Old World, transported from the past into the new millennium on a magic carpet of imagination, modern technology and academic investigation" (Baldwin 2004). The Liquid Sound Temple is the picture of a financially viable modern spa—thanks to good funding and a sustainable vision steeped in art. Furthermore, the success of the complete Toskanaworld project reveals how modern German spa culture continues to challenge itself not only to capitalize off its rich cultural past, but also to reconceive spa vacations in intellectually creative and valuable ways. Bad Sulza has responded successfully to the demands German unification brought. As a reinvented town in the former GDR,

Bad Sulza has gained recognition in its ability not only to bring together East and West, but also to harken back to the past, bring together disparate elements of cultural, historical, and social importance, and envision a new future. The cultural reframing of its natural environment, its brine and scenic setting, and an imagined otherworldliness, complete with the ancient oracle tradition of Epidaurus and modern multimedia and UFO-shaped buildings, have enabled it to market itself as standing apart from other small towns, spas, and tourist attractions in the region and to move beyond just a national, German-German vision of unification to answer a global need for innovation for wellness seekers.

Notes

1. Even during GDR times, most tourism to the rural areas of Thuringia was, as Coles explains, "domestic in nature" and included health tourism to spas and excursions to the mountains and lakes as common leisure and tourist activities (2003: 219). International tourism to the GDR was heavily restricted and regulated. Only heritage sites deemed worthy of attracting foreign visitors received state funding; therefore, many sites and commercial hotels in operation were in disrepair at the time of unification (Mellor 1991; Hill 1993). Translations in the following are my own unless otherwise indicated.

2. Since its inception, Bad Sulza has been featured in numerous travel, spa, and wellness magazines. For a comprehensive list, see: http://liquidsound .com/index2_fla_eng.html, accessed 2 February 2012.

3. Coles suggests there is "uneven development of tourism in the east" (2003: 221) and the new states "have enjoyed markedly different trajectories since Unification" (220).

4. To receive the designation of *Kurort* or *Heilbad,* a location must have a thermal spring on site or special atmospheric conditions with therapeutic qualities (Maretzki 1989: 25).

5. "Tuscany of the East" is a lingering touristic description of the region that refers to the countryside's gently rolling wooded hills, dark valleys and water, and many days of warm sunshine, reminiscent of Italy.

6. The European Fund for Regional Development (EFRE) subsidized the complete Toskana Therme project with DM 19 million. All pools are fed with local warm thermal saltwater from the underground Trias Sea, which enables a weightless kind of floating.

7. In 1950, the healthcare section of Wismut took over the spa facilities in Bad Sulza and further expanded them, building new bathhouses in 1959 and the sanatorium for treatment of chronic respiratory illnesses and rehabilitation, begun in 1964 and completed in 1969. These modern facilities counted among the best in the GDR and treated uranium miners, who were exposed to dangerous levels of radon and quartz (Tagliabue 1991).

8. In 1828, while visiting the city, Johann Wolfgang von Goethe recommended the brine be used for healing purposes.

9. Unification brought material advantages: over €1250 billion, primarily from the West, was invested into the eastern regions by the German government (Cooke 2005: 2).

10. The history of Bad Sulza is found on its official website: http://www.bad-sulza.de/de/node/20, accessed 2 February 2012.

11. Salve.TV consists of a regional television broadcasting station for the towns of Erfurt, Weimar, Apolda, and Arnstadt as part of the enterprise group "toskanaworld Ltd." The name Salve.TV is directly linked to Weimar's 1999 claim as *Kulturhauptstadt* (cultural capital), where Salve became its trademark. Salve.TV has received numerous distinctions for its creative and informative television and Internet pieces, including several that document aspects of the KBS Medical Spa.

12. The film is viewable at http://www.youtube.com/watch?v=6vXO2wdqVhg.

13. For more information on Asclepius, see Papadakis 1973, Tick 2001, and Houston 1996: 128–129.

14. De Vierville (2000) briefly addresses the history of bathing in his article. His workshop, "Dreams and Rituals in Healing Waters," offered annually at the Toskana Therme, draws clearer parallels between ancient dream temples and Liquid Sound: http://www.alamoplazaspa.com/training/germany/, accessed 2 February 2012.

15. For a description of the Asclepieion, see Risse 1990: 56.

16. For more information regarding the history of dream temples, see Brandon 1969.

17. Following his dismemberment by the Maenads, Orpheus's head floats downstream singing, while all of nature mourned him.

18. The English translations of Paul Scheerbart's *Glass Architecture* are by James Palmes. See Scheerbart and Taut 1972. The German original is available online: Paul Scheerbart, *Glasarchitektur* (1914), http://gutenberg.spiegel .de/buch/1752/1, accessed 2 February 2012.

19. Scheerbart's aphorisms appear in his letter to Bruno Taut of 10 February 1914 (Scheerbart 1920).

20. This account is based on personal interviews held with Remann in 2001 and 2002, in which he described the initial inspirations for Liquid Sound. His emphasis that "nothing happened" is echoed in his encouragement of newcomers to experience Liquid Sound without preconceived perceptions: "there is nothing to do, but to do nothing."

References

Baldwin, Leigh. 2004. "Necessary Hype: Three Spa Writers Talk Trends." *Experience ISPA Spa Reading.* http://www.experienceispa.com/conferences/ articles/necessary.html, accessed 2 February 2012.

Baranowski, Shelley, and Ellen Furlough, eds. 2001. *Being Elsewhere: Tourism, Consumer Culture and Identity in Modern Europe and North America.* Ann Arbor: University of Michigan Press.

Belmore, H.W. 1954. *Rilke's Craftsmanship: An Analysis of his Poetic Style.* Oxford: Basil Blackwell.

Berendt, Joachim-Ernst. 1987. *The World is Sound: Nada Brahma.* Rochester, V.T.: Destiny Books.

Brandon, S.G.F. 1969. *Religion in Ancient History.* New York: Scribner.

Bundesministerium für Wirtschaft und Technologie, (BMWI). 2000. *Tourismus in Deutschland.* Magdeburg: Gebr. Garloff GmbH.

Coles, Tim. 2003. "The Emergent Tourism Industry in Eastern Germany a Decade After Unification." *Tourism Management.* 24 (2): 217–226.

Coles, Tim E., and Dallen J. Timothy, eds. 2004. *Tourism, Diasporas and Space.* London and New York: Routledge.

Cooke, Paul. 2005. *Representing East Germany Since Unification: From Colonization to Nostalgia.* Oxford: Bloomsbury Academic.

Curl, James Stevens. 2000. "Scheerbart, Paul." *A Dictionary of Architecture and Landscape Architecture.* Oxford: Oxford University Press, 684.

de Vierville, Jonathan. 2000. "Taking the Waters: A Historical Look at Water Therapy and Spa Culture Over the Ages." *Massage & Bodywork* (February/ March). http://www.massagetherapy.com/articles/index.php/article_id/ 323/Taking-the-Waters, accessed 2 February 2012.

Firman-Pitt, Sara. 2001. "Spa Culture and the Soulful Life." *Spas.About.com Articles.* http://spas.about.com/library/weekly/aa071501a.htm, accessed 2 February 2012.

———. 2008. "Between Two Waves: The German-Ozark Connection." http:// www.waterjourneys.net/html/between.html. Also under Goethe's legacy for water and spa, http://www.visionsparetreat.com/2008/09/goethes-leg acy.html, accessed 2 February 2012.

Freud, Sigmund. (1930) 2010. *Civilization and Its Discontents,* Complete Psychological Works of Sigmund Freud Series, translated by J. Strachey. London: W.W. Norton & Company.

Gardner, Kay. 1990. *Sounding the Inner Landscape.* Stonington, M.E.: Caduceus Publications.

Haag Bletter, Rosmarie. 1975. "Paul Scheerbart's Architectural Fantasies." *Journal of the Society of Architectural Historians* 34 (2): 83–97.

Hall, Derek R. 1998. "Central and Eastern Europe: Tourism, Development and Transformation." In *Tourism and Economic Development. European Experiences,* edited by Allan M. Williams and Gareth Shaw, 345–374. Chichester, UK: Wiley.

Hill, R. 1993. "Tourism in Germany." In *Tourism in Europe: Structures and Developments,* edited by Wilhelm Pompl and Patrick Lavery, 219–241. Wallingford: CAB International.

Houston, Jean. 1996. *A Mythic Life: Learning to Live Our Greater Story.* New York: HarperCollins.

Krutsch, Peter. "Intendant in Badelatschen." *Leipziger Volkszeitung Wochenend-Journal.* 10 January 2003. http://www.mickyremann.com/lvz.htm, accessed 2 February 2012.

MacCannell, Dean. 1989. *The Tourist: A New Theory of the Leisure Class.* New York: Schocken Books.

Maerten, Renate. 2001. "Studying Liquid Sound: How 'Bathing in Light and Music' Can Change Your Mind. And Your Spa, too." *Spa Management* (September): 66–69.

Maretzki, Thomas W. 1989. "Cultural Variation in Biomedicine: The *Kur* in West Germany." *Medical Anthropology Quarterly, New Series* 3 (1): 22–35.

Masson, David. 1951. "Patterns of Vowel and Consonant in a Rilkean Sonnet." *The Modern Language Review* 46: 419–430.

McGahey, Robert. 1994. *The Orpheus Moment: Shaman to Poet-Thinker in Plato, Nietzsche, and Mallarmé.* Albany: State University of New York Press.

Mellor, Roy E. H. 1991. "Eastern Germany (The Former German Democratic Republic)." In *Tourism and Economic Development in Eastern Europe and the Soviet Union,* edited by Derek R. Hall, 142–153. London: Bellhaven Press.

Middleton, Christopher. 1998. "Mallarmé, Rilke, and the Orphic Trace." *Revue Po&sie* 85: 148–158.

Naraindas, Harish. 2011. "Of Relics, Body Parts and Laser Beams: The German Heilpraktiker and his Ayurvedic Spa." *Anthropology and Medicine* 18 (1): 67–86.

Nollman, Jim. 2002. *The Man Who Talks to Whales: The Art of Interspecies Communication.* Boulder, C.O.: Sentient Publications.

Papadakis, Theodore. 1973. *Epidauros: The Sanctuary of Aesclepios.* Munich: Verlag Schnell and Steiner.

Przybyszewski, Stanislaw. 1965. *Erinnerungen an das literarische Berlin.* Munich: Winkler.

Rilke, Rainer Maria. (1919) 1978. "Primal Sound" (Ur-Geräusch). In *Where Silence Reigns: Selected Prose.* Translated by G. Craig, 51–56. Houston and New York: New Directions Publishing.

———. 1989. *The Selected Poetry of Rainer Maria Rilke.* Translated by Stephen Mitchell. New York: Vintage.

———. 1998. *The Duino Elegies and the Sonnets to Orpheus.* Translated by Stephen Mitchell. New York: New Directions Publishing.

Risse, Guenter B. 1999. *Mending Bodies, Saving Souls: A History of Hospitals.* Oxford: Oxford University Press.

Scheerbart, Paul. 1914. *Glasarchitektur (1914).* http://gutenberg.spiegel.de/buch/1752/1, accessed 2 February 2012.

———. 1920. "Glashausbriefe," *Frühlicht,* supplement of Stadtbaukunst 3: 45–48.

Scheerbart, Paul, and Bruno Taut. 1972. *Glass Architecture and Alpine Architecture,* edited by Dennis Sharp, translated by James Palmes. New York: November Books Limited.

Sewell, Elizabeth. 1971. *The Orphic Voice: Poetry and Natural History.* New York: Harper and Row.

Tagliabue, John. 1991. "A Legacy of Ashes: The Uranium Mines Of Eastern Germany" *The New York Times,* 19 March. http://www.nytimes.com/1991/

03/19/news/a-legacy-of-ashes-the-uranium-mines-of-eastern-germany .html, accessed 2 February 2012.

Thornton, Fiona, and Hans Brutscher. 2001. "What is a Spa? Historical Background and Modern Influences." http://web.archive.org/web/20050921 171546/http://spas.about.com/library/weekly/aa070801.htm, accessed 15 July 2013.

Tick, Edward. 2001. *The Practice of Dream Healing: Bringing Ancient Greek Mysteries into Modern Medicine.* Wheaton, I.L.: Quest Books.

Tomatis, Alfred. 1991. *The Conscious Ear: My Life of Transformation Through Listening.* New York: Station Hill Press.

Walker, Barbara. 1983. *The Woman's Encyclopedia of Myths and Secrets.* San Francisco: HarperCollins.

Weisz, G. 2001. *Spas, Mineral Waters, and Hydrological Science in Twentieth-Century France.* Isis 92 (3): 451–483.

Williams, Allan M., and Vladimir Balaz. 2000. *Tourism in Transition: Economic Change in Central Europe.* London: I.B. Tauris.

✣· Chapter 5 ·✣

Berlin through the Lens

Space and (National) Identity
in the Postunification Capital

SUSANNA MILLER, JENNIFER RUTH HOSEK,
TAMARA NADOLNY, HEIDI MANICKE,
FLAVIA ZAKA, TREVOR BLAKENEY,
AND JUDE HIRMAN

The twentieth anniversary of the fall of the Berlin Wall was publicly celebrated in many ways. Most of these events naturalized the triumph of capitalism—read as democracy—and suggested a linear path toward a united nation and people. Yet, geographical, social, and cultural unification did not match the political. In Berlin, divisions reside in streets and construction sites, housing complexes and affluent homes, and in cinema.

The long history of nation-building through film is well known, and the notion of city as metonymy for nation is not new. Yet, the Berlin urban imaginary is a salient case in point. Following on Weimar and the Third Reich as they did, the postwar Germanies had well-developed film traditions (Meurer 2000). Their governments recognized the importance of movies in the articulation of cultural identities (Feinstein 2002; Poiger 2000). During the era of peaceful coexistence, East and West German filmmaking received considerable financial and institutional support through the Deutsche Film-Aktiengesellschaft (DEFA, the state-run film studio of the German Democratic Republic, GDR) and the Filmförderungsanstalt (German Federal Film Board, film agency of the Federal Republic of Germany, FRG), respectively. The 1980s and 1990s saw a shift in the funding landscape in relation to political changes, resulting in, for example, filmic Berlin being articulated through box offices successes and through what came to be dubbed "Europudding" cinema for its representation of shiny, happy similarity across the member states (Bomnüter and Scheller 2009; Halle 2008; Rentschler 2000).

These political and cultural histories are engendering Berlin's multiple relationships to film today. Increasingly, the reinstated German capital and aspiring *Medienhauptstadt* (media capital) features festivals and competitions, funding, and moviemaking infrastructure. Results include quantifiables such as film sales and new investment in media and less measurable correlates such as increases in cultural, human, and material capital, for instance in the form of urban renewal, new residents, and visitors (Hosek 2010). The success of the movie industry at marketing the city has translated into blockbuster-style productions meant for international mainstream consumption as well as independent works meant for domestic audiences and cinema scholars. Since the mid-1990s, Berlin has not only been competing with Hamburg and Munich as German, European, and global film mecca, but has also increasingly become home to and subject of Berlin-specific film (Halle 2006).

Achtung Berlin!—New Berlin Film Award (AB) is at the forefront of this growth of Berlin film and Berlin in film. Begun in 2005, the annual series presents contemporary films with links to Berlin and Brandenburg. These connections may be financial, for instance, regional stipends or other funding, or geographic—the city or region must be the headquarters of the production company or the place of residence of at least one producer or director. If none of these conditions are met, then the work must feature recognizable, local screening locations. The latter criterion is intriguingly overdetermined, due to its definitional instability; for instance, what comes across as recognizably "Berlin" depends greatly on the familiarity of the jury and the audience with the city (Schäfer 2010).

AB and its showpiece, the Made in Berlin-Brandenburg competition, have always presented support of the new capital region as their raison d'être. The festival receives sustained support from the mayor and culture minister, Klaus Wowereit, as well as from city coffers.[1] That AB's mandate is so explicit, pragmatic, and locally focused may seem surprising in comparison with other European film traditions, in which capitals have long and uninterruptedly been central to each national cinema. Yet, the representation of Germany on film and furtherance of German film had traditionally been handled rather modestly in West Germany, for both financial and historical reasons. Germany's Berlinale film festival had provided an excellent example of such reserve toward overtly Germanophilic cinema; since unification, this premiere international festival has gradually been following a similar course to that of AB. Officially antifascist, East Germany had no such ideological limitations, but other political and financial constraints shaped its scope.

In 1951, the occupying U.S. military government founded the Berlinale as a "Showcase of the Free World," with its primary venue, the movie theater Zoo Palast, in Charlottenburg, the luxurious heart of West Berlin. From 1979 to 2001, under the direction of the Swiss Moritz de Hadeln, the festival allowed limited space for films made in Germany, by Germans, and/or about German themes. German director Dieter Kosslick inaugurated *perspektive deutsches kino* (Perspective: German Film), a section aimed at integrating more German works, particularly those of young filmmakers, into the festival. The Berlinale's new geographical centering speaks to the increased profiling of Germany as well. Its most representative events take place at the new Potsdamer Platz, a square upon which the Wall between East and West once stood, and that now represents German consumer culture and economic strength.[2] More evidence of the active promotion of German movies is the new iteration of LOLA@Berlinale, part of the concurrent European Film Market program. In 2012, the Berlinale and Glashütte Original are also beginning a "Made in Germany—Perspektive Fellowship" for German directors, which will address the concern that so few can continue to find funding for their work past their second or third release.

Thus, both AB and, increasingly, the Berlinale showcase German film in the wake of unification and of what is often called German normalization, a rethinking of history that sees Nazi actions as part of a now ostensibly worked-through past and in relation to the atrocities of other polities. AB's West German creators and *Wahl-Berliner* (Berliners-by-Choice), Hajo Schäfer and Sebastian Brose, embody this new consciousness in their eagerness to create an event that addresses what they see as an inappropriate lack of German content in Berlin's festivals. The Berlinale and AB differ in size, scope, and prestige; their thematic difference is that the latter focuses on Berlin as uniquely luminous in the German constellation, both in its role as a new-old capital that metonymizes Germany and as a microcosm in its own right. The movies shown in AB illuminate this new national space as few other cultural forms.

With the aim of reading city space in AB films, we worked with Hajo Schäfer to select twelve films that feature Berlin as a protagonist. These works depict internationally, nationally, and overwhelmingly locally known urban sites in multifaceted ways and in varied relation to the protagonists. Careful viewings and heated debates often extending far beyond regularly scheduled class time yielded our analysis of the multifaceted representation of the new Berlin in these films, a reading that seeks to account for interpretations among AB's largely Berlin-centered audiences. As our interest in the multidirectional dialectics between filmic Berlin and its protagonists and between urban spaces and experiences grew, we sought the perspectives of urban thinkers such as Georg Simmel and Edward Soja, whose theories resonated with the concerns that drive these films.

We asked ourselves: would Simmel consider AB's urban space a *Großstadt* (metropolis), with all of its attendant attributes and impacts? "Die Großstädte und das Geistesleben," ("The Metropolis and Mental Life") famously considers how space affects the mental states and practices of its dwellers (Simmel 1903). Simmel's metropolis is marked by money economies, strict, formal schedules, autonomy, and instrumentalization. The interaction between the "social-technological mechanism" of this impersonal environment and its inhabitants engenders struggle (Simmel 1950). Individual urban dwellers respond to such environments by creating what are lived as unique identities in what could be experienced as urban uniformity and mechanization. Simmel's "great historical formation" is the city, whose "peculiar condition" engages this deepest dialectical tension of modern life most saliently. Edward Soja's work interacts with Simmel's city, casting it as modern ground par excellence. Notable here is Soja's notion of synekism—"the stimulus of urban agglomeration"—a force arising in concentrated, massed heterogeneity that shapes human development to dynamic effect (Soja 2003: 6). Celebrated crucible for art, culture, and creativity, this same geography also forges inequities (Soja 2010).

Alternatively, should we consider the Berlin of these films as more of a *Kleinstadt* (small town)? In Simmel's *Kleinstadt*, the "rhythm of life and sensory mental imagery flows more slowly, more habitually, and more evenly" (Simmel 1950: 410). Unlike in the *Großstadt*, everyone is acquainted with one another and identity is defined relationally within rather narrow parameters. There is no need to develop intellect or other individual characteristics or skills as weapons in order to cultivate and defend individuality. Here, order is practiced through commonly acknowledged and agreed upon material, social interactions, not through punching the factory timecard. The continued robust existence of these norms demonstrates their popular acceptance, generally under conditions shaped primarily by the more dominant community members. There is no particular gain for a radically individual personality in the small town, because clearly defined standard roles exist by which each troupe player is known and somehow accepted as long as they play along. These very roles enable the immediate understandings intrinsic to relationships. The *Kleinstadt* is a setting for emotional connections, where the heart takes precedence over the head.

While Simmel and Soja have much to offer our analysis with regard to the dialectics of space and identity, neither adequately describes the new capital as seen in and through AB films, in which Berlin is neither entirely *Großstadt* nor entirely *Kleinstadt*. Therefore, we propose the term *Dorf* (village) to suggest a hybrid notion of urban *Kleinstadt* that also draws upon the long-standing trope of *Berlin als Dorf* (Berlin as Village) common in popular idiom. *Dorf* has a slightly self-deprecating valence in this phrase as uttered by Berlin inhabitants, a valence that recognizes the limitations inherent in provincial, inwardly focused attitudes (Poschardt 2010). The term is judgmentally descriptive and/or analytic, rather than geographically specific, which reflects the diverse mixture of *Wahl-Berliner* who arrived primarily from small- to medium-size towns in southern Germany after 1990. In contrast, the term *Kiez* (or *Kietz*), a word for neighborhood unique to Berlin, could describe Berlin's actual infrastructure as shown in these films in the sense that these geographically circumscribed urban spaces are seemingly self-contained and independent. However, *Kiez* is inadequate as an analytic term for our filmic Berlin, because although it implies a common social reference system linked to a geographic space, it also connotes a de facto openness toward social difference that careful analysis demonstrates lacking in these films. While their Berlin might style itself a *Kiez*, upon closer examination we find *Dorf* more accurate.

Our term draws on Simmel's *Kleinstadt* by incorporating its tradition of affective relations while simultaneously highlighting the contradictory practices of openness within and blindness toward its geographic and demographic monoculture. We see these practices as legitimated by a notion that we are calling operative heterogeneity, which we describe further below. In addition, our term *Dorf* springs from common usage, in turn based on precisely situated geographies and social roles in the new Berlin. German unification is frequently heralded as unproblematic, yet our analysis of these filmic narratives reveals another story. A façade of unity hides landscapes of privilege and niches of survival shaped by the interplay of space and identity. By plotting spatial access in relation to mobility, elective subculture, privatization, and otherness, we show that while the Berlin of these films often plays an idealized *Kiez*, its exclusionary self-absorption is better described with recourse to our conception of *Dorf*. We further suggest that, seen as a national metonymy, the *Dorf* is a notion that buttresses uncritical mainstream unification narratives and feeds into traditional ideas of Germanness.

Flâneuring Mobility: (Un)limited Access to Urban Spaces

Whereas mobility often marks dislocation, necessity, and want, it is enabled by and characterizes privilege in most of the AB films. Generally defined as rights, advantages, or immunities granted to a person or group of persons, privilege here is accorded by certain dominant demographic categories, such as male, white, of Christian background, native German-speaking, and formally educated. The mobility in question is captured in the figure of the flâneur, that Baudelarian-Benjaminian detached, privileged viewer with a curious eye who establishes short term connections with all that he sees as he wanders through the city streets (Frisby 1994). This unique combination of looking and moving—*flânerie*—is a frequently represented practice in AB films. Walkers, bicyclists, and even the audience itself play the role, passing fluidly through and fleetingly partaking of the cityscape. These characters benefit from the privilege concretized in their mobility as they redraw the sprawling capital as a *Dorf*, free from urban pressures and dangers.

Austern Ohne Schale (Oysters Without Shells, 2009) features best friends Mia and Jules, who are emotionally and psychically restrained by a fluid interplay of hopes, fears, and disappointments. *Flânerie* gives structure and purpose to their days and nights. The two wander arm in arm in the streets of their neighborhood, Prenzlauer Berg, without concern for time or safety. Privilege is both catalyst for and enabler of their movement. They are visually marked as sufficiently monied, white, educated, able-bodied, and attractive, all community-defining characteristics of the prime demographic of this trendy quarter. Intense urban renewal has characterized Prenzlauer Berg since 1990, gentrification seen in high-end renovations of late-nineteenth-century apartment buildings into condominiums; skyrocketing rents; and installations of upscale consumer locales such as eateries, boutiques, and pet-project art galleries. Statistically speaking, its inhabitants are some of the whitest, most highly formally educated, and most reproductively active in Germany; underemployment is high and living standards are often supported by private Western German family funds.[3]

The young women move in a filmic vision of this quarter that highlights what remains of the bohème and the seedy. They pass and frequent modestly renovated buildings and homey, unique commercial sites that characterize the seemingly protected, noncompetitive, neighborhood-oriented places that mark Prenzlauer Berg as *Dorf*. These youngish inhabitants are the human embodiment of and symbiotic with this Berlin space. Disciplined not by the working grind, but by practices of belonging, Mia and Jules spend their time delighting in café outings and diversionary display-case trinkets in a modern interpretation of the strolling figure in Benjamin's Paris arcades. These characters produce nothing, consume little, and seem uninfluenced by the personality-shaping economic and social discourses of the city and its other dwellers.

Jules and Mia embody and practice freedoms impossible in both the city and the *Kleinstadt*; rather, it is in the *Dorf* of *Austern* that these protagonists symbolically own the streets. Benjamin's flâneur is assumed male, and feminist analysis has long articulated dangers that limit access to public spaces (Feministisches Kollektiv 2008). Jules and Mia's liberty is enabled by a filmically produced *Dorf* geography. Although Prenzlauer Berg is intimately connected, both historically and physically, to the larger city that surrounds it, the turf of these flâneurs is visually and aurally separated from the city. There are no establishing shots of powerful, mysterious skylines, no distant takes of the shiny, internationally known television tower at the famous square, Alexanderplatz. *Austern*'s Berlin is glimpsed in the time-worn cobblestones pounded by their stilettos, in eye-level, medium-range tracking and tightly filmed reaction shots in the familiar people-sized surroundings of sidewalks, shops, cafés, and *Imbiss* (small, fast food establishments).[4]

The filmic disconnect from the larger geography of the capital expresses itself in the practices and attitudes of the characters. At ease in their familiar environs, the young women seem to imagine no danger in pursuing and being pursued on the streets. They connect to strangers with an ease of emotionality unexpected in the metropolis. For example, at loose ends in the early hours of a morning, the young women begin chatting with a young man seated at one of the ubiquitous wooden tables of a late-night *Imbiss,* a scene which smoothly transitions into a cozy threesome in Jules and Mia's nearby apartment. The male character then fades from the plot. During another scene that ambivalently connotes community-wide trust on one hand and street sex work on the other, one of the protagonists takes a ride from a man she does not know who rolls to a stop next to her. While the openness, directness, and intimacy of potentially dangerous interactions such as these put the young women at odds with big city standards, their relatively impersonal fluidity, spontaneity, and eccentricity would be unacceptable in the *Kleinstadt*, which furthers normativity. Neither the rules of the metropolis nor the time-tested standards of the small town shape their practices as they move smoothly among lovers and friends in public and private, real and imagined spaces, all on a flexible time schedule. *Austern*'s protagonists live and create Berlin as *Dorf* through their *flânerie* enabled by their particular and unarticulated privilege.

Marcus Lenz's darker, gritty take on the flâneur in *Close* (2005) re-lies on *Dorf* logics to lend credibility to its narrative. The transient and jobless Jost takes from others what the absence of privilege has not af-forded him. His lack of property and authority bother him, as exempli-fied by his demand to keep the lighter lent to him by a security guard and the violent scuffle that predictably ensues. While wandering on foot in the city, he finds himself in what looks to be a newly gentrifying part of northeastern Prenzlauer Berg. The scaffolding on a building provides Jost easy access, which at first suggests that dangers inhere in the radi-cal makeovers of this urban site. Yet, the characters of *Close* inhabit a Berlin where, prompted by a knock on the window, a stranger is not only welcomed into private spaces but into beds, a Berlin in which the pros-pect of sharing a drink with a former mugger barely merits hesitation. Jost engages with the fragile recluse Anna in a manner that blurs the line between home invasion and romance, and this violent engagement ends up reconnecting Anna to the world outside her apartment. In this Berliner *Dorf*, actual danger does not exist as it would in the city. This is not a *Kleinstadt*, for Jost's utter rebellion against the social order would be unacceptable there. In these films, Berlin's possibilities for diverse life practices and what Zygmunt Bauman might term liquid mobility suggest a metropolis, while the emotional and intimate proximity among inhab-itants and environment and the safe, familiar surroundings conjure a small town (Bauman 2005).

In these ways, perambulation enables intimate and multifaceted ac-cess to the city; flâneuring by bicycle is a similarly vital practice, as seen in the romantic comedy *Der Letzte macht das Licht aus!* (The Last One Out Turns Out the Light!, 2007), the documentary, *Sieben Tage im Leben meiner Freunde* (Seven Days in the Lives of My Friends, 2005), and the feature *Netto* (2005).[5] For instance, *Der Letzte* follows a group of East-erners, construction workers unemployed since the fall of the Wall, who are brought together by a work-placement program that prepares them for jobs in Norway. These characters possess more privilege than con-struction workers of the global South and less than higher-class white Germans. They can access spaces inhabited by the latter through two-wheeled mobility.

Bicycling also allows Eastern and/or impoverished characters com-mand over the expansive geography of Berlin. In *Der Letzte*, rides are effortless, even when bicyclists pass widely spaced city landmarks in mo-ments. The many AB viewers familiar with Berlin's landscape would un-derstand that these trips would take hours in real time; this is not just a pragmatic editing technique but an active suturing of the city, perhaps incorporating a neorealist nod to Tom Tykwer's *Lola Rennt* (Run Lola

Run, 1998). With the capital shrunk to a more manageable size, areas dominated by the privileged are accessible to these East German characters. In *Der Letzte,* a focused Silvio navigates across the city in minutes, allowing him to catch his girlfriend at a Charlottenburg bus station in the West without breaking a sweat. In *Sieben Tage,* one artsy-alternative couple pedals from deep in what was West Berlin along a lightly trafficked and expansive Unter den Linden boulevard all the way to Prenzlauer Berg on ancient bicycles, making record time at an effortless snail's pace. Moreover, pedal-powered transport furthers extensive interactions between characters and their urban surroundings. Bicyclists do not move through a lonely, sprawling city dictated by pocket watches, strict appointments, and regimented movement. Although their liminal existences may be curtailed by inadequate economic resources and sometimes by Easternness, when on two wheels, these protagonists live in a privileged, comfortable, and geographically accessible *Dorf.*

A subjective camera sometimes places the audience in the role of flâneur through first-person access to the lives of the inhabitants. Mimicking the traditional roving human spectator, this electronic eye flits effortlessly from one subject to the next. The *flâneurie* of *Neun Szenen* (Nine Scenes, 2006) juxtaposes stasis and mobility in a manner that emphasizes *Dorf* interconnectivity. Seven of the scenes are single-take and shot with a completely static camera. Out of at first seemingly unrelated vignettes, a larger plotline begins to emerge about relatively insignificant tensions between older and younger generations whose members are otherwise relatively similar. The tales, which are told statically when the camera is indoors, come together climatically near the end through the eye of a highly mobile handheld camera that follows the characters at close range as they meet and disperse outdoors in Prenzlauer Berg's beloved Weinberg park. The indoor takes allow the audience full-shot access to the private lives of these Berg inhabitants. And it is when a freely flâneuring camera ranges across the open, safe, equally accessible space of the park that these individual sketches are pulled into a bigger picture of shared and meaningful, if unspectacular, *Dorf* life.

Audience takeover of the subjective, flâneuring camera exemplifies the tendency of these films to legitimate the *Dorf*'s homogeneity. While AB has become the second largest Berlin-based film festival, it remains primarily a local phenomenon.[6] Its audience is relatively affluent or has access to family wealth. They are white, youngish Berlin inhabitants with cultural capital who are (being) educated and identify as the creative class and against commodity fetishism. Frequently inhabiting Prenzlauer Berg, they generally hail from the Western Germany. Their demographic characteristics and life practices echo those of many AB filmmakers and the sympathetic protagonists in AB films. Viewer privilege mirrors filmic privilege. Seeing themselves in the lives of characters such as those of *Neun Szenen,* audiences legitimize their focus on and membership in the privileged *Dorf.* Critically, this *Dorf* is presented as so diverse and complex, so emotionally charged and intellectually stimulating as to be a world in itself; there is no need to engage beyond it. These films help to engender deep, multifaceted connections between identity and space in their viewers. They not only belong in Berlin; they are Berlin.

All three examples of *flânerie*—the strolling and bicycling of characters and the camera/viewer as active spectator—rearticulate space in the capital. Leveraging privilege available on the basis of participation in dominant class, ethnicity, creed, age, and other categories, characters and viewers use movement and observation to create yet more license in the form of the *Dorf.* Walkers are symbolically free of the confines of both political and social rules, namely wealth-based hierarchies, sexual norms, and disciplining features of property and authority. The bicycle aids in shrinking the whole city to the proportions of a *Dorf* in which access is easy. The camera pulls viewers into the *Dorf* and solidifies its standard of privilege and homogeneity as seemingly diverse. With membership in this de facto elite club, identificatory characters and viewers create their new Berlin in this unspectacular, nonmonumental, person-sized, daily-life oriented, but not truly affordable or accessible neighborhood space.

Elective Subcultures: Privileged Rebellions in the *Dorf*

Thus, these films deal in homogeneity disguised as heterogeneity. Perhaps because this narrative logic recalls dominant consumer and political domestication of difference, it is surprising that AB's Berlin as *Dorf* nevertheless contests Berlin as modern northern capital shaped of, by, and for the rich and famous. AB films reject dominant, market-driven images of the contemporary urban center, presenting the city as a site of counterculture instead. Careful assessment of characters engaged in such activities reveals that privilege is necessary to access this counterculture. Yet these narratives challenge what are generally understood as determining features of urban life by undercutting the notion of technology as *sine qua non* and by framing the ascendance of market-driven urban planning as an assault on authentic culture.

Technology has long been a defining feature of the urban world. Instantaneous telecommunication is only one of the ways that distance seems to have been overcome in what David Harvey calls space-time

compression (Harvey 2006). Such shifts have changed how people relate, for in the networked society, individuals are (to be) constantly connected.[7] Information technology is reputed to have altered the nature
of capitalism; no longer characterized by mass production of goods, the
"new" capitalism relies instead on informational goods, signs, and symbols (Geyh 2009). Efforts to increase consumer demand have produced
marketing itself as a major urban industry without not-in-my-backyard
backlash.

Although forms of technological modernity are ever more thickly
connecting people and cities, they are rarely depicted in AB films and
never without critique.[8] *Sieben Tage* follows the lives of seven ostensibly
diverse characters looking for meaning and rootedness in contemporary
Berlin, their lives focused around the *Dorf* of Prenzlauer Berg. The near
total absence of technology comments on its very ubiquity. Whether at
home, work, in public or private realms, these figures emanate a self-
sufficiency that renders technology redundant. Most indoor scenes are
staged with a minimalist aesthetic; a glimpse of the electronic equipment of a musician is surprising because unique and yet quickly fades
in importance, because for him these are simply tools unworthy of verbal or visual focus. In a time in which smaller and faster seems directly
correlated with better, the presence of a personal computer built in the
1980s or 1990s, perhaps incapable of instant connectivity, speaks for the
viability of a very different lifestyle.

In complementary contrast, *Auf Nummer Sicher* (Hedging Bets, 2008)
focuses on technologies of (spatial) control in a dystopian near future.
Berlin inhabitants enthusiastically have computer chips implanted to increase their connectivity to the web of flowing information that helps
form the urban landscape. Cameras and sensors grant the government
and corporations omnipresent access, disciplining by means of panop-
ticon. The geographical hot spots of control in the narrative represent
precisely these powers. Scenes are shot at the governmental buildings
along the bend of the Spree River and near the Brandenburg Gate, in
offices at the Media Spree corporate/consumer park, and at the newest
central nightlife locations. Counterculture is impossible even were it to
seem desirable, and resistance, not to mention rebellion, is futile. Rather
than aiding in the creation of a connected society, the chip primarily
functions to weed out undesirables; technology hierarchizes and divides.

Another countercultural critique against the new modern capital targets urban planning based in purely economic logics. What in many films
is dismissal and symbolic avoidance of market structures becomes the
depiction of an active struggle in *SubBerlin* (2009). This documentary

chronicles the story of one of Berlin's most legendary nightclubs. Tresor's birth and growth are portrayed as a profoundly organic process. The documentary frames the inception of the club as a serendipitous event, led by instinct, not meticulous calculation. Former club visitors, workers, and owners tell of DJs coming from all over Germany and the world to participate in and support the countercultural space: a transnational flow of non-alienated labor. Those engaged in the project were from diverse backgrounds: grassroots East-West and transnational unification on symbolically democratic, even anarchic terms. The club is presented as a site of true postmodernity, its parent owners having planted the seed and watching as *Dorf* members embraced and furthered the heterogeneous life that grew.

In contrast, Tresor's death is presented as far from organic. The film opens and closes with a menacing wrecking ball bearing down on its walls. The once-empty meeting ground that for a time nourished Tresor's robust existence has become a central site in the middle of the city near the ongoing reconstruction of the commercially important Potsdamer Platz, which had been destroyed during World War II and which had lain barren for decades as part of the no man's land between the two Berlins. Market-driven property values eventually preclude favored access to those relatively less privileged. The filmic Tresor perpetually embodies a martyred *Dorf* based on diverse human interaction, not capitalism or consumerism. While Tresor indeed made way for bigger business, the documentary makes no mention of the reopening of the club, meticulously recreated to capture the original atmosphere, this time available for private parties. Nor does it tell of the evolution of the Tresor brand, to include a website, peddling merchandise as well as promoting their record label (Tresor Berlin Official Website). *SubBerlin* consistently distances the utopian urban *Dorf* it depicts from the organizing logics of profitmaking and privilege. From one perspective this logic is compelling, yet even the first Tresor depended on the latter, for dancing until dawn is a practice of luxury for most urban dwellers.

The countercultures in *Sieben Tage* and *SubBerlin* are driven by empowered characters who restrain the embrace of extreme technology and who identify outside of the hierarchy defined by extreme capital and the spaces that it delimits. *Auf Nummer Sicher* articulates a similar critique by presenting an urban dystopia birthed by unbridled market-driven technology. Through distinct processes of volitional erasure, these films create or suggest a *Dorf* distanced from modernity for modernity's sake, that contrasts starkly with a Berlin, in which on every corner the next shiny invention vies for purchase. In such ways, AB films overtly proclaim that the *Dorf* and its inhabitants are instead about human contact and authentic lifestyles, yet these subculture lifestyles are also buttressed by privilege that is concretized in geography.

Privat(izing) Spaces: Transportation and Housing

In the examples above, privilege enables shared geographies of political, intellectual, and creative freedom and catalyzes emotional connection. The filmic *Dorf* reinforces a particular Prenzlauer Berg inhabited by those who, as it turns out upon close examination, have inherited license rather than having actively struggled for their certain degree of it. The heterogeneity of the neighborhood is mythic. Belonging to the GDR in recent history, the Berg that these films cite is also home to those lacking privilege, yet insiders and outsiders inhabit parallel worlds. These simultaneous lives are thematized in a few of the films through motorized transportation and housing. Mobility and spatial privatization function as barometers of social equity, as well as municipal and even national unity.

The mass implementation of public transportation in Berlin that began in the 1870s revolutionized the way inhabitants moved through space and brought with it a platform for human interaction and cultural development that continues today. AB films recognize this interaction between public mobility and *Dorf* creation. While these films exhibit a striking dearth of positive representations of monumental sites, that quintessential landmark, the Berlin light rail system, is the most meaningful exception. In *Die Helden aus der Nachbarschaft* (Heroes of the Neighborhood, 2008), Easterners and Westerners are always divided except when using the trains and trams. Niko, the son of privileged Westerners now residing in gentrified Prenzlauer Berg, and Easterner Attila both ride public transit not out of desire but necessity; Niko is too young to drive and Attila presumably too poor. Despite their ambivalence toward such modes of transportation, in this shared public realm the characters grow and learn from one another. They develop mutual understandings through their short conversations, generated as they participate in this space in which they are valued as social equals.

The two symbolize an ideal development of East-West relationships in larger Germany and the effects of this connectivity are robust. Niko rides the Ring-Bahn—touted concretization of German unification in mass transit form[9]—to Café Keese in Western Berlin, where he spontaneously rescues Attila's shy East German girlfriend, Rosine, from the pranks of his privileged, Western friends. In public spaces of transport, empathies are forged through brief shared moments among Berlin inhabitants who usually inhabit parallel worlds in much the same geography. Such common transport can expand the largely invisible confines of the *Dorf* by furthering connections across privilege.

The flip of connections afforded by public transit is the disconnectedness furthered by increased privatization of quotidian space. If public transportation is cultural stimulus, AB films show how new trends of private mobility further cultural decline. Wealthy citizens such as Niko's parents are almost exclusively depicted in contained, private spaces, controlled environments allowing only constricted experiences and loose social bonds (Wray 2008: 64). These characters do not inhabit the street, the café, or the grocery store. They access the city in private automobiles to retain what they perceive as cultural and economic capital. In commodity-driven societies, shabby public transportation has the potential to lower the symbolic worth of its riders (Jeschke 1997). In privately owned vehicles, characters control their image by controlling their environment.

For the overtly privileged, private living spaces are also critical expressions of their parallel *Dorf.* In *Helden,* the curtains of wealthy homes are drawn, avoiding any involvement with people outside their class or circle. Housed in blocks organized in the Berlin courtyard system, their apartments look onto the street in front and onto the more modest quarters across and to either side of the courtyard in back. Their closed mien contrasts with that of the Easterners living in the back courtyard apartments. The uncovered windows that display Attila metonymize privacy as a privilege, an ideology, and of limited value. The open manner in which the eastern characters live may be objectified into spectacle, but, in contrast to the isolation of the wealthy Westerners, this practice furthers deep connections to their environment. *Helden* unsettles the status of the *Dorf* of privilege by suggesting the value of heterogeneity and the stickiness of interpersonal connections, for it is those of less privilege, the Easterners in particular, whose relationships have complexity and affective longevity.

Separation in private, proximate worlds is also critiqued in films such as *Der Letzte* and the ironic narrative manifesto *Sprit* (Gas 2009). In the former, Norbert has purchased a house in the Berlin suburbs and a car, as did so many East Germans with savings freshly converted into DM after the fall of the Wall. This desire for private, privileged space has been theorized in relation to the American Dream: "For the first time in history, a civilization created a utopian ideal based on the house rather than on the city or nation"; this ideal is an aggregation of millions of private dreams that seemingly bear no relationship to each other (Wray 2008:

63). The materialistic individualism expressed through the ownership of freestanding, private living space is shown even more frequently in these films through the car. The mobility of the privately owned vehicle means that the control, security, and status of the dream home can be ever-present.

In *Sprit*, automotive mobility becomes a fetish; masculinity is equated with car ownership, virility with a full tank. Kai's life is driven by his addiction in a time of depleted oil reserves when gasoline costs seven Euros per liter. Everything important to Kai runs on premium unleaded—his car, his job as a mechanic, and even his relationship with girlfriend Maja. His mobility is sexualized through and through; his relationships with Maja and his car are intertwined in numerous cruising scenes, while an involuntary bicycle ride leaves him pallid and emasculated. His increasing obsession and his social alienation are cast in sexual registers. While stealing fuel, Kai stumbles upon a couple making love in a car. In contrast, scenes in which he transfers stolen gasoline recall masturbation. Kai's lonely vision is driven by being unable to fill up and culminates in a vivid mirage of Maja entering another man's car at the gas station. Running on empty, he chases down the car and viciously beats its driver, finishing the act by taking his gas. Throughout this scene, bicycle lane and central train station signs feature prominently, suggesting viable alternatives. Yet Kai's allegiance is to solitary mobility. As his car redlines, the addict commits suicide by purposely crashing on a tree-lined boulevard in the East, permanently disconnecting himself from human or other community.

These films show (dis)unity among inhabitants through their interactions with and in private spaces of housing and transport. They illustrate the privilege that attends ownership of such private space, while at the same time suggesting its relationship to emotional and intellectual impoverishment. In the public realm, characters without privilege gain opportunities for connection to heterogeneous spaces and inhabitants, enriching their lives and forging unity. At first blush, privilege appears synonymous with freedom and seems to be able to rearticulate the potentially dangerous and anonymous city as *Dorf*. These films suggest its deeper potential for division. Privilege and privatization thwart unification by creating a town of insiders in a city of outsiders.

Privat(izing) Spaces: Othered Sexuality

Privatization drives inhabitants apart and maintains existing rifts; it creates and shores up outsider status. When it extends from homes and transit to other public space, the powerful come to own Berlin both literally and through dissemination of their standards and attitudes. Several AB films narrate the relationship between private space and sexuality. Faced with chauvinism in public spaces and the inaccessibility of personally defined private spaces in a city dominated by privilege, characters with non-normative sexual practices seek to forge their own niches for security and unhampered expression.

In these films, the primary spaces of danger are private, while public and semipublic spaces enable more safety and self-expression. While the home is mythically linked to security and acceptance, here it is a space in which pressure to conform stifles individual expression. Home has long been a de facto confining space of danger for women, serving as a "microcosm of the political order, with the male head of the household as the ruler" (Duncan 1996: 128). *Folge der Feder* (Follow the Feather, 2005) depicts a situation in which a man threatens the autonomy and safety of women in the home. Hêlin travels from Turkey to Berlin for an arranged marriage, with an ulterior aim of finding her estranged mother and sister. Once in the city, she flees from her fiancé's house. Later scenes when she visits her former betrothed, Kenan, suggest what life would have been had she stayed with him as his wife in Berlin. At first accommodating and kind, Kenan quickly moves to control Hêlin physically and to transform their home into a prison. Only aid from outside the house can help her; Hêlin's mother comes and negotiates her terms of release.

Traditionally a patriarchal organizing structure of family life, the home is often also "an extremely heterosexist and alienating site for gays" (Duncan 1996: 137). For instance, in *Evet, ich will* (Evet, I Do, 2009), a romantic comedy depicting a series of tradition-breaking Berlin romances, Tim and Emrah hide their intimate relationship from Emrah's family, fearing rejection due to cultural prejudice. Emrah only admits the truth upon meeting his arranged bride in the small living room of his family's apartment in a densely populated housing complex. After this revelation, the family's acceptance of Emrah's sexuality hinges on never being confronted by it. The result is about containment not only within ideational boundaries, but also within spatial ones. Nothing can take place within the small, shared, private space without becoming common knowledge. Emrah comes under the closest surveillance and sanction within his home.

These films depict successful annexations of space as well. When Tim proposes marriage in a cocktail lounge with a largely gay clientele in *Evet,* he privatizes a commercial space. Here, Tim and Emrah's lifestyles are not contested because this particular space that remains public to all who possess enough economic leverage embraces the counternormative, and chauvinists would feel uncomfortable crossing the threshold. This supportive environment encourages the expression of Emrah and Tim's romantic affections; Emrah lets his guard down enough to respond with "Yes, I do." In the same film, Dirk and Özlem create a comfortable, romantic spot on a university lecture room floor, away from the judgment of her Turkish parents. During such interludes, the characters control the spaces that they have sought out and shaped. However, they do not attain long-term safety and acceptance free from the threat of chauvinist intervention. Ownership of space that shelters is rare. Hêlin's lesbian sister in *Folge der Feder* is the exception that highlights how ownership of space facilitates ownership of self-expression. Ayda practices her sexuality at will in her apartment, the privilege of the private shielding her from judgment and opposition, even from Hêlin when she is a guest.

These films suggest that private space protects when controlled by the individual who needs safeguarding. Yet leverage derived from private spaces is incapable of fundamentally changing society's terms. AB characters do not perform non-normative, identity-constituting practices in public. Instead, they rely on commercial countercultural, annexed, and private space to shelter them from familial and societal proscription. These spaces do not further broad emancipation, because they do little to foster changes in social structures. Struggles for civic emancipation—especially for equal rights as citizens—are crucial to destabilize the norms that govern public space (Young 2005). These narratives focus on individual negotiation of overt bigotry. Such punctuated mitigation tends to stabilize the covert homogeneity of the *Dorf,* because this structurally bigoted space need not alter radically for non-normative characters simply to assimilate. Moreover, in each of the examples, it is the Turkish element of German culture that disrupts the affective harmony. In this way, the tensions of the community are cast not as internal—for instance structural sexism, racism, and heteronormativity—but external elements that should be overcome. In the end, the problems are the attitudes and positions of the Turkish heritage outsiders, not those of the German insiders.

These AB films reveal how privatization tends "to depoliticize space and shrink the public spheres" (Duncan 1996: 127). While in some cases, such as at the gay lounge, privatization can rearticulate city spaces as more accessible, it often functions to divide according to lines of privilege, that of class in particular. Members of poorer minorities are thrust more forcefully into those very spaces that are depicted as (potentially) dangerous, such as the private family home, and the mainstream public realm in the sense that they do not have access to financial resources that could buy them alternatives. The films do not undermine the public/ private binary, open these spaces for contestation, nor offer models for queering public spaces (Duncan 1996). Rather, the characters practicing non-normative sexualities seek to carve out niches through annexation or private ownership. These options may be satisfying, but they are also limiting. The resultant separation from the mainstream allows little resistance to the structural chauvinism of the *Dorf*, with its de facto homogeneity wrapped in a veil of putatively significant distinctions.

Privat(izing) Spaces: Life on the Hyphen

Some AB films, including many that we treat here, focus on visible minorities, who exist as outsiders in circumscribed parallel worlds. Most of the other AB films nearly erase these minorities from the privileged *Dorf* and simultaneously articulate and embrace differences among insiders. While Berlin's largest group of visible minorities has Turkish heritage, it is largely privileged outsiders with insider status that populate AB works in the role of other. *Sieben Tage* presents the cosmopolitan migrant Cecilie, a Danish exchange student, who has full access to the *Dorf* and the city, at times as a privileged flâneur. She lives within walking distance from what appears to be the open air market at Kollwitz Square in Prenzlauer Berg, shopping there although she comments that the meat is unaffordable. She dines in the revolving restaurant in the television tower on Alexanderplatz on a date with a young University of Potsdam media studies professor; now living in Berlin, he is one of the many Westerners who have moved into posts in the former East. Cecilie's complaint about the service asserts her insider status; she legitimates it by pointing out that she has been a guest since 1989. Although by nationality foreign to the *Dorf* and the city, and by personal history foreign to the East Berlin that ended before she arrived, Cecilie seems to have unlimited access to the city. This may seem surprising, for Alexanderplatz and its tower have a long and important pre-1989 legacy that Cecilie did not experience. She could be considered an outsider. However, this member of the European intelligentsia exemplifies Soja's desirable stranger who is welcomed into the urban agglomeration. Although she brings nothing tangible to the urban space and could thus be read as parasitic, she bears cultural capital, credited with carrying the new philosophies, innovations, and positive intellectual change of which Soja writes (2003). This widely perceived potential to affect the city sets her apart from deeply marginalized characters.

The seemingly inclusive attitude that governs the treatment of outsiders by *Dorf* insiders is based on the latter's definition of heterogeneity, a definition that imputes significance to their own intragroup differences. Simultaneously and necessarily, insider interactions with outsiders such as visible minorities are fleeting and not constitutive of the *Dorf* community. Under such conditions, that is, when insiders define themselves both as heterogeneous and accepting of this same heterogeneity, these insiders may passively blame outsiders such as visible minorities for their own marginalization. To be sure, characters embodying dominant categories are never shown committing outrightly racist acts; indeed, at times they are overly accommodating. In *Evet*, Dirk's German mother dons a headscarf to meet Özlem's pious family. Although intended to show respect, this act may leave us wondering why, if white Germans are so accepting, the migrants and their children live in outlying districts rather than near the Winterfeldt market in the heart of bourgeois Schöneberg in Western Berlin, where Dirk's parents shop. The answer is that films such as *Evet* do not thematize structural inequities organized by social hierarchies. For instance, in *Evet*, the Turkish-German family lives in its cramped private space in a nondescript suburban high-rise seemingly just as contentedly as Dirk's parents do in their spacious, centrally located apartment. Indeed, these narratives imply that all individuals can choose where to live and, by extension, that they identify with that chosen site. In other words, these stories cast voluntary identification with space as norm rather than as privilege, without recognition of how such identification depends on space being representative of and supporting its inhabitants. When in play, these logics legitimate the normativity of the new Berlin as *Dorf*.

Under these circumstances, access for outsiders hinges on their bending to constraints imposed by privileged insiders. When marginalized inhabitants do gain access, it is frequently through adoption of an "authentic" German as chaperone and concomitantly borrowing small amounts of his or her privilege. If outsiders take to the streets without chaperones, they never gain access to mainstream life in the *Dorf* or they have limited freedoms in the city. Theirs is simply not the same vibrant capital as that available to privileged characters. Hêlin's nocturnal Berlin of *Folge der Feder* offers little embrace or contestation. For instance, she rarely encounters anyone and no one questions the legitimacy of her presence; even visually, she is simply insignificant in the urban landscape. Turks and Turkish-Germans in *Evet* access a similarly deserted city and seem to rely on safety in numbers. Similarly, while perhaps not visible minorities per se, East Germans seldom navigate crowded streets in downtown either; instead, they meander through empty zones in the

East. Likewise, in *Sprit*, Kai continually drives through the same stretches in the East. Although he frequently approaches and even passes through the new Tiergarten tunnel, he cannot continue much beyond the mouth of this symbolically laden monumental project that dives underground in former West Berlin, now also the majestic heart of the new capital. He always turns back. Even when access is hypothetically available, it is de facto strictly limited; these outsider groups are seldom able to access the Berlin of the privileged.

When outsiders are invited into the *Dorf*, they pay concessions. They are often exoticized to increase the (multi)cultural capital of the space, for instance in *SubBerlin*, where African-American DJs sell a way of life and legitimize Tresor's subculture that flourished in central areas of post-1989 eastern Berlin. That *Folge der Feder* aims for a non-Turkish heritage audience is clear in that even characters with the same first language communicate in German with each other in order to make key plot points more broadly intelligible. At the same time, the film markets its narrative and its protagonists through traditional and mystic Islamic and Kurdish/Turkish imagery set in arid and other non-urban, non-German surroundings. These dreamlike sequences and magical realist filmic elements remain largely unintelligible to the uninitiated viewer. Characters also join in on this superficial appreciation of the other. Exotic geographies are offered for enjoyment, not comprehension; they are beautiful but remain unexplained. The domesticated outsider is allowed access when commodifiable for the "real" German insider.

In these films, strangers in Soja's sense of the term are depicted as working to integrate into the *Dorf*. One means of fitting in is through language. Personages code-switch—for instance between the German and Turkish languages—and align themselves with more desirable migrant groups. Most have linguistic competence in German. Legitimation of the *Dorf* depends on certain beliefs about language. Much like the absolution sought through the use of hyphenated national terms (e.g., Turkish-German), dominant notions of bi- and multilingualism assume that the speaking subject has complete and comfortable access to both sides of the hyphen. Yet, bilingualism does not guarantee integration and AB films that focus on outsiders recognize this. They repeatedly present linguistically assimilated but culturally and geographically isolated outsiders. Hêlin, her mother, and her sister all speak perfect German, yet are not true *Dorf* members, although they do have more access than outsiders who do not have their skill set. Even East Germans are marginalized in *Der Letzte* and *Helden* making it clear that fluency does not guarantee inclusion.

For most minorities, *Dorf* access is limited. AB films focused on marginalized characters often show them confronted with exclusion fueled by veiled intolerant attitudes. The survival of these outsiders in Berlin is dependent on their willingness to negotiate, concede, and conform to the limits placed on acceptance by insiders—for instance, by adopting a German escort in the form of a kind female friend or a potential lover, limiting their own access, and inhabiting the role of exotic novelty. Alternatively, they can seek to subvert the exclusive attitudes shaping their treatment. By turning what insiders view as handicaps into strengths—for instance, by using the most expedient language or cultural role available at a given time—the outsider may gain leverage. This power, however, does not translate into the outsiders' acceptance or incorporation on their own terms. Even with effective coping strategies, the *Dorf* remains largely unattainable for the outsider.

Eastern Space and Space for Easterners

Depictions of the second main group of minority others suggest that one must not be altogether counternormative to be excluded from the new capital. Despite political status as equal members of the new Germany, East Germans are still treated as outsiders. The East-West division inheres more than two decades after unification (Dürr 2003). So-called *Ostalgie*—nostalgia for the East—is central to this exclusion. The ostalgic trope that focuses on East German commodities as fetish trivializes substantive connection to the past and the present. AB films that involve Easterners suggest that *Ostalgie* is in fact nostalgia for access, not things. They critique the exploitation of people, places, and histories and show characters trying to cope with a still unfamiliar capitalist society. By doing so, films such as *Helden, Netto,* and *Der Letzte* call the success of unification into question and suggest the exclusionary character of the *Dorf,* arguably more explicitly than films with Turkish-German outsiders.

Anthropologist Dominic Boyer calls *Ostalgie* "a symptom less of East German nostalgia than of West German utopia ... in which East Germans' neurotic entanglement with authoritarian pastness allows those Germans gendered western to claim a future free from the burden of history" (Boyer 2006: 363). He argues that *Ostalgie* is a Western myth. Refusing to admit that postunification changes disadvantaged many East Germans, it envisions the West as a hero that saved the East from its authoritarian past.

It is exactly this notion of West as savior that is refuted by AB films such as *Helden,* which centers on an eponymous television show that draws from the *Ostalgic* impulse. The Western host, Erika, and her Western producers search for the next quaint, entertaining Eastern story. Their cameras are meant only to capture the follies of Easterners and are blind to favorable depictions. The first segment filmed centers on Attila, a firefighter from the East. Able to digest everything from an entire drinking glass to coins, he is depicted as an endearing sideshow freak who, we recall, lives in a back courtyard apartment with uncovered windows, exposed to Western eyes. The story of Rosine, the local baker, who after unification helps to realize her father's dream of baking the world's largest *Pfannkuchen* (a sort of jelly donut), is similarly trivialized and packaged for consumption.

However, these characters resist caricature, even if the Western producers, who inhabit the front houses of the Prenzlauer Berg and whose trendy offices occupy some of the most expensive newly designed real estate in the capital, do not see it. Weary of the continuing challenges of post-Wall life, the despairing Rosine stands on her window ledge, threatening to jump. Erika rushes to the scene to capture this moment on film on her terms. There, she is confronted with what she can only see as an embarrassing affront: her husband, Rosine's psychiatrist, fondling his patient at the latter's demand with the promise of dissuading her. Erika abandons the scene and no cameras witness Rosine's jump and Attila's rescue as he lifts her unharmed from a well-placed safety net, in so doing defining the shared courtyard as a site of success, rather than defeat.

Attila and Rosine's unusual practices are comprehensible in context. Attila's swallowing ability afforded him a life of adventure touring in the East. The dream of Rosine's father first became possible with the fall of the Wall and, in this sense, critiques the limitations of the East German system. That their culinary tour de force was difficult to achieve post-Wall speaks little better of the new. Even more relevant, this gargantuan project expresses a daughter's gargantuan love for her father and emblematizes the *Ich AG* (Me, Inc.) welfare-to-work program devised and promoted by federal and city administrators. Despite these motives that dovetail with Western sensibilities, Rosine's successful project did not enable her entrée into the new Germany. This past and what remains are not only weighing on Rosine's mind, but they also occupy the majority of the common back courtyard in the form of a giant frying vat. Not seen from the gentrified streets and front windows of the *Dorf*, this inset and bolted-down dream insists on the substantive form of *Ostalgie*, a desire for access to the conditions necessary for aims to be realized, and on the influence of history on contemporary practices.

Netto similarly depicts *Ostalgie* in a form that critiques Western materialism, with characters longing instead for access to previous standards of employment, affordability, and familial stability. The word play of the title metonymizes the theme. *Netto* refers to the situation of the protagonist Marcel, who has insufficient net worth in an environment in which money dominates access to all types of geography. *Netto* is also the name of a low budget grocery chain owned by the Western firm Edeka that expanded rapidly northeastward from 1990. Marcel's nostalgic obsessions underscore the weight of his contemporary struggles; this father has been unemployed since the fall of the Wall and certainly knows Netto. Depicting a character suffering the real shortcomings of the new capital, the film nevertheless suggests the destructive effects of nostalgia on individuals—even when such nostalgia is for valuable aspects of life such as financial and familial health. The Marcel we first meet is obsessed with the past, struggling against alcohol, mistrustful of West Germans, and caught in inertia. Born around 1990, Marcel's son Sebastian embodies (the necessity of) a solution.

In these films, the Eastern characters do not gain access to places of Western privilege per se, but rather they variously increase their geographic scope by means of human interactions. In *Helden,* Rosine and Attila solidify their personal connection and reappropriate their own history as Attila eats a piece of the *Pfannkuchen* pan at a well attended, public event that brings people together in the courtyards of the underprivileged. Marcel escapes the confinement of his Eastern mindset and his groundfloor Prenzlauer Berg apartment through a growing relationship with Sebastian. He manages a visit to his former partner, Angelika, and her new partner, Bernd, in a large modern house surrounded by green. Early in the film, Marcel places his Western rival in relation to Schöneberg; Bernd and Angelika's house seems to be at an even more upscale Western address, perhaps in the wealthy quarter Grünewald, for Bernd mentions rollerblading around a nearby lake. Marcel's bicycling return east to northern Prenzlauer Berg through the night under the lights of what appear to be the Unter den Linden bicycle path between West and East Berlin is filmed as a slow-motion, melancholy epiphany. Morning finds him on Behmstraße (Behm Street) where it crosses the regional and light rail train lines looking north. After a brief, fantastical, and supportive appearance by his musical idol, who remains unnamed, Marcel chooses life and turns 180 degrees to stride down Schwedter Steg (a pedestrian bridge) toward downtown, which is marked in the distance by the television tower at Alexanderplatz. This bridge was constructed to reunite East and West Berlin from Behmstraße to Mauerpark (Wall Park) across from the newly recompleted rail loop that features in *Helden* and that has symbolically united the city. *Netto* does not promise that this middle-aged, blue-collar East German will manage to find a well-connected place in the *Dorf* and new city, but his surroundings and directionality as he saunters off in a high distance shot opens the possibility.

In close dialogue with *Netto, Der Letzte* depicts its group of Eastern protagonists resolutely setting off by automobile together from the Landesberger Allee (Landesberg Boulevard) light rail stop at the Tempodrom event venue for work in Norway. Based on an intensive discussion between Jennifer Hosek and Jörg Foth in October 2011, we read this site for how it underscores the erosion of space and place. Shortly after unification, at the time of the hotly debated removal of the enormous Lenin statue from what is now Platz der Vereinten Nationen (United Nations Square), Lenin Allee (Lenin Boulevard) was rechristened Landesberger Allee, an earlier name that alludes to the nearby town of Altlandsberg but also resonates with the German referents for many nearby northeastern sites in Poland. This busy, modern area between the nearby city center and Prenzlauer Berg and the now-ghettoizing Eastern bedroom communities of Hohenschönhausen and Marzahn remained rather tranquil long after 1990. However, the old stockyards and slaughterhouse complex, whose façade can be seen across the street as the car starts moving, is now the site of a high-end living project replete with condominiums. The tough-guy construction team leader who leaves his family behind could be speaking for all of the protagonists when he grumbles that they should hurry up and leave before he starts crying. That these long-time Berliners leave from precisely this place suggests not a lack of desire to stay, but rather lack of space in the *Dorf* and the city and a lack of opportunities to shape the places that exist.

Conclusion

AB films seldom showcase internationally or even nationally known landmarks in Berlin. Although their depiction is sometimes a requirement for local and regional funding, when these representative areas are featured, they are often critiqued rather than celebrated, styled as ridiculous or metonymically connected to a filmic villain or other danger. These Made-in-Berlin-Brandenburg films rely more heavily on overdetermined, understated, and selectively legible sites such as the stockyards of *Der Letzte,* and less known, insider places of the sutured middle of the new Berlin in and near Prenzlauer Berg. Although this area continues to gentrify, its filmic version is seldom presented in upscale glory; rather, corners and edges that remain grungy and gritty, yet homey, safe, comfortable, and bohemian become the core geography of the *Dorf* of the *Wahl-Berliner* about whom and for whom these films are made.

This mythic *Dorf* reminds that the new capital has come to embody many dichotomies: weighty history and inexorable modernization; financial poverty and cultural richness; a meeting place of East/ern and West/ern. AB films capture Berlin's pulse in ways unique to the medium. They thematize the pleasures and pains of this new-old capital as it grows—awkwardly and elegantly, haphazardly and systematically. Our twelve examples were chosen for having particularly strong ties to the city. Rather than depicting a beacon for a unified nation, their Berlin is fragmented and reveals another organizing dichotomy: space and its inhabitants. Our analysis has explored this oscillation through transportation, movement, and the figure of flâneur; outsider status as embodied in racialization, non-normative sexual identity, and Easternness; and (class) privilege and selective blindness. Marketed as a vibrant, inclusive, heterogeneous metropolis, the surface hides pockets of inclusion and exclusion and deep social rifts. Connections flourish within homogeneous groups and homogeneous spaces, mythologies of heterogeneity and opportunity notwithstanding. And seen in this way, another dichotomy becomes visible. From one perspective, Berlin is defined by the privileged, the insiders, with seemingly full access to prime urban space. And yet from another perspective, surrounding what emerges as privileged *Dorf,* a second grouping is outnumbering the first, their access to *Dorf* and city limited. Owning little, these outsiders rely upon geographical and temporal niches that they can seldom define or defend. Based on such recognitions, one may have space to hope that this city is a *Baustelle* (construction site).

Notes

1. According to the coordinator of film for the state of Berlin, Dietrich Reupke, Medienboard Berlin Brandenburg GmbH (Media Board Berlin-Brandenburg, Ltd.), an institution commissioned by the states of Berlin and Brandenburg, finances AB with between 50,000 and 70,000 Euros yearly. Email correspondence with Reupke (March 2012). Translations in the following are our own unless otherwise indicated.
2. We thank Carrie Smith-Prei for reminding us of this. We also thank both of the editors for their extreme patience with and support of this unusual writing project.
3. For an overview of Prenzlauer Berg demographics over the last decades see Dörfler (2010) and Sußebach (2007).
4. See de Certeau, especially the chapter "Walking in the City" (1984).

5. In this reading, we consider full-length documentary and fiction together and our study does not explicitly account for generic influence in its readings, instead taking the position that all of these texts construct Berlin fictions. Our decision was influenced by the fact that the documentary films generally focus on themes intimate to the filmmakers and present stylized visions of what might be termed "reality." Ethical concerns about representation of an other or elision of larger concerns and truth claims that are common to the documentary genre were of little significance for *Sieben Tage Im Leben Meiner Freunde*; *SubBerlin*'s very selective vision of Tresor's demise highlights its debt to fiction genres.
6. The assessment in this paragraph is based on Jennifer Ruth Hosek's discussions with AB organizers, attendance at many film screenings, study of the literature on Berlin demographics, and AB documentation.
7. Bauman quoted, in Gregory (2004: 81). AB documentation.
8. Bauman quoted, in Gregory (2004: 81).
9. Jean-François Lyotard, *The Postmodern Condition* (1984; Geyh 2009: 9).
10. On the symbolic meaning of the rail loop in historical perspective, see Dietrich Bohrer's rail system documentary series, including Bohrer 1992 and Bohrer 2003.

References

Auf Nummer Sicher. 2008. Dir. Jonas Dornbach. Kinoherz Film Produktion.
Austern Ohne Schale. 2009. Dir. Jette Miller. Faunesse Film.
Bauman, Zygmunt. 2000. *Liquid Modernity.* Cambridge: Polity Press.
Benjamin, Walter. 2002. *The Arcades Project,* edited by Rolf Tiedmann, translated by Howard Eiland and Kevin McLaughlin. Cambridge: Harvard University Press.
Bohrer, Dieter, ed. 1992. "S-Bahn Berlin: Wieder Grenzenlos Nordsüd-Tunnel/ Stadtbahn." Bohrervideo.
———. 2003. "Wieder Mit Ringbahn: Eine Ost-West-Geschichte." Bohrervideo.
Bomnüter, Udo, and Patricia Scheller. 2009. *Filmfinanzierung. Strategien im Ländervergleich: Deutschland, Frankreich und Großbritannien.* Baden-Baden: Nomos.
Boyer, Dominic. 2006. "*Ostalgie* and the Politics of the Future in Eastern Germany." In *Neoliberal Historicities,* 361–378. Durham, N.C.: Duke University Press.
Close. 2005. Dir. Marcus Lenz. Sabotage Film Produktion/DFFB.
de Certeau, Michel. 1984. *The Practice of Everyday Life.* Translated by Steven Rendall. Berkeley: University of California Press.
Der Letzte macht das Licht aus! 2007. Dir. Clemens Schönborn. KaminskiSteihm Filmproduktion.
Die Helden aus der Nachbarschaft. 2008. Dir. Jovan Arsenic. Heldenfilm.
Dörfler, Thomas. 2010. *Gentrification in Prenzlauer Berg?: Milieuwandel eines Berliner Sozialraums seit 1989.* Bielefeld: Transcript Verlag.

Duncan, Nancy, ed. 1996. *Body Space: Destabilizing Geographies of Gender and Sexuality.* New York: Routledge.

Dürr, Tobias. 2003. "On Westalgia." In *The Spirit of the Berlin Republic,* edited by Dieter Dettke. New York: Berghahn Books.

Evet, Ich Will. 2009. Dir. Sinan Akus. Luna Film.

Feinstein, Joshua. 2002. *The Triumph of the Ordinary: Depictions of Everyday Life in East German Cinema 1949–1989.* Chapel Hill: University of North Carolina Press.

Feministisches Kollektiv. 2008. *Street Harassment: Machtprozesse und Raumproduktionen.* Vienna: Mandelbaum.

Folge Der Feder. 2005. Dir. Nuray Sahin. Moneypenny Film Produktion/DFFB.

Frisby, David. 1994. "The flâneur in Social Theory." In *The Flâneur,* 82–110. New York: Routledge.

Geyh, Paula. 2009. *Cities, Citizens, and Technologies.* New York: Routledge.

Gregory, Derek. 2004. *Colonial Present.* Oxford: Blackwell.

Halle, Randall. 2006. "German Film, European Film: Transnational Production, Distribution and Reception." Screen 47 (2): 251–266.

———. 2008. *German Film after Germany: Toward a Transnational Aesthetic.* Urbana-Champaign: University of Illinois Press.

Harvey, David. 2006. *Spaces of Global Capitalism: Towards a Theory of Uneven Geographical Development.* London: Verso.

Hosek, Jennifer Ruth. 2010. "Materialities of Urban Film Space: Interpolating a European Capital." Talk held at the German Studies Association Conference. Oakland, C.A.

Jeschke, Carola. 1997. "Angsträumer in Städten." In *Verkehr ohne (W)Ende,* edited by E. Giese. Tübingen: dgvt-Verlag.

Lyotard, Jean-François. 1984. *The Postmodern Condition: A Report on Knowledge.* Minneapolis: University of Minnesota Press.

Meurer, Hans Joachim. 2000. *The Split Screen: Cinema and National Identity in a Divided Germany 1979–1989.* Lewiston, N.Y.: Edwin Mellen.

Netto. 2005. Dir. Robert Thalheim. HFF.

Neun Szenen. 2006. Dir. Dietrich Brüggemann. HFF.

Poiger, Uta. 2000. *Jazz, Rock, and Rebels: Cold War Politics and American Culture in a Divided Germany.* Berkeley: University of California Press.

Poschardt, Ulf. 2010. "Unser *Dorf* soll schöner werden." *Die Welt Online,* 1 October. http://www.welt.de/die-welt/kultur/article9997215/Unser-Dorf-soll-schoener-werden.html, accessed February 2011.

Rentschler, Eric. 2000. "From New German Cinema to the Post-Wall Cinema of Consensus." In *Cinema and Nation,* edited by Mette Hjort and Scott MacKenzie, 260–277. London: Routledge.

Schäfer, Hajo. 2010. "On Berlin Film Culture and German Unification." Talk held at *Globalization and (Dis)Unifications: Europe's Berlin Republic Turns 20.* Queen's University, Ontario.

Sieben Tage im Leben meiner Freunde. 2005. Dir. Christian Shidlowski. Keyframe Produktion.

Simmel, Georg. 1903. "Die Großstadt und das Geistesleben." In *Die Großstadt. Vorträge und Aufsätze zur Städteausstellung. Jahrbuch der Gehe-Stiftung Dresden,* vol. 9, edited by Th. Petermann. Dresden: Gehe-Stiftung Dresden.

———. 1950. "The Metropolis and Mental Life." In *The Sociology of Georg Simmel,* edited by D. Weinstein, translated by K. Wolff, 409–424. New York: Free Press.

Soja, Edward W. 2003. "Writing the City Spatially." *City* 7 (3): 269–281.

———. 2010. *Seeking Spatial Justice.* Minneapolis: University of Minnesota Press.

Sprit. 2009. Dir. Marco Raab. Zahlbach Films.

SubBerlin. 2009. Dir. Tillman Künzel. Filmlounge.

Sußebach, Henning. 2007. "Bionade—Biedermeier: Der Berliner Stadtteil Prenzlauer Berg ist das Experimentierfeld des neuen Deutschlands. Doch wer nicht ins Raster passt, hat es schwer im Biotop der Schönen und Kreativen." *Die Zeit Online* 46: 44.

Tresor Berlin Official Website. http://tresorberlin.com, accessed 29 March 2010.

Wray, J. Harry. 2008. *Pedal Power.* Boulder, C.O.: Paradigm.

Young, Iris Marion. 2005. *On Female Body Experience: Throwing Like a Girl and Other Essays.* Oxford: Oxford University Press.

The Amputated City

The Voids of Hoyerswerda

GWYNETH CLIVER

Neustadt (New City), the burgeoning but sleepy workers' settlement at the center of Brigitte Reimann's novel *Franziska Linkerhand* (1974), is deemed an amputated city by the lover of the title character (Reimann 1998b: 359). He believes the city's purported function, the realization of a Marxist utopian ideal of urban community, has been sacrificed to the ceaseless demand from the authorities to build as many economical housing units as rapidly as possible. The reader knows by this point in the narration that Linkerhand, an architect helping to plan the city, shares her lover's frustration. She and her colleagues have failed to convince their superiors to convert socialist urban development theories into practice and to construct a utopian city as they have conceived it in the numerous models that clutter their workspace. Instead of celebrating the construction of a thriving cultural center as they have optimistically designed it, the architects witness with emotions ranging from abhorrence to cynicism to resignation the gradual disappearance of the space designated for this center under the weight of one identical *Wohnblock* (high-rise apartment building) after another. Linkerhand considers the monotony of this concrete landscape to be a betrayal of her own aesthetic ideals and of the socialist project in general and blames the high rates of alcoholism, hooliganism, pregnancy, and suicide she observes in Neustadt on the boredom and isolation she attributes to the lack of shared community space. Neustadt, as it is and not as it is planned, perverts the notion of city, as it offers none of the cultural or communal interaction the modern subject expects in an urban environment; instead, it provides its inhabitants only with a series of "Fernsehhöhlen" (TV caves), which divide their residents from one another physically and mentally (358).

It is no secret to scholars of Reimann that Neustadt is a thinly disguised pseudonym for Hoyerswerda, a small town northeast of Dresden. In fact, the development east of the Black Elster River, which includes the majority of Hoyerswerda's *Plattenbauten* (residential high-rises erected in the German Democratic Republic, GDR), is called Hoyerswerda-Neustadt. Known during the GDR as the second socialist city, Hoyerswerda had been chosen by the government to be an intentionally designed workers' community. Reimann moved to Hoyerswerda in 1960 and lived there until 1968, and the birth of Neustadt in her novel very closely follows the history of Hoyerswerda's development. Numerous markers in the novel reveal Hoyerswerda to be Neustadt's inspiration, from the bilingual German-Sorbian signs, indicating the presence of the Slavic minority indigenous to the region Lausatia, to the *Kombinat* (combine), alluding to Schwarze Pumpe (Black Pump), the giant energy-producing combine responsible for Hoyerswerda's population boom in the 1950s and 1960s. The Hoyerswerdaer Kunstverein (Art Club) included excerpts from *Franziska Linkerhand* about Neustadt in their tract, *Hoyerswerda—Literarische Spiegelungen* (Literary Reflections, 1998). It is Hoyerswerda that Linkerhand and her colleagues are designing, that can offer its residents only "a door you can lock behind yourself, the old Game of Life between table and bed, nothing more" (Reimann 1998b: 359).[1] Hoyerswerda is the amputated city to which Linkerhand's lover refers. Reimann's turn of phrase is ambiguous; either she anthropomorphizes the city, in which case it is an amputee with its theoretical function as urban community severed from its physical reality, or it is itself that which has been severed, a city amputated from society. This chapter will explore the various manifestations of Reimann's metaphor.

By describing Hoyerswerda as amputated, Reimann captures early in its urban life the voided essence of a town little known outside of Germany. According to Andreas Huyssen's 1997 essay, "The Voids of Berlin," spatial voids can play a central role in historical representation. Huyssen considers the signifying power of the empty spaces in Berlin-Mitte (Central Berlin), left after the destruction of the Wall and now vanished under high-rise construction and monuments. While they lasted, the voids in Berlin, in particular the swath of No Man's Land stretching out south of the Brandenburg Gate, lay in testimony to a ruptured past and resisted the Disneyfication of historical tourism and the commercialism of free-market capitalism. Huyssen's spatial voids provide onlookers used to monuments and museums with the opportunity to confront discord and contradiction and to construct historical narrative themselves. If Reimann's assessment of Hoyerswerda as amputated is correct, then the void(s) created by this severance—like Huyssen's voids in Berlin—have stories to tell about urban design during the GDR period and the historical experience of planned socialist cities since German unification. This chapter will identify a number of voids in the urban "text" of Hoyerswerda and relies on a variety of sources—fiction and creative non-fiction in which Hoyerswerda plays a role, historical architectural tracts, visual observations of the author, promotional materials published by members of the community, and journalist reports on the city—in order to consider the literary, historical, social, and cultural significance of these voids.

Text after text about Hoyerswerda, from the literary to the journalistic to the civic, employs images of and allusions to void, lack, deficiency, or emptiness. Although the most frequent examples occur in texts published since German unification, the notion of Hoyerswerda as voided began earlier, as seen above in *Franziska Linkerhand*. In a piece of travel literature, *Reisebilder: Ansichtskarten aus der DDR* (Travel Images: Postcards from the GDR, 1973), published not long after Reimann's novel, East German Richard Christ relates a series of impressions of the city, as imparted to him by residents. The list includes a number of optimistic remarks concerning the technical improvements the new construction provides its inhabitants, but the passage ends with the claim that "well, something is missing ... atmosphere, for instance." The citizens believe the city lacks a "cultural climate," and that its inhabitants live "in involuntary asceticism: no cinema, no café, no bar" (Christ 1973: 181).[2] Reflections on Hoyerswerda published after unification almost uniformly repeat this representation of Hoyerswerda as voided. A publication of the city celebrating the fortieth anniversary of the founding of Hoyerswerda's Neustadt (1993) recounts the failures of the authorities to complete the construction as planned in the following terms: "could not be carried out," "impermissible underestimation," "unsuitable for expansion," "lack of the originally planned central urban cultural and commercial facilities, which were never realized," and "discrepancy" (*Anspruch und Wirklichkeit* 1993: 7–8). All of these articulations remind one of the absence of something desired or planned that never came to fruition. In Günter Grass's *Ein weites Feld*, (Too Far Afield, 1995) writer Fonty vows never to return to Hoyerswerda after having been invited there to read by its Kulturverbund (cultural club), in spite of "nothing but the best memories" and his having been warmly received, because the area itself seems to have been "sucked dry"; it offers "nothing but chasm and moonscapes" (509). Here, Grass's choice of expression suggests the removal of the good ("sucked dry") or absence incarnate ("chasm"). In a work of travel literature, Irina Liebmann describes a visit to Hoyerswerda after the pogrom of 1991 to search for the former home of Brigitte Reimann.[3]

She finds the *Innenstadt* (downtown) "strangely empty," then "astonishingly empty," and finally "empty as if God-forsaken" (1997: 73, 77, 88). Similarly, as Liebmann drives through one housing complex, she notes that "there was nothing to see but concrete and empty streets. Among a few stores, obviously closed for good, [she] found an open Italian restaurant, which was completely empty" (82–83). More direct than Grass, Liebmann characterizes Hoyerswerda repeatedly by its emptiness. Not only literary works, but journalistic ones as well, associate Hoyerswerda with absence. The surprisingly numerous number of English-language newspaper reports on Hoyerswerda perpetuate this imagery of lack or emptiness. Any description of the current economic climate in the city must evoke the large volume of *Leerstand* (vacancy) in the apartment units (for example, Biernath 2005: 1). The *Economist* declares that Hoyerswerda "must be one of Germany's ugliest towns …, utterly devoid of a sense of community" (Havlat 2002: 15). Wilhelm Klauser says Hoyerswerda has "lost its center of gravity" (2009: 28). Citizen Joachim Bramborg went so far as to tell *The New York Times* that his hometown is "a dead city" (Zielbauer 2002: A3). Even the most optimistic accounts of the city's recent history admit the constant presence of want, shortcoming, absence, or, to return to Huyssen's metaphor, the void.

For Huyssen, voids are "saturated with invisible history, with memories of architecture both built and unbuilt" (2003: 58). The empty spaces in the center of Berlin during the transitional nineties recalled an unidealized past, resisting the general nostalgia of the post-Wall period. Some nostalgics advocate the revival of castles and churches and emphasize the narration of a history prior to World War I, a history more easily made harmonious by its chronological distance. This brand of nostalgia is exemplified by the demolition of the headquarters of the GDR (Palast der Republik) and the reconstruction of the royal castle. Others reduce the period of German division to the amusements and quirks of everyday life, an act of looking back known as *Ostalgie,* a conflagration of the German word for "nostalgia" (*Nostalgie*) and that for "east" (*Ost*). In addition to counteracting both of these nostalgic drives, the voids of Berlin withstood the siren of the high-rise, cyber-world of late capitalism, typified by the development on Potsdamer Platz, which for Huyssen replaces history with the eternal present. Huyssen accuses nostalgics and capitalists alike of lacking inspiration and of fetishizing image. In order to shape post-Wall Berlin into a city capable of attracting large numbers of tourists, urban planners on both sides are reproached by Huyssen for concerning themselves most with "how best to decorate the corporate and governmental sheds to better attract international attention: not the city as multiply coded text to be filled with life by its dwellers and its readers, but the city as image and design in the service of displaying power and profit" (63). In reaction to what he considers the profit-driven banalities of both the conservative and the futurist strains of the (re)construction debate, Huyssen encourages an emphasis of the voids themselves, which strive toward a memory of twentieth-century Germany and its disjoint-edness and its unease. He praises Daniel Libeskind's annex to the Jü-disches Museum (Jewish Museum) for being unique in its attempt to express, structurally and explicitly, the fissures and discomforts of the city's twentieth-century past (71). He mourns the construction on top of No Man's Land for having squandered an opportunity to have the space become a "memorial as empty page right in the center of the reunified city" (58). In sum, the void for Huyssen is an empty marker of history, a tabula rasa that allows for continuous, spontaneous, and democratic readings of the urban text by visitors and residents alike.

Of course, Huyssen's effort to promote No Man's Land as a monument was purely intellectual—and doubtless, intentionally so—as the filling of voids in the popular and densely populated capital with federal build-ings, memorials, and commercial enterprises was inevitable. His theory gains new import, however, when applied to voids that do not disap-pear, to deconstruction rather than reconstruction, to holes that replace buildings rather than the other way around, to the figurative holes left when a community is neglected or despised. The voids gradually turning smaller, less successful communities across the East into ghost towns provide a practical testing ground for Huyssen's theory. Hoyerswerda's modern history, from its development during the GDR to its decon-struction since reunification, is one of voids: the gap between Marxist theory and socialist praxis, the lack of history and the avoidance of tra-dition, shrinking population, and demolition. Hoyerswerda provides a compelling example for considering the narrative power of empty lots, vacant buildings, and abandoned industries, and their defiance of the dominant historical or memory paradigms being written by reconstruc-tion efforts in the flagship cities of the East.

Hoyerswerda has played a role in the construction of historical narra-tives since the beginning of its modern incarnation; in fact, its very ex-istence as city derives from a conscious drive for historical production. Before its having been chosen in 1955 as the site of the "second socialist city," Hoyerswerda was, with fewer than seven thousand inhabitants, scarcely larger than a village. It grew to approximately 72,000 residents by German unification. Intended as the residence for tens of thousands of employees of brown coal mines and of Schwarze Pumpe, an enor-mous combine located approximately twelve kilometers from the city, Hoyerswerda became a self-congratulatory emblem of the GDR's industrialization, social engineering, and planned urban design. An examination of the rhetoric of a text contemporary to its development, written by the head of the administrative organization overseeing planning and construction during the early years, reveals how Hoyerswerda's growth was to tell a certain story about socialism and to provide physical evidence for its success. Hoyerswerda's design was to substantiate certain socialist axioms: that the state not only should but can provide the masses an improved lifestyle, that a starkly unified community supports private individuation, and that the modern and progressive thrust of socialism would establish it as the social and political system of the future. Architect Richard Paulick writes in 1960, "We can allocate the living spaces of our working population not only according to economical but also to lifestyle needs. It is already possible for us to satisfy demands for hygiene and comfort to the greatest degree" (355). The rapid construction in Hoyerswerda of *Wohnblöcke* and *Plattenbauten* comprised of prefabricated materials would soothe the stress felt by the government due to a dire housing shortage in the wake of World War II; modern conveniences built wholesale would provide masses of workers a dignity of lifestyle previously denied them. The layout of housing complexes would bolster community spirit: "Each housing complex has a dual-tracked comprehensive polytechnical high school with afterschool, infant care, and preschool ... In each housing complex are a self-service store for everyday items, a laundry and shoe-repair drop-off, a post office with a newspaper stand, a lottery ticket booth" (Paulick 1960: 356). Whereas space outside living quarters would foster a sense of community, individuality would blossom behind closed doors in the private paradise of a single unit per nuclear family. With a number of these mini-communities surrounding a projected city center, Hoyerswerda was to demonstrate to the world the progressiveness and hence superiority of socialist design: "In the shortest possible time, an industrial center will develop from a backwards agrarian district. Already in 1960, 'Lausatia' is no longer synonymous with 'backwoods,' but rather with the most rapid tempo in the construction of socialism" (Paulick 1960: 355). In the space of two decades, Hoyerswerda's physicality was to project the socialist mission, its universal applicability, and its inevitable future dominance. Unlike previous examples, take for instance the GDR's "first socialist city," Eisenhüttenstadt (or Stalinstadt), Hoyerswerda was to do this without a central square (*Zentralplatz*) designated for militaristic and political parades. Instead, its architecture and planning would convey its socialist mission by means of the most modern and comfortable living quarters for workers (Durth, Düwel, and Gutschow 1998b: 531). While the reconstruction and renovation of war-damaged premodernist housing in Berlin and other cities were neglected, new construction in Hoyerswerda and other similarly planned socialist communities—such as Halle-Neustadt, Eisenhüttenstadt, Schwedt, and satellite neighborhoods of major cities, like Marzahn and Hellersdorf in Berlin—was meant to signal to citizens that the GDR was capable of fulfilling its promise of a socialist utopia and that this fulfillment would succeed by means of communal urban design that strove toward the future and rejected the past.[4] Hence from the inception of its major expansion in 1955, the design of Hoyerswerda was intended as—indeed, *chosen* to be—a focal point for historical production.

Not only the housing units, but also the shared community spaces were designed to relate certain socialist ideals. The city center, whose original plan was never completed, was to include a central square connected to the park, a monument to Marx and Engels, the headquarters of the administration, shopping facilities, a hotel with a restaurant and cafés, a central post office, and a movie theater. A cultural center would provide space for music, dance, and the visual arts, and professional artists would produce their crafts alongside amateurs. To preserve its status as a space for rest and recreation (*Erholungszentrum*), the city center would be reserved for pedestrians and cyclists and would be heavily landscaped (Paulick 1960: 357). In addition, a Sorbian Square would be built, in which the seat of the ethnic minority's administration and recreational facilities would provide it with a gathering space as well as representation and would promote the preservation of its culture and language (Durth, Düwel, and Gutschow 1998a: 492). Many of the ideals espoused by this design faltered, however, and the city center the citizens of Hoyerswerda finally gained looked very reduced in scope: the cultural center did not appear until 1975, the park between the Altstadt (old town) and Neustadt disappeared under monuments to the Red Army and additional apartment buildings, and the proposed center for Sorbian culture was rejected by authorities under the justification that it would be too expensive (Durth, Düwel, and Gutschow 1998a: 494). Instead, additional living complexes were added to answer the demands of an ever-growing population, resulting in a sea of *Plattenbauten* with little nature or community space to relieve the monotony.[5]

Further analysis of Reimann's novel suggests that at least some residents bristled at this monotony even from Neustadt's earliest years. Ever sensitive to an alienation resulting from this uniformity, Reimann's protagonist Linkerhand mocks herself repeatedly for continuing to use the term "street" to designate the labyrinth of paths created by the negative space left between apartment high-rises. For Linkerhand, a path that disorients cannot be called a street; similarly, a collection of apartments that isolates residents and impedes community cannot be called a city. Recently, the German language has idiosyncratically employed the English *City* to distinguish the urban centers of midsized and large *Städte* (the traditional German word) from the metropolitan area as a whole. Travelers arriving at train stations are directed to the *City*, and the inducted understand that by following this direction they will enter the city center, which houses the most popular tourist or commercial destinations. Reimann's Neustadt is amputated because it is a *Stadt* without the *City*. Instead of a community, it is merely a collection of some tens of thousands of residents.

This history of the city's idealistic conception and bureaucratic faltering forms the background for the escalating frustration Linkerhand feels regarding her work as an architect of Neustadt, a frustration that derives primarily from her gradual acknowledgment that the city center would not be realized. A utopian vision of urban community recedes as the Neustadt planners receive diminishing promises from superiors:

> Bait? Weak. The city center should now be yet, possibly, probably, in the next year or the year after. The first construction sheds on the circular square. Not bad, huh? The second, the tastier bait … twelve million for a theater are granted—or at least as good as granted. Twelve. Laughable. A multiple-use hovel for theater, cinema, concerts, conferences, lousy acoustics, wooden seating, coat checks like monks' quarters, if at all … As if he could tempt me with his city center, discussed a hundred times, rejected and planned again, election promise of two years ago … And my walking path, the comforting, breathing, hundred-eyed double row of pavement and shop windows, where you can be alone among people, and where one step, one glance can be the beginning of a story that might be written, one that's possibly already done even before you spell out the first sentence—my passageway under a glassy sky? Dropped and deceased, at very best still seen only in model form, white and pleasing in an exhibition … or a war of nerves against traders and investors for every lousy joint, every boutique, soda shop, ice cream parlor. (Reimann 1998b: 515–516)

Linkerhand comes to realize that the city center she had envisioned would probably exist only as archival evidence in model form, and whatever small progress that could be made would only occur after epic battles of will between the architects and the accountants. For Reimann's protagonist, the recognition of the inevitable absence of Neustadt's city center represents more than its actualization probably ever could. Were the center to be built, it would be yet another pedestrian zone with shops, gathering spots, cultural activities, along with the complaints, disappointments, strife that inhabit any space in which humans live. Indeed, her lover Trojanowicz points out to her the fallacy in utopian vision. Linkerhand tells him that she and her colleagues have failed in their obligation to design "not only houses, but also relationships, contact among residents, a social organization," but Trojanowicz tells her that they "overestimate themselves ... exorbitantly overvalue the meaning and influence of architecture" (540). Realized, the city center could only be just that, a city center with its unforeseen, nuanced, imperfect, but actual future. As a void, however, the city center becomes a placeholder, a variable on which to place and interpret cultural significance. The very absence of the city center allows this imagined but never constructed space to maintain and cultivate its utopian drive; only as long as it remains unbuilt can the city center fulfill the socialist ideal of bringing workers the highest degree of "hygiene and comfort," as Paulick has declared above, simply because the inherent disparity of the ideal and the real prohibits the practical existence of the former.

In other words, the absence of the city center signifies another of Hoyerswerda's voids: the gap between theory and praxis in socialist urban planning. The theory was nothing less than the possibility of constructing a city that would make the socialist ideal manifest for real people. Volker Braun describes this gap in his short essay "Die Leute von Hoywoy" (The People of Hoywoy, 1971). The narrator returns to Hoyerswerda and wonders where all of his acquaintances have gone, whether they have left or merely changed unidentifiably: "Would I recognize them, here on the concrete? Are they who they were? Haven't they long had other expressions and movements, white smocks or electronic machines?" (1976: 100). Braun, who participated in the construction of Schwarze Pumpe, employs a clearly satirical tone to indicate his recognition that the futuristic utopia promised by the second socialist city had not come into full fruition:

> Had they not built this city from different materials as ever before, with different vanishing lines, different structures? Hadn't they sat on enormous pieces of furniture? Hadn't they eaten from tables less easily tipped? Hadn't they rocked themselves to sleep on featherbeds? ... Had they not already done a number of things as wonderful as these? Hadn't they taken factories that were junk or were becoming junk into their own hands and now they functioned fantastically, at least at first glance? Hadn't they socialized land and divided it into scraps, and then put it back together again under almost inexplicably better conditions? Hadn't they chased the false teachers from their podiums while know-

ing nothing themselves: and hadn't they become clever all on their own—like magic?! (100–101)

By imitating the inescapable smugness of the present in relation to the past's failures, Braun's satire exposes the fallacy in the naïve optimism of his younger self and his former comrades.

The people Braun remembers from his time in Hoyerswerda, those idealist youths certain of a better future, have disappeared: "Are they perhaps present, and I didn't recognize them?" (Braun 1976: 101). Braun expresses his incredulity at their absence in the form of a question in order to implicate himself in the history as well; perhaps it is not they who have changed—the people, the ideals, the city—but he, in the manner in which he views them. For Braun, Hoyerswerda has become a mere mockery of the socialist promise of its origins. His first-hand observations reveal the crux of Hoyerswerda's condition as amputated city. The "socialist"—at least in the idealistic interpretation of the word by the Marxist urban planners—was removed from the "second socialist city." From Linkerhand's perspective, this severance occurred at the hands of bureaucrats concerned only with the bottom line; from Braun's satirical perspective, it was the inevitable outcome of unrealistic utopianism itself.

Reimann's novel, although without Braun's satirical voice, similarly attempts to reconcile the disconnection between the stated goals of socialist urban planners and the realities of their accomplishments. Although Linkerhand promises a young *FDJler*, a member of the GDR's youth organization, that Neustadt will one day become a metropolis (in German: *Großstadt*, "great city"), she has already long despaired of the possibility for a realization of this objective (Reimann 1998b: 477). Instead, she feels betrayed not only by her superiors who have resigned themselves to mediocrity for the sake of frugality but also by her educators for inspiring her with unattainable ideals: "How long can one live as a henchman in a house factory? I thought, we've been deceived, even by Reger, who dismissed us from college with a social mission …, who swaddled us in a cocoon of ideals and illusions … Here, in Neustadt, our ideas prove to be ineffectual. Between idea and possibility stand regulations and code figures" (Reimann 1998b: 269). Although Linkerhand's intellectual sensibilities lead her again and again to criticize, both privately and openly, the seemingly mercenary acquiescence of her peers, her ongoing participation in everyday life in Hoyerswerda forces her reason to admit the whole utopian endeavor as she was taught it as illusory academic hot air. Her supervisors, too, those whom she accuses of resignation, acknowledge their own disillusionment regarding the gap between ideal and reality. One, Landauer, explains to Linkerhand, "We don't build our cities for multiple generations anymore. Nonetheless, I had hoped to build a city that would not just house two or three generations—a city that offers them more than just a modified space in which you can put a table and a bed. And, picture it, I had already imagined myself retired, walking through my city and on Sundays drinking a mocha on this terrace or, ever better, in a sidewalk café. Have you been to Paris?" (Reimann 1998b: 154). Evoking Paris, Baudelaire's quintessential bourgeois city, Landauer exposes himself to have believed himself charged with the development of the next great world metropolis, the ideal socialist city ready to represent for the twentieth century what Paris does for the nineteenth. Instead, he is building Neustadt, "just a provisional measure," merely a series of temporary housing quarters (344). Even Schafheutlin, Linkerhand's supervisor and unlikely friend, whom she considers to be hopelessly conciliatory, finally exposes to her a common dissatisfaction at Neustadt's deficiencies:

> Hmm, do you really believe I wouldn't also rather build as we planned and built it for ourselves on a hundred evenings? Do you really believe that I have never wished, like Landauer, to walk sometime through my city, to sit in a theater or on terraces, to observe the people, and to be able to think, that's your doing, this is what you've lived for, and it was worth it ... Do you really believe your dreams are foreign to me, just because I've learned not to declare them anymore? I've sat there just like you a dozen times and have had to swallow disappointment, and you will also sit there a dozen times, and you will learn to take blows without pathetic outcries ... Go back to work. No more discussion, please. The decision has fallen to a higher level. (591)[6]

The divergence of practice from theory and the architects' resulting frustration, as seen in the quotations above, develop over the course of the novel as the story of Neustadt/Hoyerswerda. Physical housing buildings do in fact appear, but what becomes more tangible even, precisely by its absence, is the community these physical buildings alone are unable to embody, along with the edicts of unnamed superiors who block every attempt to fill this void.

Perhaps the inability for urban designers to establish a community in Hoyerswerda derived, at least in part, from their denial of the city's history and tradition. Although very small, a town did exist prior to Hoyerswerda having been chosen as the second socialist city. A market hamlet in the largely agrarian, Catholic Sorbian Lausatia, Hoyerswerda can be traced as far back as 1744 in written chronicles (Schmidt 1998: 5).[7] Numerous accounts of the founding of Hoyerswerda (Neustadt) reveal that developers and politicians interested in the combine's success relied on a rhetorical strategy of denial of or even disdain for the Sorbs and their farming traditions in order to justify the appropriation of large areas of their natural and agricultural landscape. A fictionalized representation of this treatment of the Sorbs can be found in Jurij Koch's novel, *Landung der Träume* (Landing of Dreams), in which a young journalist paraphrases a dignitary at the combine's groundbreaking ceremony: "[He] spoke of the construction of the development of the land … He conjured an image of the cheerful future with factories and smokestacks on the heath, on which cities would be erected, cities with highrises and shops. Historical justice would finally arrive and put an end to the backwoods backwardness of the populace" (1982: 238). The Sorbs, by mere virtue of having remained agrarian in an industrialized world, are considered rubes. A quotation considered earlier, in which the head of Hoyerswerda's urban development, Richard Paulick, calls Hoyerswerda a "backward agrarian district" and equates Lausatia with "backwoods," proves another prescient example in the current discussion (Paulick 1960: 355). Reimann's heroine also dismisses the indigenous population as foreign, curious, and uncultivated. As she enters the region for the first time on the train, Linkerhand observes a few Sorbian women as distant Others, whom she will never come to know despite her lengthy stay in their home:

> At a station, whose name was already displayed bilingually, three old farmers' wives got on the train, made hugely round by uncountable ankle-length black skirts, wearing green woolen headscarves … They held their covered baskets on their laps, on their green half-aprons, stared ahead, and conversed leisurely, with long pauses, in a language incomprehensible to Franziska …, and they reminded her of figures from Brother Grimm fairy tales, as if they had climbed out of a distant past in forgotten costumes. (She never learned to tell these old farmers' wives apart). (123)

These women are so foreign to Franziska's sensibilities that she cannot (or will not) distinguish even their facial features. She never comes to know the Sorbs because she has no need for them; her ambition to "realize an urban planning ideal" precludes the involvement of essentially agrarian lifestyles, just as it does the home gardens that spontaneously appear on future building sites to irk her and her colleagues (Reimann 1998b: 531–532). Socialism is to be the economic and political system of the future, and Hoyerswerda is to be its model city; acknowledgment of the past beyond trifles like the bilingual signs could undermine the forward thrust of the design plans.

Reimann, unlike her protagonist, recognizes this lack of historical tradition in Hoyerswerda in a 1960 diary entry, in which she concedes the advantages of the new living quarters for the workers at a time of a desperate housing shortage but simultaneously mourns the city's relentless futurism: "The whole city Hoyerswerda was unpleasant to me in its oppressive newness (although I know too well what the pretty, comfortable, sunny apartments mean for our new town and its residents, who mostly come from close and constrictive situations); it has no tradition, no atmosphere. It's just modern" (Reimann 1998a: 35). Reimann's experience of the city exposes a fundamental contradiction in this frequently perceived lack of tradition in Hoyerswerda. Although she seeks some connection to the past and therefore apparently does not consciously eschew its importance, her complaint reveals nonetheless her own dismissal of a very real cultural tradition in the region. The Sorbs remain invisible even in her professed fervent desire for a respite from "newness." Similarly, Volker Braun has "the fatal feeling that nothing stays as it was here, that everything floats away and changes" (1976: 100). For Braun, the past in Hoyerswerda is ephemeral, so that the city becomes a signifier for an ever evolving, constant present. That Hoyerswerda's history eludes its observers and critics derives precisely from the city's role from the conception of its Neustadt as a locus for socialist historical production; in order to maintain a strong narrative of now and later, it was necessary to ignore the past, which became an empty verbal signifier against which to contrast the present and the future in the developing narrative: a mere cipher.

Once the future came, in a form irreconcilable with the initial plan, the roles of the past and future in the narrative were reversed. After the two Germanies unified, after the coal mines were closed and the scope of the combine vastly reduced, after economic downturn with soaring unemployment rates befell the city, after its slow decline to a ghost town became evident, the future could no longer maintain its signifying power for Hoyerswerda. It no longer seemed tenable. The present with its economic and social hardships and violence, and the past with the community's role as chosen and planned socialist city, became the historical narratives being written by any reference to Hoyerswerda.[8] Now the present and the past were the content and the future had become the cipher, the empty verbal signifier representing a non-time in the city's history. Braun reaches the same conclusion in "Die Leute von Hoywoy (2)," a follow-up to the aforementioned text of the same title and written in response to the pogrom in Hoyerswerda in 1991.[9] Braun asks, "What had evolved amid the lazy peace, the state-inflicted boredom? ... They had become sedentary. They had ceased moving into the future, into the world" (1998: 65). Suddenly, this city that had been defined by its future-oriented design had become aggressively reactionary. Indeed, this ideological turn to look back that Braun sees while reflecting on the possible origins for the crime also began to manifest physically on the surface of the city, if not in the sense of a conservative drive toward historical reconstruction (what could it reconstruct?), at least in the sense that it no longer expressed any orientation toward the future. Rather, Hoyerswerda began to reveal a decided trend toward aging and decay, and a gradual march toward urban death. The life and energy of the city had left the future and moved into the past.

This observation is not merely theoretical. All demographic and economic studies of the city confirm this course. As quickly as Hoyerswerda had grown, so quickly does it now seem to be shrinking. In the twenty years since unification, the city has shrunk from approximately 72,000 inhabitants to approximately 40,000 in 2007 (de Quetteville 2007: 18). Some demographers consider the latter statistic generous, as the withering population has led to city lines being redrawn; the population within the city lines as they were in 1990 may indeed be even lower. This trend is not expected to abate, which is no astonishing revelation when one considers that the bulk of emigrants are young people fleeing the unemployment rate that continues to be staggeringly high. Since the closing of Schwarze Pumpe after reunification, Hoyerswerda has consistently ranked among the most employment-deficient cities in the federal republic.[10] On a main thoroughfare in the Altstadt, almost every storefront has a "to let" sign in the window.

In combination with an already low birth rate across Germany, the loss of young women, who are leaving at a faster rate than the men, portends further demographic decline; without the promise of a next generation, Hoyerswerda is now the home of a swiftly aging population and threatens to become a ghost town.[11] Indeed, in Future Atlas 2007, a study by a Swiss think tank, Prognos, in which all 439 cities and regions in Germany were ranked according to their *Zukunftschancen* (chances for the future), Hoyerswerda emerged as the lowest-ranked urban district at 430, under the heading "very high risk for the future." In demography, it ranked last; in 2007, Hoyerswerda was losing population faster than any other city or region in the republic. And so absence has become the primary development in Hoyerswerda since unification: absence of people to be sure, but also absence of youth, of prospects, of vitality. And this absence has made itself manifest physically: as apartments become vacant, buildings are demolished; as schools become devoid of children to teach, their doors are closed. This was not always the case. In the 1990s, money from the West flowed into the city as it did into others; the shopping center on the central square of the Neustadt was turned into a western-style mall, a large and modern swimming facility appeared on the outskirts of town, and Globus—a wholesale discount store not unlike a Super Walmart—opened a branch on the edge of the Altstadt. But these developments were unable to halt the soaring employment loss that had resulted from the vast reduction of Schwarze Pumpe and other GDR industries. Hoyerswerda, an unpopular recipient for welfare due to its notoriety as a Neonazi hotbed, saw this influx of funds diminish. It became easier—and many would argue, more sensible—to ignore Hoyerswerda than to revive it.

The people who remain in Hoyerswerda do not suffer from denial about the city's prospects. The last decade has seen the city, along with others around the former GDR, come to terms with its reality as a *schrumpfende Stadt* (shrinking city). Spaces that had been vacant lots due to the demolition of *Plattenbauten* have been turned into parks, and buildings on the outskirts of town are more or less ignored while buildings in the central part of town are being renovated presumably in an effort to encourage the population to condense. A 2010 tour guide of Hoyerswerda even seems to assume its readership has come to the city to examine the remnants of its socialist design and to witness its not-so-gradual decline (Biernath 2005: 1). The excursions in this guide divide the city into the same units as the GDR's original plan and describe their development, and its maps identify not only the *Sehenswürdigkeiten* (sightseeing spots, literally "things worthy of being seen"), but also mark the spaces that had once held now-demolished buildings with little *x*'s. In contrast, however, the parks and renovated *Plattenbauten* in the city center are not highlighted in this guide. The author, Peter Biernath, ends his guidebook by referring to Brigitte Reimann, asking whether "the only thing that remains of Hoyerswerda [is] a novel that, by means of its provocative nature, completely and uncomfortably mirrors the state of disintegration into which the individual, the state, and the society of the GDR ... had devolved?" (73).[12] Biernath's somewhat hyperbolic rhetorical question captures the signifying power of the absences left by a city in decline. The utopian ideals of Hoyerswerda's original plans, betrayed and abandoned, appear hopelessly anachronistic more than twenty years after the collapse of the GDR, and the city, as it still stands today, is defined more by this outdated past than it is by its present.

One must be careful not to simply equate this turn to the past with nostalgia. Nostalgia, "a longing for a home that no longer exists or has never existed" as Svetlana Boym defines it, unquestionably contributes to a certain amount of interest in the past in Hoyerswerda (2001: xiii). But where nostalgia "desires to obliterate history and turn it into private or collective mythology, to revisit time like space, refusing to surrender to the irreversibility of time that plagues the human condition," the voids of Hoyerswerda achieve precisely the opposite (Boym 2001: xv). They reveal—even revel in—the transience of historical moments, and the void observer, in contrast to Boym's nostalgic, is left to contemplate the irreversibility of time. Indeed, as Julia Hell and Andreas Schönle ascertain with regard to analogous ruins, "[r]uin gazing ... always involves reflections about history: about the nature of the event, the meaning of the past for the present, the nature of history itself as eternal cycle, progress, apocalypse, or murderous dialectic process" (2010: 1). Voids, like Hell and Schönle's ruins, are "transhistorical" (1). They connect the gazer with the ebbs and flows of history in their generalized forms—the rises and declines of empires, the continuous and often brutal reassertion of nature over humanity, the periods of peace and the periods of conflict—while nostalgic longing requires historical specificity. The nostalgic resists the march of history by desiring the return to a specific and personal moment. The observer of Hoyerswerda's voids, meanwhile, resembles more the ruin gazer than the nostalgic, not because they do not point to a specific moment in history—the forty-year life of a small nation could not be more historically specific—but because the observer's reflections do not derive from an attempt to defy history and regain this moment, but rather from an effort to comprehend its place in the inevitable temporality of civilization. Consider again, for instance, the x's in the tour guide. A nostalgic guide would focus its reader's attention on what remains of the past; this guide, however, inspires void gazing by pointing out what no longer remains.

Thus, Hoyerswerda lingers as a gradually disappearing monument not to Hoyerswerda per se but to the cycle of time itself. The empty lots, once underneath the familiar gray-and-beige housing blocks, lie as a foil to the Frauenkirche (Church of Our Lady) in Dresden, once a pile of rubble and now again a structure. The abandoned *Wohnblöcke* contrast with the sanitized and gentrified old edifices in Prenzlauer Berg and Friedrichshain, neighborhoods in former East Berlin popular among young professionals, intellectuals, and artists. The craters in the earth left by decades of coal mining, spreading across the landscape surrounding Hoyerswerda, mismatch the beautifully restored parks of Potsdam. Rejuvenation projects throughout the former GDR carefully preserve or revive artifacts that seem to have easily digestible cultural or aesthetic significance, either because they represent broadly celebrated artistic endeavors, or because any historical complexity is overshadowed by beauty. The Frauenkirche may be rebuilt because it is beautiful and any abuse to which its original construction might have contributed lies in a distant enough past so as to be quaint. The Palast der Republik had to fall because it was ugly and the wounds it signifies still gaped for many. By choosing one and not the other, as we know, the players in power decide, however, to sanitize history as well; the uncomfortable disappears and the celebrated is memorialized. But in Hoyerswerda, history is too short for the whitewashing of memory. Nothing new or re-new is materializing in the space from which the uncomfortable, the now despised, is disappearing. No old, illustrious past—at least not any acknowledged one—existed to return and take the place of it. Until the trees and wildlife reclaim their right of residence, the physical signs of absence in Hoyerswerda remain, challenging the dominant historical paradigms being written in Dresden and Weimar, in Potsdam and Berlin.

The entire city of Hoyerswerda, then, could be seen as an inadvertent example of James Young's countermonument. Young describes Jochen and Esther Gerz's pillar in Harburg, Germany, a temporary installation reminiscent of the smoke stack of a gas chamber, on which visitors etched their names as a vow to remain vigilant, until the column disappeared under the weight of a critical mass of signatures decrying fascism. Young attributes the power of the work to its inherent transience and fluctuation. He writes, "With audacious simplicity, the countermonument thus flouts any number of cherished memorial conventions: its aim is not to console but to provoke; not to remain fixed but to change; not to be everlasting but to disappear" (1993: 30). Permanent monuments eventually become "archaic, strange, or irrelevant altogether," but temporary countermonuments attest to the evolution not only of human experience itself but of our memory of this experience as well (Young 1993: 47). Young inquires, "How better to remember forever a vanished people than by the perpetually unfinished, ever-vanishing monument?" (31). It would be callous indeed to equate the shrinking of Hoyerswerda due to economic hardship with the attempted extermination of the Jews, but the aesthetic analysis of the provisional nature of the countermonument has useful application here. Hoyerswerda, as it shrinks, narrates a story of the disconnection between ideal and real, the circularity of history, the impermanence of human efforts, and the complexity of the past.

Countermonuments strive against the Benjaminian auratization of the artwork at the expense of the act of remembering itself. The Gerzes' installation bothered locals with its "ugliness," but Young questions their objections: "But what repels the critics is not clear. Is it the monument's unsightly form or the grotesque sentiments it captures and then reflects back to the community? As a social mirror, it becomes doubly troubling in that it reminds the community of what happened then and, even worse, how they now respond to the memory of the past" (1993: 35).

Ugliness and unpleasantness are central to the role of the countermonument in confronting its onlookers with the disjointedness, contradictions, and even horrors of the past and demanding their attention to the same in the present. The choices of construction—whether of buildings, parks, or monuments—inevitably narrow the possibilities available for the interpretation of memory. The empty spaces of deconstruction, like temporary installations, however, tell silent stories of the past. Returning to Huyssen, they democratically give observers agency in constructing historical narrative.[13] By doing so as well, the voids of Hoyerswerda linger as countermonuments, both resisting the dominant memory narratives being written in other cities by the filling of voids through construction and reconstruction, and democratically drawing from the observer a spontaneous and individualized interpretation.

Neustadt and its development are described by Trojanowicz in *Franziska Linkerhand* as *Unbekannte Größen* (unknown quantities): variables, placefillers (Reimann 1998b: 497). Neustadt is a city, but one borne out of nothing. What past it has is deemed ignorable; as far as she, her colleagues, and the authorities are concerned, it has grown out of what had been a wooded emptiness. Neustadt might have been located in any number of places across the GDR, and in fact similar settlements did appear in Eisenhüttenstadt, Halle-Neustadt, Schwedt, and Wolfen, among others. If Neustadt is x, they are y, z, a, and b. Had the formula been designed properly, had the city not "missed its mark" in terms of function, as Trojanowicz put it, the variable might have become a known value (Reimann 1998b: 359).[14] Instead, Neustadt fails to define its function and remains an unknown quantity, a cipher that fills a space in the equation without any defined value.[15] For Reimann and during the GDR in general, Hoyerswerda lacks a known value because it could not develop a sense of community or define its urban function beyond providing workers with a place to sleep, and because it has largely overlooked or denied the indigenous tradition of the region. Today, Hoyerswerda continues to act as a cipher, but now in a very different equation. With little prospect for a future and with its notoriety, the city has become a placefiller in a national narrative about economic woes in the former GDR.[16] Playing a similarly metonymic role in this narrative as Flint, Michigan, does in the United States, the name Hoyerswerda has become synonymous in German parlance with rightwing fundamentalism, unemployment, and demolition.[17] Hoyerswerda is no tourist destination, except perhaps for a very few with a specialized interest in the GDR's social or physical history. The reality of day-to-day life of the approximately 30,000 people who continue to reside there does not—cannot—coincide with the image the city has developed by its relatively frequent representations the media, including in this chapter itself. The known Hoyerswerda is all surface, a Baudrillardian simulation of a reality that cannot truly be known.[18] The city's ability to narrate the kinds of disjointed, ruptured, and complex stories about its GDR past and the realities of a unified Germany, as Huyssen advocates, derives precisely from its role as an empty signifier without a defined signified, as an unknown value in an incompletely defined formula. In Huyssen's Berlin, the voids are defined by the constraints that enclose them, both spatially or temporally. Neither type of limitation defines Hoyerswerda's voids, however, because the available space and time only expand. Whereas the possibilities for No Man's Land have given way to the actualities of Potsdamer Platz and the Memorial to the Murdered Jews of Europe, the variables represented by Hoyerswerda's voids remain unknown.

A sign, seen by the author in 2004 on a lot across from the mall on which a residential building once stood, reading "Space for Your Ideas!," takes on a far different significance than its intended commercial one when considered in light of the reflections in this chapter (see figure 6.1). The realtors or city officials who erected the sign in the hopes of attracting new business and life to Hoyerswerda were undoubtedly announcing the lot as a space for the imagining of possible futures. But left as a lot growing weeds, we had instead a space for the contemplation of possible pasts: what might have stood here, who might have lived here, and what could have occurred to lead to their present absence.[19] Another

Figure 6.1. "Space for your ideas!" (seen 2004). Photograph by Gwyneth Cliver.

Figure 6.2. On an outer wall of the closed Konrad-Zuse-Gymnasium (seen 2004). Photograph by Gwyneth Cliver.

sign, reading "Hoywoy unfolding," discovered by the author on the outer wall of the Konrad-Zuse-Gymnasium (a secondary school) two years following its closing in 2002, further illuminates the suggestive power of absence (see figure 6.2). The designer's choice of words reveals perhaps a somewhat awkward command of English; Hoywoy "unraveling" might have been more idiomatically correct. But the particular choice of words assists in our study here; as Hoyerswerda unravels, a story unfolds: a history of the city, of the attempts and failures of socialism, and of the attempts and failures of unification. This history, narrated by the city's spaces of absence, will not endure forever; the city will continue to shrink and large portions of it will succumb to nature. For the time being, the spaces themselves, left for the curious to observe, provide an alternative historical narrative to those being generated by reconstruction efforts elsewhere.

Notes

1. All translations from the German are the author's unless translated editions of works are cited.

2. This list of impressions is imparted in a literary style, without quotation marks or information identifying the original source(s). It is unclear whether these are direct quotations, paraphrasings, or aggregates of the statements of multiple individuals.

3. Hoyerswerda is also infamous in a united Germany for a truly outrageous pogrom that occurred there in 1991, the first attack on foreigners in the former GDR following unification. Fire was set to an apartment complex housing immigrants and the nation watched as television reports showed German citizens passively watching and sometimes even cheering the act. For more information, see for instance Kohl (2011), Book (2011), Smee (2006), and Kinzer (1991).

4. The *Plattenbauten* were, in fact, very popular in the beginning and people tolerated long waitlists to escape the *Altbau* (old housing), which was commonly considered backwards, because most toilets were shared among units and the buildings lacked central heating.

5. For a comprehensive history of the planning of Hoyerswerda's Neustadt in particular and GDR urban planning in general with accompanying primary documents, see Durth, Düwel, and Gutschow's two-volume *Architektur und Städtebau der DDR* (Architecture and Urban Development in the GDR).

6. "ja, glauben Sie denn, ich würde nicht auch lieber bauen, wie wir es geplant haben und für uns gebaut an hundert Abenden? Glauben Sie, ich habe mir nie gewünscht wie Landauer, später einmal durch meine Stadt zu gehen, in einem Theater, auf Terrassen zu sitzen, den Leuten zuzusehen und denken zu dürfen: das ist dein Werk, dafür hast du gelebt, und es hat sich gelohnt … Glauben Sie, mir sind Ihre Träume fremd, nur weil ich verlernt habe, sie zu deklamieren? Ich habe dutzendmal so dagesessen wie Sie jetzt und Enttäuschungen schlucken müssen, und Sie werden noch dutzendmal so dasitzen, und Sie werden es lernen, Schläge einzustecken ohne pathetische Schreie … Gehen Sie an Ihre Arbeit. Keine Diskussion, bitte. Die Entscheidung ist auf höherer Ebene gefallen."

7. Irina Liebmann mentions having read accounts of the city's existence extending back at least six hundred years (88).

8. See, for example, Book (2011), Kohl (2011), Jaschensky (2010), Kulisch (2009), de Quetteville (2007), Cowley (2006), Smee (2006), "Still troubled" (2005), Landler (2004), O'Brien (2004), Havlat (2002), and Zielbauer (2002).

9. For more information, please see note 3.

10. The 2007 Prognos report places Hoyerswerda at 196th of 439 regions in Germany in terms of the vitality of its job market (Prognos 2007). This statistic itself is probably misleading, as so many young people have left Hoyerswerda and the average of age of the population is very high (Jaschensky 2010). The city no longer appears on its own in the 2010 rankings, as it had by that time been merged with Bautzen for statistical purposes.

11. Reimann prophesied this event as early as 1968: "The coal is running out. Maybe Hoy will be a ghost town like the deserted golddigger settlements in twenty years" (Reimann 1998a: 35).

12. "Ist das einzige, das übrig bleibt von Hoyerswerda, ein Roman, der durch seinen provokanten Charakter ein kompletter und unbequemer Spiegel des Zustandes der Zerrüttung ist, worin Individuum, Staat und Gesellschaft in der DDR ... geraten waren?"

13. Julia Hell and Andreas Schönle discern a similar phenomenon of signification in the human fascination with ruin gazing. The arguments can be taken to be analogous, as both ruins and voids represent endings, destruction, deconstruction, and decay—the negative flipsides to a modern notion of the progress of civilization. Remarking on the subjectivity of ruin gazing, not unlike that of void gazing, Hell and Schönle emphasize, "The beholder defines the ruin" because the ruin "bespeaks a potential vacuity of meaning" (2010: 7, 6). Like the void, "[t]he ruin ... enables individual freedom, imagination, and subjectivity" (8).

14. "die Stadt [verfehlt] ihre Funktion"

15. Similarly, Hell and Schönle's ruin "is a ruin precisely because it seems to have lost its function or meaning in the present, while retaining a suggestive, unstable romantic potential" (2010: 6).

16. The author, having had lived in Hoyerswerda herself over a decade ago, is frequently confronted with this notoriety. When one mentions the city to Germans, especially West Germans, the response is almost invariably—paraphrased—"Ach, Hoyerswerda! Wie kann man da leben?" (Oh, my! Hoyerswerda! How can anyone live there?)

17. One can observe this metonymic role quite clearly in the titles of two articles, one in *Zeit Online*, "Niemand will das neue Hoyerswerda sein" (Nobody wants to be the next Hoyerswerda), and one in *Süddeutsche.de*, "Mehr Hartz IV für Berlin, weniger für Hoyerswerda" (More State Support for Berlin, Less for Hoyerswerda) (Schwickert 2012, Sinn 2009). For further examples, see Jaschensky (2010), Kulish (2009), Cowley (2006), "Still troubled" (2005), Landler (2004), O'Brien (2004), Havlat (2002).

18. Hell and Schönle remind us that the postmodern condition insures that "so many of us experience the rawness of ruinous reality primarily as a media effect" (2010: 5).

19. In fact, the space has since been converted into a statue garden.

References

Anspruch und Wirklichkeit. 1993. Hoyerswerda: Stadt Hoyerswerda, Einwohneramt.

Baudrillard, Jean. 1994. *Simulacra and Simulation.* Translated by Sheila Faria Glaser. Ann Arbor: University of Michigan Press.

Benjamin, Walter. 1968. "The Work of Art in the Age of Mechanical Reproduction." In *Illuminations,* edited and introduction by Hannah Arendt, translated by Harry Zohn, 217–251. New York: Schocken Books.

Biernath, Peter. 2005. *Architektour Hoyerswerda: Stadt—Bau—Kunst.* Hoyerswerda: Kulturbund e.V. Hoyerswerda.

Book, Simon. 2011. "20 Jahre Hoyerswerda: Eine Stadt kämpft um ihren Ruf." *Spiegel Online* 22 September. http://www.spiegel.de/politik/deutschland/ 0,1518,786697,00.html, accessed 6 January 2012.

Boym, Svetlana. 2001. *The Future of Nostalgia.* New York: Basic Books.

Braun, Volker. 1976. "Die Leute von Hoywoy." In *Es genügt nicht die einfache Wahrheit: Notate,* 100–101. Frankfurt: Suhrkamp.

———. 1998. "Die Leute von Hoywoy (2)." In *Wir befinden uns soweit wohl, wir sind erst einmal am Ende: Äußerungen,* 65–66. Frankfurt: Suhrkamp.

Christ, Richard. 1975. *Reisebilder: Ansichtskarten aus der DDR.* 2nd ed. Berlin and Weimar: Aufbau Verlag.

Cowley, Jason. 2006. "Dresden: In the east, the Cup does not overflow." *Observer Foreign Pages* 25 June: 29.

de Quetteville, Harry. 2007. "E German towns 'left to poverty.'" *The Daily Telegraph* 9 April: 18.

Durth, Werner, Jörn Düwel, and Niels Gutschow. 1998. *Architektur und Städtebau der DDR.* Vol. 1. *Ostkreuz: Personen, Pläne, Perspektiven.* Frankfurt and New York: Campus Verlag.

———. 1998. *Architektur und Städtebau der DDR.* Vol. 2. *Aufbau: Städte, Themen, Dokumente.* Frankfurt and New York: Campus Verlag.

"Gemeinden in Deutschland nach Fläche, Bevölkerung und Postleitzahl am 31.03.2011 (1. Quartal)." Table. *Statistisches Bundesamt Deutschlands. Gemeindeverzeichnis-Informationssystem (GV-ISys).* http://www.destatis.de/ jetspeed/portal/cms/Sites/destatis/Internet/DE/Content/Statistiken/Reg ionales/Gemeindeverzeichnis/Administrativ/Archiv/GVAuszugQ/1Q_ 31032011__Auszug.psml, accessed 24 June 2011.

Grass, Günter. 1995. *Ein weites Feld.* Göttingen: Steidl Verlag.

Havlat, Konrad. 2002. "Borderline cases." *The Economist,* 365 (8302): 15.

Hell, Julia, and Andreas Schönle, eds. 2010. *Ruins of Modernity.* Durham, N.C. and London: Duke University Press.

Huyssen, Andreas. 2003. *Present Pasts: Urban Palimpsests and the Politics of Memory.* Stanford: Stanford University Press.

Jaschensky, Wolfgang. 2010. "Leben nach der Platte." *Süddeutsche.de,* 12 September: n. pag. http://www.sueddeutsche.de/politik/unser-osten-demog raphie-leben-nach-der-platte-1.996590, accessed 7 February 2012.

Kinzer, Stephen. 1991. "A Wave of Attacks On Foreigners Stirs Shock in Germany." *The New York Times,* 1 October: A1.

Klauser, Wilhelm. 2008. "Reicht ein Großwohnbau als Zeichen?: Fragwürdiger Abbruch und Umbau in Zentrum von Hoyerswerda." *Bauwelt* 99 (6): 28–33.

Koch, Jurij. 1982. *Landung der Träume.* Halle-Leipzig: Mitteldeutscher Verlag.

Kohl, Christiane. 2011. "Eine Stadt bekämpft den rechten Pöbel." *Süddeutsche. de,* 15 September: n pag. http://www.sueddeutsche.de/politik/neonazis-in-ostdeutschland-eine-stadt-bekaempft-den-rechten-poebel-1.1144416, accessed 7 February 2012.

Kulisch, Nicholas. 2009. "In East Germany, a Decline as Stark as a Wall." *The New York Times,* 19 June. http://www.nytimes.com/2009/06/19/world/eu rope/19germany.html, accessed 7 February 2012.

Landler, Mark, and Victor Homola. 2004. "In Germany's East, a Harvest of Silence." *The New York Times,* 22 August: 10.

Liebmann, Irina. 1997. *Letzten Sommer in Deutschland: Eine romantische Reise.* Cologne: Kiepenheuer & Witsch.

O'Brien, Kevin J. 2004. "Last Out, Please Turn Off the Lights." *The New York Times,* 28 May: 1.

Paulick, Richard. 1960. "Hoyerswerda: eine sozialistische Stadt der Deutschen Demokratischen Republik." *Deutsche Architektur* 9 (7): 355–374.

"Prognos Zukunftsatlas 2007—Deutschlands Regionen im Zukunftswettbewerb." 2007. Prognos AG. http://www.prognos.com/fileadmin/pdf/Atlanten/Zuk unftsatlas_07/Prognos_Zukunftsatlas_2007_Auf_einen_Blick.pdf, accessed 9 June 2014.

Reimann, Brigitte. 1998. "Diese Stadt Hoyerswerda." In *Hoyerswerda—Literarische Spiegelungen,* 34–35. Hoyerswerda: Hoyerswerdaer Kunstverein—Freundeskreis der Künste und Literatur—e.V.

———. 1998. *Franziska Linkerhand.* Berlin: Aufbau Verlag.

Schmidt, Martin. 1998. "Vorwort." In *Hoyerswerda—Literarische Spiegelungen,* 5–7. Hoyerswerda: Hoyerswerdaer Kunstverein—Freundeskreis der Künste und Literatur—e.V.

Schwickert, Martin. 2012. "Niemand will das neue Hoyerswerda sein." *Zeit Online,* 18 January. http://www.zeit.de/kultur/film/2012-01/kriegerin-intervi ew-wnendt, accessed 7 February 2012.

Sinn, Hans-Werner. 2009. "Mehr Hartz IV für Berlin, weniger für Hoyerswerda." *Süddeutsche.de,* 9 November. http://www.sueddeutsche.de/wirtschaft/ifochef-sinn-mehr-hartz-iv-fuer-berlin-weniger-fuer-hoyerswerda-1.143165, accessed 7 February 2012.

Smee, Jess. 2006. "Exodus from east leaves land of broken promises to the wolves and neo-Nazis." *The Guardian,* 15 November. http://www.guardian .co.uk/world/2006/nov/15/germany.mainsection, accessed 7 February 2012.

"Still troubled." 2005. *The Economist,* 376 (8441): 58, 25 August. http://www .economist.com/node/4323186, accessed 9 June 2014.

Young, James. 1993. *The Texture of Memory: Holocaust Memorials and Meaning.* New Haven, C.T. and London: Yale University Press.

Zielbauer, Paul. 2002. "As Eastern Germany Rusts, Young Workers Leave." *The New York Times,* 25 December: A3.

Part III

❥ ◆ ❦

Theories

Chapter 7

Sounding out Erfurt

Does the Song Remain the Same?

HEINER STAHL

Does a city have a particular sound? Of course most cities sound similar—by day, the hubbub of markets and malls, the quieter buzz of green spaces, and the noise of traffic and police sirens; and by night the musical beats of the clubs, pubs, and street corners. Most cities, however, have a unique sound that sets them apart. All sounds produced by and in a city blend together to form the scales, cadences, and descants of a complex musical composition (Schafer 1973). This chapter will outline at first how sounds mold an urban landscape by forging a space consisting of a multitude of acoustic events. Secondly, it will demonstrate how, within this setting, a sound functions as a marker, or signifier, of the changes occurring within the city itself.

The analysis focuses on the city of Erfurt, a medium-sized city of approximately 200,000 inhabitants, located near Weimar in the center of Germany. Choosing an auditory perspective allows an examination of the political, social, and infrastructural change in the transition from a socialist to a postsocialist cityscape. Especially in the 1990s, Erfurt underwent a radical process of restructuring, evolution, and, in some respects, emulation of changes occurring elsewhere. These reflections on Erfurt's development, encompassing the time period from roughly the mid-1960s to 2013 aim at applying the concepts of *soundscape,* *acouphene,* and *phonotope* as a theoretical framework. Considering the acoustic dimensions of an urban entity supports the adoption of a distinctive approach at the point where urban studies, the theory of media and communication, and contemporary history converge.

The Canadian composer and scholar Raymond Murray Schafer coined the term *soundscape* to understand and to conceive better the presence, structure, and interconnectedness of any kind of sound-emitting source

(Schafer 1973). Secondly, Michel Serres defines *acouphene* as a mode of contention between the internal world and the sounds of the world outside, where individual experiences become the focal point of analysis (Serres 1998). The *phonotope*, suggested by the German philosopher Peter Sloterdijk, broadens Serres's concept of the *acouphene* by linking it to the socially generated construction of noise, especially in terms of the blocking out of unwanted sounds. Creating a *phonotope*, therefore, fosters the insulation of individuals from groups and, in turn, supports the creation of acoustic comfort zones (Sloterdijk 2004). Central to Sloterdijk's approach to the insulated zones of convenience is the capacity of individuals and communities to filter sound, just as it is crucial to the tactics and politics of filtering affiliated with Schafer's concept of *soundscape*. These three terms, briefly touched on here, prove helpful in illuminating what sorts of sound emissions are linked to specific but acausal noise effects. Noise is, first of all, an unwanted sound. Therefore, it can be understood as a loose and flexible, even uncontainable and illimitable arena of social negotiation. Furthermore, noise serves as a projection screen on which yet unregulated acoustic events are related to practices and procedures of filtering, appropriation, and scaling. Sounds can be characterized as physical stimuli and shared sensory background (Thibaud 2011), created in places and locations. The case of Erfurt reveals that the deficient management of unwanted sounds did challenge the means of standardization associated with the socialist notion of normality and rule. By means of this approach, sound and noise advance from the margins of scholarly interests into ongoing discussions within contemporary history and media and communication studies.

More recently, Jürgen Müller has brought sound within the scope of historical research. He argues that historians still dismiss accounts of sound, and what was heard throughout various historical epochs, without recognizing its analysis as a valid approach to examining the past (Müller 2011: 4). Müller stresses the point that working with past and present forms of hearing, or cultural techniques of listening, is a worthwhile challenge—although it is still uncommon in research methodologies. Müller lists information, orientation, experience, and communication as the main categories for analysis, and suggests that these be embraced with enthusiasm as part of the "aural turn" toward this theoretical approach (Müller 2011: 27). In keeping with Müller's claims and following on the "sound" issue of *Studies in Contemporary History*,[1] as well as in line with Gerhard Paul's panel on "Sound History" at the 2012 meeting of the Association of German Historians, I attempt to define sound and noise as key indicators in the analysis of the shaping of a community within a given historical and political context. The constellations of sound and noise constitute a useful approach to reconsidering post-socialist cityscapes, Erfurt in particular. For the purpose of this study, I have chosen to outline the process of transition and change in the city from the 1960s to 2013 by looking at private and public transport as just one aspect of city life. I start with the contemporary urban traffic policies and developments in the domain of public transport in Erfurt in the first decade following the year 2000. I will then compare these measures to the socialist urban traffic policies of the 1970s, before arguing how an auditory perspective can be adopted when assessing the tangible transformation of an urban cityscape over a given period of time.

The Sound of Erfurt: Auditory Experience of Road Traffic Noise and Public Transport

If you happen to live in a city, there is a strong chance that you find your neighborhood too noisy at times. Many people in this situation would usually just close their windows when the ambient noise produced by inner city traffic gets annoying. If the disturbance becomes too great, we might even resort to earplugs to block out these sounds.

In this respect, my own experience of living in Erfurt is no different. Beginning at around 6 each morning, the constant hum of traffic on the Stauffenbergallee, known during the GDR-era as Wilhelm-Pieck-Straße, travels across the river to reach my apartment. This is the sound of the 28,000 cars that pass over this stretch of road every day.[2] These figures have been calculated on the basis of a comprehensive traffic and noise data collection conducted in 2006, updated three years later by the Erfurt Council's Department of Environmental and Natural Conservation for the purpose of reporting traffic noise across the city, although it is likely that the number of vehicles per day—individually perceived by myself—has increased since then. According to the Noise Action Plan, the level of traffic noise that reaches my flat is, on average, 74 dB (decibel) during the daytime and 65 dB at night. Provisions to combat this sound pollution have not yet been implemented by the municipal departments. The most expensive measure would be to move the lanes about fifteen to twenty meters apart, thereby decreasing the level of noise by 5 dB (Erfurt Noise Action Plan 2009: 30). This would reduce sound pressure by almost half, volume by two-thirds, and sound intensity to a quarter of its previous strength while further reducing public annoyance in this section of the inner city road ring. From the point of view of city planners, however, the nearby riverbank is an obstacle that imposes increasing financial constraints to such a project. In addition, in this district the population actually affected by noise pollution is containable to a discrete number of households.

Traffic is an obvious source of unwanted sounds that must be filtered. While strolling with students, Michael Southworth suggested that we explore the connections between the ecology of everyday life and the experience of loudness in urban space. In order to get the full picture of the evolving conditions within a city, he proposes to include the sensual dimension of meandering through the urban space into all forms of assessment. For Southworth, the human aural perception of sound and noise plays a significant role in experiencing urban districts (Southworth 1969: 52). A *soundscape*, according to Raymond Murray Schafer, is—in its idealized shape—natural, or at least manually and not mechanically created. In the second place, it can be technically engineered and technologically forged. Following on Schafer's distinction, it can be claimed that a modern and, to an even greater extent, a postmodern *soundscape* is made up of multiple layers of acoustic events. To set the stage for an analysis of traffic noise and the soundscape in Erfurt, I first take account of an interwoven net of competing sources, such as mobile phone ringing, the rattling of cooling and heating systems, and music seeping from retail shops.

Erfurt's main train station provides an excellent case with which to examine more closely the concept of the *soundscape*. Recently, while waiting for a train, I heard the usual announcements about the day's timetable vibrating through the arrivals and departures areas. These were given by a recorded female voice stating, "The next train to arrive at platform one is the 6:18 A.M. to Frankfurt." As the echoes of such acoustic data were bouncing wildly around this space of travel and transition, I could not help but wonder about its auditory shape.

The French philosopher and communication theorist Michel Serres asserts that everything audible echoes within places where both listening and regulation take place (Serres 1998: 145). He singles out the human body, nature and environment, and collective social associations as the main sources of noise. Using the term *acouphene*, Serres describes the experience of ringing in the ears, or tinnitus, as a mode of internal contention with sounds outside the ear (Serres 1998: 139). By internalizing the babble of social life in this manner, a person's capacity to endure strong background noise becomes a continuous, even painful challenge. Addressing this, the act of regulation is a system of imposed filtering, which the individual has to accommodate, to adjust properly, or to defy emphatically. Regulation can foster cultural, political, or sensory readjustment. Jacques Attali connects filtering initiatives, for example music policies in the media and the selection of songs at public festivals, to how communities negotiate, manage, and monitor noise. Attali exposes the tactical filtering of sound as a key feature of socialist and communist music policies (Attali 1977: 16). When considering the cultural politics of music, Attali argues that socialist party officials deemed it necessary to regulate, because sound and music had the ability to question state authority and legitimacy. Furthermore, it could be claimed that noise exposure and noise pollution—when fully perceived as a side effect of industrial production and of urban housing construction—may have exceeded the efforts of the socialist bureaucracy to fortify its public welfare statements with practical provisions. Accepting this argument leads to querying whether socialism is louder than capitalism. In order to determine this, it is necessary to reconsider fully the scale to which sensory experiences were screened during periods of political transition. Noise serves as a means by which to explore diverse consequences and transformations during such a period. In a city in transition such as Erfurt, it marks social difficulties with which the community has to cope. On the one hand, noise mirrors what action is required to stabilize social cohesion, and on the other, it signifies insistently the new sound of the multioptional society, embodying the Western model of liberal freedom (Gross 1994).

Mapping a cityscape from an acoustic perspective is challenging in light of the significant political transition of Germany in 1989/90. I aim to link sources of sound and techniques of experiencing sound to reveal the auditory narrative of a particular space—in this case, Erfurt's main train station. First, while such a conjecture might be polemical, the station appears to be calmer and quieter in 2011 than it would have been in 2006, 1996, 1986, or 1976. In my experience, it produces a much more comfortable auditory space and environment.

Secondly, we have to assume that the *soundscape* of the station corresponds with the physical changes to the architectural structure. In proceeding to comment on how a city's past and present are captured in its *soundscape*, I will lay a theoretical foundation from which to consolidate and consider other facts gathered from disciplines like engineering, urban planning, acoustics, and medicine that have not yet been included in mainstream historical research studies.[3] Previously, while the GDR railway service—which retained the name Deutsche Reichsbahn (German Imperial Rail)—was in charge, the echo of train brakes reducing speed resonated through the hall, waiting room, and entrance. The aesthetical transformation of Erfurt's train station, publicly launched in September 2001, more than ten years after Germany's major political transition, has been centered around the obliteration of features since denigrated as socialist. Aiming toward reconciling historical roots in the Prussian and

Imperial German railway service with a current, liberal conception of achievement, accessibility, and the art of civil engineering, the crucial reconstruction activities started in February 2003, and within just two months, the middle section of the station had been fully demolished. By 2008, Erfurt Hauptbahnhof (Erfurt Main Station) had been completely renovated, and it now serves as a transport hub for highspeed trains on route from Frankfurt Airport to Berlin, Leipzig, and Dresden, as well as for connecting regional centers. In addition, railway tracks began gradually to be replaced. The Deutsche Bahn (German Railway Service) began comprehensively to raise noise containment walls and continues voluntarily to install noise protection windows in about two thousand apartments alongside 4.5 kilometers of railway tracks.[4]

The manner in which this space has changed could definitely be regarded as a reinvention. The massive gray stones and dark, dull interior of the building have been replaced by steel arches and a metal-framed roof that supports a transparent ceiling, bringing light and a sense of openness into the structure. This transformation signifies an ideological shift in the powers that determine the appearance and substance of railway service. If a train station is recognized as a multisensory place, as a specific *lieu de mémoire,* it is accessed and experienced through at least one auditory layer (Nora 1990; Ritter 2010). In the case of Erfurt, the visual alignment of the train station as a space is not in line with the narration stored in its acoustic and auditory shape. The shape remains noisy due to the visitor's perception formed by ingrained expectations of such a location. Both expected and unexpected sounds open up corresponding banks of knowledge within the individual's consciousness when reentering space. In my experience, tolerance to and annoyance at a level of noise disturbance in different places can remain static and long-lasting, depending on the individual's auditory experience and the personal disposition toward taking this sensory dimension into account.

Similarly, individuals walking through a city interpret all sorts of sensory data—visual, aural, olfactory, tactile, or gustatory—to understand the unique passage of traffic and people or the layout and structure of streets and buildings. When considering persistence and change within the *soundscape* of a city, public transport is a constant and ubiquitous source of sound and noise at the same time as it offers a wide range of individual auditory experiences over time. The amount of noise emitted and the sources of annoyance induced by noise seem to have remained stable at a high level despite the fact that the population of the city is constantly decreasing (Erfurt Noise Action Plan 2009). Erfurt has lost nearly 10 percent over the past decade, from 220,000 in 1989 to approximately 200,000 in 2010.⁵ Therefore, urban shrinkage does not necessarily lead to a calmer, quieter environment.

During population growth in the 1970s and 1980s, socialist public transport planning aimed at allowing commuters to reach their workplace at an affordable price and in a comfortable amount of time. However, when planning the design of the system, decision-makers were torn between implementing a comprehensive public transport solution and allowing space for private motor vehicle traffic. Competing notions of socialist modernity can be attached to each mode of traveling (Betts and Pence 2008: 10). Engineer Florian Geier, Head of Infrastructure and Track Management at Erfurt Public Transport, stated that in the 1980s, a tram would call at the main station every thirty-five seconds during peak traffic hours.⁶ As the fleet of trams was steadily upgraded from 2000 onward, older models being replaced with newer and quieter trams, the reduction of noise pollution was a side effect. Considering this, the variety of measures concerning public transport and traffic management has led to a form of noise containment that has shaped the auditory experience of Erfurt in the second post-*Wende* decade. In 2011, each tram that arrived at the interchange point at the train station during rush hour was separated by two minutes. Until 1989, the timeslots of the tramway were much tighter. The decrease in frequency and the exchange of the fleet have fully effaced this previous marker of Erfurt socialist soundscape, reducing the noise emissions emerging in Erfurt's main station area.

Sound and Noise: Communicating Narratives of Evolving Cityscapes

Transition and motion clearly indicate stages of evolution, and noise is a by-product. Rossitza Guentcheva posits that noise is positively framed when notions of progress and modernity are attached to the sounds of factories (2004). Accounting for the relevance of sound to a cityscape, it is apposite to understand noise to be a vital layer of community space. This significantly contradicts most stories of urban planning and reshaping, which equate noise regulation with success. Sound brings opportunities to reframe experience within a community, allowing the potential for change from within. This goes along with modes of resisting external forces, for example bureaucratic and political players who attempt to impose order on a population whose sound production cannot be unilaterally contained. Sound and noise interact to form a community-shaped constellation (Arkette 2004). Sophie Arkette, referring to the concept identity construction, claims that acoustic profiles and sound markers are in a state of constant transition: "Each community has sets of sound markers which reinforce its own identity; each district has its own sonic profile" (Arkette 2004: 162).[7] Arkette certainly makes a fair point in connecting sound to identity formation; for instance, music appears currently to be a commonplace identifier for popular culture and adolescent subcultures. The sources of noise and sound, and expectations toward both, are linked to individual filtering tactics, and strategies of self-training, involving deeply stored assumptions about unwanted tones and tunes. Arkette's concept of the sonic profile remains rather loose and volatile in its reference to present developments, however. It neglects the dimension of the individual, stored assumptions, and the inscribed sociocultural arrangements concerning noise. These points have to be clearly marked in any sound profile. Especially when applied to a cityscape, I would suggest properly illustrating its historical dimensions in order to consolidate this approach to auditory experience in the past.

Erfurt's contemporary sonic profile, at least in terms of traffic noise, is built up by several initiatives put into place in the past. In 1969, a comprehensive and integrated plan for traffic capacity was implemented across the city, following the 1967 creation of the Office of Traffic Management, which acted at the community level. The Erfurter Generalverkehrsplan (General Traffic Plan for Erfurt) was adjusted over the ensuing years. Those managing the effort worked in close collaboration with the College of Traffic Engineering, a division of the Dresden Technical University. Erfurt was thus becoming a testing ground for innovations concerning traffic management. After a major administrative reshuffle in the mid-1960s led to stricter accountability to various central ministries based in East Berlin, Erfurt's traffic planning workgroup collaborated, albeit distantly, with the Department of Building and the Department of Housing Estate Planning. Hermann Saitz worked in the Department of Traffic Planning, reporting to the Erfurt Public Construction Authority and the mayor of the city council from the late 1960s onwards.[8] In an interview, Saitz stated that managing traffic at the time meant calculating potential traffic volume capacities, with no consideration for the types and levels of noise being directed at certain parts of the city. He revealed that the main aim of his community think-tank was to confine approximately 80 percent of the traffic that passed through Erfurt to 20 percent of the city's major streets, so that it should only affect 5 percent of residents.

By the late 1970s, connecting the newly built suburbs and council estates on the northern and southern peripheries of the city with the industrial hotspots became a high priority, with the aim of reducing the length of a worker's daily commute (Siedentop et al. 2005: 225). An expansion of the public transport infrastructure in the form of new roads and tramway tracks, as well as the purchasing of tramcars, were the primary focal points of the scheme as it moved into the 1980s.[9] A key challenge at this time was the reorganization of traffic flow that passed through the town center from satellite communities on the way to huge industrial enterprises, such as the publically owned metal-works and plastics factory, situated two and a half miles north of the city center. Outdoor noise exposure peaked three times daily during shift changeover. Complementary to this texture of the soundscape was the noise exposure in the working environment that proved to be even more detrimental than the ambient sound level outside the gates of the production site. The engineering standard concerning noise reduction, implemented in October 1963, displayed several regulatory holes. The most crucial one was that this technical norm was focused on the materiality of products and fully excluded social nuisance.[10]

Triggered by the inclusion of environmental protection policies in the second version of the GDR constitution around 1968 and in preparation for the GDR Landeskulturgesetz (law on homeland and cultural preservation), launched 14 May 1970, the Ministry of Health encouraged a case study about the effects of increasing traffic on the socialist population and the environment. Therefore, in 1968, the county of Erfurt's Department of Hygiene and Public Health—a regional administrative unit superior to the municipal health authority—started measuring noise across the city, as well as across other communities in the region. Findings were classified according to the type of noise and degree of loudness in different areas of the city. The Department had gathered enough data to draw up a "noise map" of the city by the end of 1968 (see figure 7.1), showing that in the northeastern sector, where production sites are bordering or mixed into housing areas, and alongside the main road, the amount of noise exceeded 70 dB during the day.[11]

This conversion from planning to understanding noise to a ready-made study in the form of a chart was very quick indeed. However, the Department of Hygiene and Public Health of the county of Erfurt had been concerned about noise pollution before this term was even coined. Confirming this, in June 1970, R. Ullmann, who continued to head and manage the county's Department of Hygiene and Public Health for two successive decades, suggested in a letter to the public health officer of the communal authority, Elisabeth Völlkopf, that the findings of the 1968 study may be used as benchmarks against which to judge the improvements or deteriorations that had occurred in the interim (*Stadtarchiv Erfurt* 1970: 1). The road traffic regulations and the standard approval

178   *Heiner Stahl*

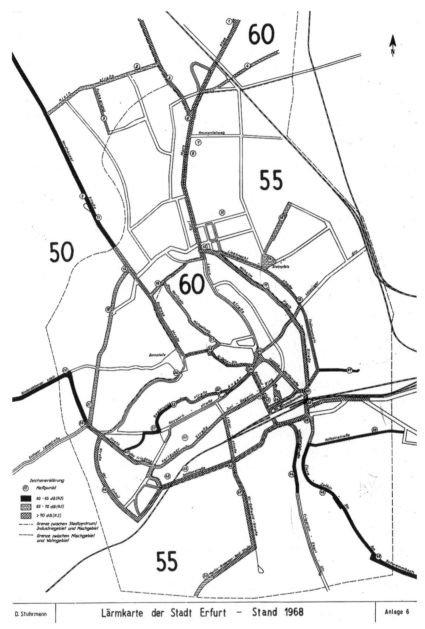

Figure 7.1. Noise Map of the City of Erfurt, 1968. Stadtarchiv Erfurt (StAE) 7/161-10, Bl. 4.

requirements for cars described in the 1968 study were outdated. The acceptable levels of sound emitted by Trabant and Wartburg cars (around 85 phon, a system of measurement that has since been replaced by the decibel dB (A)[12]) were widely exceeded by vehicles—such as the massive Robur trucks or the smaller Barkas transporters—that were on the roads at that time (*Stadtarchiv Erfurt* 1970: 2). The central argument of a presentation given at the Erfurt noise conference in 1967 pointed out that a Trabant added a noise pressure of 80 dB (A) to the ambiance, a Wartburg slightly less. The interiors of both vehicles were much louder, 93 to 94 dB (A), and the noise exposure to drivers was hence massive. For quite a long time, however, no prescriptive limits for car noise could be properly negotiated and implemented (*Stadtarchiv Erfurt* 1967: 1).

Ullmann reported that the public transport trams that passed along the narrow streets of Erfurt were already producing sound at a consistent level of 65 dB (A) during the day, and 64 dB (A) after 10 P.M. (*Stadtarchiv Erfurt* 1970: 5).[13] This is comparable to a loud conversation at one-meter distance or the humming of a vacuum cleaner. He claims that even though ever more inhabitants of Erfurt dared, in 1969 and 1970, to file noise complaints against traffic (six petitions), construction (four petitions), heavy industry (three petitions), and other sources of noise (three petitions), the city council did not recognize noise pollution as a growing problem and showed no interest in addressing the matter (*Stadtarchiv Erfurt* 1970: 8).

In contrast with those council officials who were purely concerned with predicting developments in Erfurt's vehicle and pedestrian traffic, the professionals who dealt with healthcare, hygiene, and food safety issues on a municipal level were more concerned with negative environmental trends. Through their work, they encountered different forms of environmental pollution and therefore spotted more quickly potentially harmful disturbance factors in Erfurt and were more willing to consider setting regulatory thresholds. In 1971, Gerda Lachmann, Erfurt's chief medical officer managing the municipal Department of Health and Social Issues, wrote a report informing the mayor of significant initial successes in the city, brought about by regulations that had been introduced in compliance with heritage protection laws (*Stadtarchiv Erfurt* 1971: 1). She argued that the city council would find it easier to persuade decision-makers and educate residents of the need for such measures if it continued to implement similar regulations for promoting the health of citizens. This laid the groundwork for involving local industries in voluntarily complying with the standards given for observing noise pollution along with measures concerning air, water, or sewage emissions.

Implementing Noise Reduction:
Convincing Apparatchiks and Technocrats

The need to convince stakeholders to collaborate in reforms was central to Lachmann's report. She suggested that the various municipal bodies responsible for areas like healthcare and hygiene, housing, traffic, and construction should collaborate more closely to ensure efficient results. This proved rather difficult to achieve. Lachmann's department worked at cataloguing local air polluters and simultaneously initiated a campaign to measure noise levels around the city, which led to the creation of the noise map mentioned above. This was a unique project in the socialist era, especially in light of the fact that particularly loud enterprises and institutions identified on the map had to implement special measures of filtering and reducing noise (*Stadtarchiv Erfurt* 1971: 2). As the threshold values proved to be significantly inappropriate in terms of effective noise exposure, however, Erfurt's Department of Health worked hard at persuading key regional players in the industrial sector finally to launch voluntary noise emission containment schemes. Local councils in the Erfurt area then started regularly negotiating contracts with companies to fix targets for the reduction of air and noise pollution. In particular, throughout the 1970s, the annual plans of the energy supplier and utility company VEB Energieversorgung (People's Company for Energy Supply) and the plastics producer VEB Plastina (People's Company Plastina) disclosed efforts to comply with guidelines suggested by the municipal authority. Those stipulations included undertaking comprehensive measures to adapt commonly used production technology (*Stadtarchiv Erfurt* 1971: 2). A similar contract was prepared in negotiations with the construction company responsible for building large housing estates (Wohnungsbaukombinat), but its managing director did not agree with the restrictions and penalties, especially as concerned noise reduction (*Stadtarchiv Erfurt* 1971: 3). Ultimately, the local council had to remove these clauses from this second contract in order to reach a compromise. The city council was not in the position to enforce penalties and supplementary settlements with the local companies. In this way, noise reduction measures remained unregulated. Producing goods by any means necessary and as timely as possible was valued by the industries more than mere compliance to the nascent environmental standards, and any efforts made by the company in this respect were merely acts of goodwill (*Stadtarchiv Erfurt* 1971: 3).

The Konzeption zur Senkung der Lärmbelästigung um Stadtgebiet Erfurt (plan to reduce noise pollution across the municipal area of Erfurt) stressed the importance of diverse short-term, mid-term, and long-term measures to be imposed on the management of the municipal automobile fleet, the public tram company, the independent regional coach service company, Erfurt-Bindersleben airport, the GDR railway service, and local police forces. Although some initiatives were launched immediately, Lachmann highlighted the need to direct the flow of external traffic around the city, rather than through it. She proposed compiling a list of streets that were severely affected by traffic-induced noise. In order to limit causes of noise pollution, Lachmann also suggested that the conditions of the city's road surfaces be investigated to determine whether they were made of concrete slabs, tarmac, or paving, and to schedule repairs wherever necessary (*Stadtarchiv Erfurt* 1971: 2). She also believed that being able to manage the city's noise pollution efficiently would become ever more important. She advocated for the use of improved filtering technology for engine exhausts; replacing existing trams with newer, quieter models; and taking into account noise management when designing and building new housing estates. The sixth meeting of the Socialist Unity Party (the official party of the GDR) in 1971 presented policies of caring for a good, healthy, and secure life as central goals of the socialist mission.[14] Such a claim supported and consolidated the party's massive spending policy over the next decade in favor of new community housing projects. Filtering out unwanted sound, thus creating a more comfortable *soundscape,* was not charted in this agenda.

Ancillary to traffic noise and industrial noise in the vast inner city areas in which the GDR national railway service was heavily engaged, imminent and continuous zones of noise existed. In 1974, reporting to the Ministry of Health, the Erfurt-based Institute of Hygiene and Health Protection claimed that air conditioning systems in homes and engines of track-bound vehicles, namely diesel-run locomotives, were reaching the limit of acceptable noise volumes (*BArch* 1975: 7). The document states that the GDR Ministry of Transport reacted by announcing plans to implement an investment program in order to convert, where appropriate, the locomotive traction units, vehicles pulling trains to new rails or bringing locomotives to the repair workshop or coaches to the cleaning facilities. The Institute of Hygiene also identifies zones of significantly high noise volume in the area directly adjacent to the train station and the shunting yard. Noise sources in these areas are listed as the movement of trains traveling and being arranged on the tracks, the movement of trains disposing goods for the industrial sector, and the sound of wireless voice announcements and staff communications. The noise generated by the regular rail traffic far exceeded the levels set for buildings, houses, and community estates situated near the tracks. However, the managing director of the Institute of Hygiene and Health

Protection remarked that this was not a problem as no residents had logged complaints (*BArch* 1976: 5).

A few years later, in 1977, a report on community noise in the county of Erfurt shows that the expertise of inspectors from the Institute of Hygiene and Health Protection was requested whenever construction initiatives and social housing projects were launched (*BArch* 1977a: 1–6).[15] When it came to revising the noise map of Erfurt city, a key challenge persisted in recording the fluctuating levels of noise generated by traffic (between 58 and 81 dB (A) by day, 54 and 79 dB (A) by night) and industrial sites (between 48 and 73 dB (A) by day, 42 and 65 dB (A) by night), which affected the newly built and existing residential areas nearby. The data compiled pointed to a huge variation in the traffic noise levels. The lack of soundproof windows emerged as a significant factor in the effect of noise on housing estates and the public. None of the publicly and state-owned companies across the GDR could properly fulfill existing contracts as they could not supply enough windows with noise-filtering capacity (*BArch* 1978a: 3).

The 1977 report continues by listing traffic as the dominant source of noise emissions across Erfurt. The connections to the north- and southbound F4 highway, the westbound Schmidtstedter Knoten underpass, the railway tracks, and the eastbound link of Wilhelm-Pieck-Straße were all notable zones of high noise levels. Any major improvements in exposure of residents to noise were the result of the traffic flow being redirected. The Institute of Hygiene and Health Protection could not enforce noise filtering and insulation initiatives at roadsides and was institutionally too weak to persuade decision-makers at either community or party level to promote such measures (*BArch* 1978b: 5).[16]

At this point, the county of Erfurt had designated eight zones of high priority related to noise reduction. As the other districts in the GDR at the time were not concerned with this subject, Erfurt's actions seem not only to be exceptional, but also tactical by proving expertise in competition with the more urbanized, industrial counties of the GDR. The construction of housing estates had a huge impact on the noise environment of residential areas due to the presence of large trucks delivering building materials and transferring dugout materials to disposal sites (*BArch* 1977b: 80). When the tramway beds were replaced with concrete plates, the noise level on the tram system rose by a relatively massive 8 dB (A) in densely populated areas (*BArch* 1977b: 81).[17] This nearly doubled the noise volume, more than doubled the sound pressure (voltage), and increased six-fold the sound intensity (acoustic power).[18]

All the above-mentioned reports from the 1970s on the environmental noise conditions of the district and city of Erfurt did not yet dare link noise directly to urban stress (Glass and Singer 1972). In the socialist project that was the GDR, economic activities in heavy industry, industrialized agriculture, and large housing construction emitted noise in every corner of the nation. The goals of increasing production and maintaining the socialist status quo meant that the bodies and senses of workers had to endure noise emitted by machines, powerhouses, and heating plants.[19] Assuming that the socialist project was about progress, good pay, affluence, and safety, and these aspects were controlled by means of state-imposed regulation, order, and norm, noise—in all its emerging shapes—stood in elementary opposition to this stated mission. From this angle, noise challenged this socialist normality, standardization, and rule. This marks a starting point for writing an entangled history of urban noise and provides the opportunity to link noise, labor, and modes of industrial productions across different economic systems.

Phonotopes Meet Urban Noise: Connecting Past and Present Discussions

Noise challenges measures councils implement to establish a coherent plan to manage environmental sound and silence. In the mid-1980s the Bezirks-Hygieneinspektion und -institut Erfurt (Department of Hygiene and Health of the District of Erfurt) launched several sociological studies on noise, collecting data by interviewing a sample of inhabitants of the city.[20] This collation of qualitative data gives insight into citizens' auditory perception of the cityscape. It adds knowledge about people's practices regarding noise and calculates noise exposure based on empirical data. Rowland Atkinson has chosen a similar approach. He highlights the social relevance of a sonic ecology within urban contexts (Atkinson 2007: 1914). He claims that territories can be defined by sound, and these appear to have a variety of social functions and influences. In this respect, sound and noise—as well as music—can be seen as markers of spatial and temporal territories within a city. This implies that for particular groups, the territory or *soundscape* has a profound effect on patterns of social association, physical movement, and interaction (Atkinson 2007: 1915). In contrast, George Prochnik argues that the pursuit of silence is a challenge for democracy, in that institutions of public decision-making are scarcely equipped to provide urban space with sufficient sensory retreat zones for the benefit of its citizens (Prochnik 2010: 18). From Prochnik's normative perspective, an investment in the promotion of silence is far more important than the simple implementation of slight noise reductions, which preserves noise at a given place (Prochnik 2010:

280). Prochnik defines noise as "the sound that makes us ... cease to distinguish between the beings and the objects outside us" (Prochnik 2010: 293). Combining both suggestions, Atkinson's concept of a collaborative construction of sound and Prochnik's pointing to the subject-object relation as the demarcating line concerning noise, I would claim that noise is a projection screen on which unregulated acoustic events are seen to be related to practices and procedures of filtering, appropriation, and scaling.

In addition, Amado Garcia considers sound to be the most important factor influencing the perception and communication of people in their lived environment (Garcia 2001: 5). The subjective evaluation of sound sources within an acoustic environment corresponds with sound intensity, as well as with the information contained in it. Noise and nuisance, two rhetorical siblings, refer to the context in which sound is perceived and to the social and cultural meanings attributed to it by different individuals (Garcia 2001: 5). Noise pollution is local both in source and effect, state Adams et al. (2006: 2396). In accordance with this sociocultural interpretation of sound, Jean-Paul Thibaud understands sound as a public account of the social world. Sound and noise are therefore markers of the conditions within a community and the extent to which it is bound together. Sounds can be characterized as physical stimuli and as a sensory background that is shared, concerted, and conjointly created in situations and in locations (Thibaud 2011).

The individual dimension of filtering noise is addressed by the notion of *phonotope,* introduced by Sloterdijk. It describes individual tactics of insulation, sealing, and acoustic muffling. To Sloterdijk, a location sounds like its inhabitants (Sloterdijk 2004: 377). This is why their communal space is perceived as normal, as it relates to what is known and common. According to Sloterdijk's claim, these "islands" of communal sound are self-characterizing, forming *soundscapes* of unique features. They are filled with sounds made by members and predominantly produced in the sphere of labor—at industrial sites and workshops, by manual and automated devices and tools (Sloterdijk 2004: 377). This phonotopic function, understood as a mode of group self-determination and self-regulation, is closely related to a complex pledge of consensus, as cohabitants sort through their individual views toward a common agenda (Sloterdijk 2004: 381). Sloterdijk's idea of *phonotopes* as a mode of insulation is the counterpart to Thibaud's interpretation of an urban space's sound profile as something collectively created. All statements and claims by Atkinson, Prochnik, Garcia, and Thibaud are focused on a present-time analysis of noise and sound. They lack a prolific dispute about how sound and noise are memorized and how this "echoic memory" of individuals and groups can be applied to long-term storing of auditory information within a sonic ecology of space (Baddeley 1979: 220). The rough squeaking of wheels on an uneven railway track, the mounted suspensions of tramcars grinding on concrete plates, and harsh, tinny announcements blaring from poorly tuned public address systems were the key auditory markers (Corbin 1994) of Erfurt's main station area, at central bus interchange hubs like the Domplatz (Cathedral square), and at the Centrum shopping mall at Anger during the GDR period and in the early years of unification. Based on the theory by Adams et al., those sounds would have served as the outstanding soundmarkers of Erfurt's inner city (2006: 2396). These did not change much between 1988 and 1993, or throughout the 1990s for that matter, as public transport in Erfurt remained downright noisy. However, later efforts to reroute traffic and straighten road and track beds had effectively decreased noise pollution (Erfurt Noise Action Plan 2009). The changes made to the train station and its surroundings took place as recently as the period between 2001 and 2008.

A close reading of the Erfurt train station allows for immediate access to an understanding of the auditory perspective to this historical change, a perspective as of yet uncommon. Recently, historian Jürgen Müller suggested that learning to eavesdrop on the past contributes to overcoming the structural inaudibility of historical approaches. By constructing a history of the experience of hearing, researchers gain insight into the mechanisms of power, lifestyles, patterns of action, and the forces behind historical processes (Müller 2011: 28–29). When such an approach is applied as a point of scholarly departure, the ways history is imagined, represented, and emulated as codified common cultural knowledge certainly has an auditory layer. Peter Bailey describes noise as "a broad yet imprecise category of sounds that register variously as excessive, incoherent, confused, inarticulate or degenerate" (Bailey 1996: 50). Noise does not get "our full attention until it reaches the status of nuisance or worse and our perception of its varying gradients and inflections has been blunted" (Bailey 1996: 50).

Ascertaining the listening and hearing dimension to mapping out memories of spaces and places from an acoustic and auditory standpoint provides an additional argument to acknowledge sound and noise as a storage media. There, the narratives of the sonic ecology of an inhabited space, the history of observing and tackling emissions, is connected to the forward-pressing issues of public health management in a shifting urban environment.

Conclusion

In Erfurt, the main institutions that dealt with traffic flow administration were established in the mid- to late 1970s, and the community-centered plans and schemes initiated under socialist rule remained largely unchanged throughout the 1990s. This fact reveals that the noise profile of a city does not necessarily transform significantly or even at all when a new political system comes to power and becomes involved in its management. This chapter's key claim is that the *soundscape* of a specific place is like a container. It is inherently sealed and resistant to change, while the tactics of individuals and groups in negotiating noise in general, and its harmfulness in particular, undergo phases of transition. The policies and technologies of noise control shift. On the one hand, today's state-of-the-art motor vehicle engines are quieter and run more smoothly than the models that were fitted in the Trabant or Wartburg cars of the GDR era. On the other hand, there was significantly less traffic and fewer individual commuters on the streets of Erfurt at that time, even when the population of the city had increased to well over 200,000 during the 1980s. The political transition of the *Wende* in 1989/90 did not exert immediate influence on Erfurt's inner city sound texture until the first decade of the current millennium. More recent changes to the inner city may be as important as those prior to the *Wende* when it comes to alterations to noise texture. The symbolic policies of architecture and the preservation of declining inner city areas were much more prominent in this respect. The auditory shape of a soundscape is a long-ranging process outside of the short-termed cycles of popular outrage and political business. This chapter argues that the continuous increase of noise pollution is much more obvious than any shifts toward improvement in the urban *soundscape*. The reconstruction of Erfurt's main train station was the city's flagship project of infrastructural change in the first two decades after German unification. As this project was launched in 2001, it can hardly be considered within a transitional, immediately post-1989 setting. A Tatra tramway car running on the tracks of the Erfurt public transport network before 1989 was as loud as in 1993 or 1999. This indicates that the years of political transition immediately following 1989 had only limited effects on the sonic shape of Erfurt's *soundscape* and on the nature of residents' auditory experiences during the 1990s. While the screeching sound of the tracks remained as disturbing as before, multiple options for making complaints and petitioning opened up, as civic institutions became more directly accountable. Although it took some years to upgrade the old fleet of trams, this has significantly helped to lower noise emissions across Erfurt's public transport system.

My attempt here at sounding out Erfurt's cityscape has applied a sensory approach. Examining and understanding a city's history from such an angle contributes to the genesis and consolidation of an auditory perspective within historical research and restimulates the cultural and social history of technology, societal interactions, and public spaces. Connecting the analysis of a cityscape evolving over time to a present-day and to a historical interpretation of its acoustic conditions and auditory shape is linking—noise-wise—the late socialist era with the period following 1989 to the contemporary disputes and struggles. When historians seek to open a window through which to access a period of history, they should be obliged to listen for its sounds and modes of noise production. When examining acoustic events within the soundscape of a city, it has to be taken into account what people do to limit noise exposure and annoyance. In addition, unwanted sounds have a discernible impact on people. That is why reconsidering the sensory experience of residents—whether auditory, visual, olfactory, or gustatory—from today's and from a historical perspective is worthwhile. Recalling my account of a city dweller relying on earplugs to drown out noise, we should acknowledge that a commitment to avoiding such cutting off of this sensory channel is urgently required. Metaphorically speaking, historians have to put the earmuffs aside in order to start listening to the historical processes.

Notes

1. *Zeithistorische Forschungen/Studies in Contemporary History,* Online version, 8 (2011), H. 2, *Politics and Culture of Sound in the Twentieth Century,* eds. Daniel Morat, Christine Bartlitz, and Jan-Holger Kirsch, http://www.zeithistorische-forschungen.de/16126041-Inhalt-2-2011, accessed 23 May 2013. See also *The Sound of the 20th Century,* edited by Gerhard Paul and Ralph Schock, Berlin/Bonn, 2013. Note that all translations are my own unless otherwise indicated.

2. *Lärmaktionsplan der Stadt Erfurt 2009,* http://www.erfurt.de/imperia/md/content/veroeffentlichungen/umwelt/lap_ef_09_03_25.pdf, accessed 23 May 2012: 29–30.

3. Such an incipient venture is certainly a challenge. In the last decade, scholars from different areas, such as cultural and media history (Smith 2008, Back and Bull 2003, Bull 2007, Sterne 2003, Thompson 2002, Yablon 2007), literary studies (Picker 2003, Schweighäuser 2006), urban studies, and social geography (see Thibaud 2003, 2011; Kazig 2007, 2010) have tackled

sound and noise as constituents of the urban experience. They elaborate on various empirical and methodological designs and convey inspiring theoretical approaches. In this chapter, I put aside the framing of noise in physics (see Schulze 2008) and accounts of its physiological and psychological effects (Stumpf 1890, Wundt 1902, Hornbostel and Wertheimer 1922, Dunlap 1922, and Plessner 1925/1980, 1982), as well as the strategies of noise abatement (Lessing 1908, Saul 1996, Bjisterveldt 2008, Payer 2007). In this respect, silence (see Foy 2010, Prochnik 2010, Keizer 2010) is also a worthy object of study, but it is intentionally left out in favor of clarifying these introductory remarks.

4. http://erfurt.thueringer-allgemeine.de/web/lokal/wirtschaft/detail/-/ specific/Laermschutzwaende-werden-an-Bahnstrecke-in-Erfurt-installi ert-900649201, accessed 23 May 2013.

5. Erfurt's current number of inhabitants: http://www.erfurt.de/ef/de/ratha us/daten/bevoelkerung/stadt/, accessed 23 May 2013.

6. Interview with Florian Geier, Head of Infrastructure and Track Management at Erfurter Verkehrsbetriebe, 12 May 2011.

7. Arkette applies this perspective to several city quarters of London (Foy 2010, Keizer 2010, and Prochnik 2010). The empirical cases are mainly in contemporary New York. The Paris (Zittou 2007) and Stockholm community noise reduction scheme (Berglund and Lindvall 1999) serve as a best-practice example in this globalized discussion.

8. Interview with Prof. Dr. Hermann Saitz, former Head of Traffic Management in the Bureau of City Planning of Erfurt, Erfurt 7 June 2011.

9. http://www.strassenbahn-online.de/Betriebshof/Tatra/KT4D/index.html, accessed 23 May 2013.

10. TGL stands for technical norms (T), criteria of quality and goodness (G) and conditions of delivery (L=Lieferbedingungen) and No. 10687 labels noise insulation provisions. In the first version (1963), it is bound to structural-physical protection measures taking the first steps to define sound abatement. (Bauphysikalische Schutzmaßnahmen. Schallschutz. Begriffe). See http://www.uni-weimar.de/cms/universitaet/zentrale-einrichtungen/univ ersitaetsbibliothek/recherche/normen/tgl-verzeichnis/tgl-8.html, accessed 23 May 2013.

11. See 1968 noise maps at *Stadtarchiv Erfurt,* 7/161-10, Bl. 002-Bl. 005. See 2008 noise maps, Appendix page 1–2: http://www.erfurt.de/imperia/md/ content/veroeffentlichungen/umwelt/lap_ef_09_03_25.pdf, accessed 23 May 2013.

12. The metering unit in the noise map from 1968 is dB and indicates the level of noise recorded by metering devices; dB (A) is an improved, more accurate metering unit that is calculated to match an assumed normal hearing threshold.

13. Find a comparison of dB to common sounds here: http://www.tinnitus.org .au/TAV/media/Images/noisescale.gif or see: http://www.osha.gov/SLTC/ images/a_weighted_sound_levels_small.png, accessed 23 May 2013.

14. See an overview on the effects of the housing program of the Socialist Party in various cities, Erfurt: Ott 1997; Leipzig: Tesch 2000; Schwedt: Springer 2006; Halle: Wiesener 2006; Dresden: Maaß 2006, Bernhardt and Reif 2009.
15. The institution compiled thirty-six consulting reports on planned construction projects and finished sixty-nine orders and errands that have been received by departments of street planning at borough and local level. In 1975, Ullmann stressed the positive collaboration with both institutions and the office of traffic planning at the district council of Erfurt (*BArch* 1976: 5).
16. A subsequent report in 1978 noted that assessing noise in planning schemes as an external evaluation remained a key aspect of the department duties. Noise exposure emitted by children using playgrounds across Erfurt came into the scope (see *BArch* 1978b: 5).
17. Interview with Florian Geier. He referred to that problem as well, calling it a long-lasting and unsolved challenge during the 1980s and 1990s.
18. http://www.sengpielaudio.com/calculator-levelchange.htm, accessed 23 May 2013.
19. Find an overview on the debate Kaelble (2009: 33–38), also Werner and Zimmermann (2002: 607–636).
20. These groundbreaking studies from Baumbach, Mörstedt, Schulze et al. (1990) and Schulze, Wölke, and Mörstedt (1990) were kept classified and unpublished in the GDR until 1990. They are still prominently cited in noise disturbance literature, providing a base for further research on the links between environmental noise and ischemic heart diseases.

Interviews

Geier, Florian, Head of Infrastructure and Track Management at Erfurt Public Transport Service (Erfurter Verkehrsbetriebe), Erfurt (12 May 2011).
Saitz, Hermann, former Head of Traffic Management in the Bureau of City Planning of Erfurt, Erfurt (7 June 2011).

References

Adams, Mags, Trevor Cox, Gemma Moore, Ben Croxford, Mohamed Refaee, and Steve Sharples. 2006. "Sustainable Soundscapes: Noise Policy and the Urban Experience." *Urban Studies* 43 (13): 2385–2398.
Arkette, Sophie. 2004. "Sounds Like City." *Theory, Culture & Society* 21 (1): 159–168.
Atkinson, Rowland. 2007. "Ecology of Sound. The Sonic Order of Urban Space." *Urban Studies* 44 (10): 1905–1917.
Attali, Jacques. 1977. *Bruit: Essai sur l'économie politique de la musique.* Paris: Presses Universitaires de France.
Babisch, Wolfgang. 2000. "Traffic noise and cardiovascular disease. Epidemiological review and synthesis." *Noise & Health* 2 (8): 9–32. http://www.noiseandhealth.org/text.asp?2000/2/8/9/31755, accessed 23 May 2013.

Baddeley, Alan D. 1979. *Die Psychologie des Gedächtnisses.* Stuttgart: Klett-Cotta.

Bailey, Peter. 1996. "Breaking the Sound Barrier. A Historian Listens to Noise." *Body & Society* 2 (2): 49–66.

Baumbach, W., R. Mörstedt, B. Schulze, G. Wölke, R. Ullmann, and G. Grossmann. 1990. "Neue Aspekte zur Verkehrslärm problematik im innerstädtischen Bereich (New aspects of the traffic noise problem in the inner city area)." *Zeitschrift für die gesamte Hygiene und ihre Grenzgebiete* 36 (4): 204–206.

Berglund, Birgitta, Thomas Lindvall, and Dietrich H. Schwela, eds. 1999. *Guidelines for Community Noise.* Geneva: WHO.

Bernhardt, Christoph, and Heinz Reif, eds. 2009. *Sozialistische Städte zwischen Herrschaft und Selbstbehauptung: Kommunalpolitik, Stadtplanung und Alltag in der DDR.* Stuttgart: Steiner.

Betts, Paul, and Katherine Pence, eds. 2008. *Socialist Modern. New Perspectives on East German Everyday Culture.* Ann Arbor: University of Michigan Press.

Bijsterveld, Karin. 2008. *Mechanical Sound: Technology, Culture, and Public Problems of Noise in the Twentieth Century.* Cambridge: MIT Press.

Bull, Michael. 2007. *Sound Moves: iPod Culture and the Urban Experience.* London: Routledge.

Bull, Michael, and Les Back, eds. 2003. *The Auditory Culture Reader.* Amsterdam: Berg.

Corbin, Alain. 1994. *Les Cloches De La Terre: Paysage sonore et culture sensible dans les campagnes au XIXe siècle.* Paris: Albin Michel.

Dunlap, Knight. 1922. *The Elements of Scientology Psychology.* St. Louis, M.O.: C.V. Mosby.

Foy, George Michelsen. 2010. *Zero Decibels: The Quest for Absolute Silence.* New York: Scribner.

Garcia, Amando, ed. 2001. *Environmental Urban Noise.* Southampton, N.Y. and Boston: WIT Press.

Glass, David C., and Jerome E. Singer. 1972. *Urban Stress: Experiments on Noise and Social Stressors.* New York and London: Academic Press.

Gross, Peter. 1994. *Die Multioptionsgesellschaft.* Frankfurt: Suhrkamp.

Guentcheva, Rossitza. 2004. "Sound and Noise in Socialist Bulgaria." In *Ideologies and National Identities: The Case of Twentieth-Century Southeastern Europe,* edited by John R. Lampe and Mark Mazower, 211–234. Budapest and New York: Central European University Press.

Hermann-Sinai, Susanne. 2009. "Sounds Without the Mind? Versuch einer Bestimmung des Klangbegriffes." *Deutsche Zeitschrift für Philosophie* 57 (6): 885–906.

Hornbostel, Erich Moritz von, and Max Wertheimer. 1920. "Über die Wahrnehmung der Schallrichtung." *Sitzungsberichte der Preussischen Akademie der Wissenschaften* 20: 388–396.

Kaelble, Hartmut. 2009. "Between Comparison and Transfers—and What Now? A French–German Debate." In *Comparative and Transnational History:*

Central European Approaches and New Perspectives, edited by Heinz-Gerhard Haupt and Jürgen Kocka, 33–38. New York: Berghahn Books.

Kazig, Rainer. 2007. "Atmosphären. Konzept für einen nicht repräsentationellen Zugang zum Raum." Transcript. In *Kulturelle Geographien: Zur Beschäftigung mit Raum und Ort nach dem Cultural Turn,* edited by Christian Berndt and Robert Pütz. Bielefeld: transcript, 167–187.

———. 2010. *Les ambiances de résonance culturelle et la création d' éspaces publics d'intimité.* http://ambiances.grenoble.cnrs.fr/files/Colloque%2020 09%20Rio/Col_Rio091104_ArticleRainerKazig.pdf, accessed 23 May 2013.

Keizer, Garrett. 2010. *The Unwanted Sound of Everything We Want: A Book About Noise.* New York: Public Affairs.

Lessing, Theodor. 1908. *Der Lärm. Eine Kampfschrift gegen die Geräusche unseres Lebens. Grenzfragen des Nerven- und Seelenlebens* 9 (54).

Maaß, Anita. 2006. *Wohnen in der DDR. Dresden-Prohlis. Wohnungspolitik und Wohnungsbau 1975 bis 1981.* Munich: M-Press Meidenbauer.

Morat, Daniel, Christine Bartlitz, and Jan-Holger Kirsch, eds. 2011. "Politics and Culture of Sound in the Twentieth Century." *Zeithistorische Forschungen/ Studies in Contemporary History* 8 (2), http://www.zeithistorische-forsch ungen.de/16126041-Inhalt-2-2011, accessed 23 May 2013.

Müller, Jürgen. 2011. "The Sound of Silence. Von der Unhörbarkeit der Vergangenheit zur Geschichte des Hörens." *Historische Zeitschrift* 292 (1): 1–29.

Nora, Pierre. 1990. *Zwischen Geschichte und Gedächtnis.* Berlin: Wagenbach.

Ott, Thomas. 1997. *Erfurt im Transformationsprozeß der Städte in den neuen Ländern. Ein regulationstheoretischer Ansatz.* Erfurt, http://www.uni-mann heim.de/mateo/verlag/diss/ott/platte1.htm, accessed 23 May 2013.

Paul, Gerhard. 2012. "Sound History." Panel at the 48th meeting of the Association of German Historians, Mainz. http://www.historikertag.de/Mainz 2012/de/programm/wissenschaftliches-programm/sektionen/einzelan sicht/article/sound-history.html, accessed 22 May 2013.

Payer, Peter. 2007. "The Age of Noise: Early Reactions in Vienna, 1870–1914." *Journal of Urban History* 33 (5): 773–793.

Picker, John M. 2003. *Victorian Soundscape.* Oxford: Oxford University Press.

Plessner, Helmuth. 1980. "Äthesiologie des Gehörs." In *Gesammelte Schriften, Bd. III, Anthropologie der Sinne,* 221–248. Frankfurt: Suhrkamp.

———. 1982. "Zur Phänomenologie der Musik (1925)." In *Gesammelte Schriften VII, Ausdruck und menschliche Natur,* 59–66. Frankfurt: Suhrkamp.

Prochnik, George. 2010. *In Pursuit of Silence: Listening for Meaning in a World of Noise.* New York: Doubleday.

Ritter, Rüdiger. 2010. "Tönende Erinnerung: Überlegungen zur Funktionsstruktur des akustischen Gedächtnisses. Das Beispiel der Schlacht von Stalingrad." In *Akustisches Gedächtnis und Zweiter Weltkrieg,* edited by Robert Maier, 31–42. Göttingen: V&R.

Saul, Klaus. 1996. "'Kein Zeitalter seit Erschaffung der Welt hat so viel und so ungeheuerlichen Lärm gemacht' …—Lärmquellen, Lärmbekämpfung und Antilärmbewegung im Deutschen Kaiserreich." In *Umweltgeschichte.*

Methoden, Themen, Potentiale. Tagung des Hamburger Arbeitskreises für Umweltgeschichte, Hamburg 1994, edited by Günter Bayerl, Norman Fuchsloch, and Torsten Mayer, 187–218. Münster: Waxmann.

Schafer, Raymond Murray. 1973. "The Music of the Environment." *Cultures* 1 (1): 15–52.

———. 1977. *The Tuning of the World.* New York: Knopf.

Schulze, B., G. Wölke, R. Mörstedt, R. Ullmann, and G. Grossmann. 1990. "Strassenverkehrslärm und Belästigungserlebnis (Street traffic noise and stress experience)." *Zeitschrift für die Gesamte Hygiene und Ihre Grenzgebiete* 36 (4): 201–203.

Schulze, Holger. 2010. "Hypercorporealismus. Zur Wissenschaftsgeschichte des körperlichen Klangs." In *PopScriptum 10—Das Sonische—Sounds zwischen Akustik und Ästhetik*, ed. Forschungszentrum Populäre Musik der Humboldt-Universität zu Berlin, http://www2.hu-berlin.de/fpm/popscrip/the men/pst10/pst10_schulze.htm, accessed 23 May 2013.

Schweighauser, Philipp. 2006. *The Noises of American Literature, 1890–1985: Toward a History of Literary Acoustics.* Miami: University of Florida Press.

Serres, Michel. 1998. *Die fünf Sinne: Eine Philosophie der Gemenge und Gemische.* Frankfurt: Suhrkamp.

Siedentop, Stefan, Axel Stein, Ulrike Wolf, Martin Lanzendorf et al. 2005. *Mobilität im suburbanen Raum. Neue verkehrliche und raumordnerische Implikationen des räumlichen Strukturwandels.* Forschungsvorhaben 70.716 des "Forschungsprogramms Stadtverkehr" (FoPS) im Auftrag des Bundesministeriums für Verkehr, Bau- und Wohnungswesen. Projektverbund Leibniz-Institut für Regionalentwicklung und Strukturplanung(IRS) Erkner, Leibniz-Institut für ökologische Raumentwicklung (IÖR), Dresden; Institut für Geographie der Universität Leipzig, Dresden; Berlin: Erkner, 225–230, http://www.ufz.de/export/data/1/26285_msr_c.pdf, accessed 23 May 2013.

Sloterdijk, Peter. 2004. *Schäume, (Plurale Sphärologie III).* Frankfurt: Suhrkamp.

Smith, Mark M. 2008. *Sensing the Past: Seeing, Hearing, Smelling, Tasting, and Touching in History.* Berkeley: University of California Press.

Southworth, Michael. 1969. "The Sonic Environment of Cities." *Environment and Behavior* 1 (1): 49–70.

Springer, Philipp. 2006. *Verbaute Träume: Herrschaft, Stadtentwicklung und Lebensrealität in der sozialistischen Industriestadt Schwedt.* Berlin: Christoph Links.

Stadtverwaltung Erfurt. 2009. Lärmaktionsplan der Landeshauptstadt Erfurt. Hauptverkehrsstraßen. http://www.erfurt.de/imperia/md/content/veroef fentlichungen/umwelt/lap_ef_09_03_25.pdf, accessed 23 May 2013.

Sterne, Jonathan. 2003. *The Audible Past: Cultural Origins of Sound Reproduction.* Durham, N.C.: Duke University Press.

Stölzel, Katharina. 2003. *Zusammenhang zwischen Umweltlärmbelästigung und Lärmempfindlichkeit—epidemiologische Untersuchung im Rahmen der Berliner Lärmstudie.* Diss. Humboldt Universität Berlin, http://edoc.hu-berlin.de/dissertationen/stoelzel-katharina-2004-02-04/PDF/Stoelzel.pdf, accessed 23 May 2013.

Stumpf, Carl. 1890. *Tonpsychologie.* Vol. II. Leipzig: Salomon Hirzel.

Tesch, Joachim. 2000. "Wurde das DDR-Wohnungsbauprogramm1971/1976 bis 1990 erfüllt?" *UTOPIE kreativ,* special issue: 50–58, http://www.rosalux .de/fileadmin/rls_uploads/pdfs/2000_Sonderheft_Tesch.pdf, accessed 23 May 2013.

Thibaud, Jean-Paul. 1998. "Towards a praxiology of sound environment." http://www.sensorystudies.org/sensorial-investigations-2/towards-a-praxiology-of-sound-environment/, accessed 23 May 2013. Previously presented with the title "The Acoustic Embodiment of Social Practice. Towards a praxiology of sound environment" at the conference *Stockholm, hey Listen!* in Stockholm. Stockholm: The Royal Swedish Academy of Music, 17–22.

———. 2003. "The sonic composition of the city." In *The Auditory Culture Reader,* edited by Michael Bull and Les Back, 329–341. Amsterdam: Berg. http://doc.cresson.grenoble.archi.fr/opac/doc_num.php?explnum_id=39, accessed 23 May 2013.

———. 2011. "The Sensory Fabric of Urban Ambiances Source." *The Senses and Society* 6 (2): 203–215.

Thompson, Emily. 2002. *The Soundscape of Modernity: Architectural Acoustics and the Culture of Listening in America, 1900–1933.* Cambridge: MIT Press.

Werner, Michael, and Bénédicte Zimmermann. 2002. "Vergleich, Transfer, Verflechtung. Der Ansatz der Histoire croisée und die Herausforderung des Transnationalen." *Geschichte und Gesellschaft* 28 (4): 607–636.

Wiesener, Albrecht. 2006. "Als die Zukunft noch nicht vergangen war—der Aufbau der Chemiearbeiterstadt Halle-Neustadt 1958–1980." In *Geschichte der Stadt Halle,* edited by Werner Freitag, Katrin Minner, and Andreas Ranft, 442–456. Halle: Mitteldeutscher Verlag.

World Health Organization. 2009. *Night Noise Guidelines for Europe,* ed. Charlotte Hurtley. Copenhagen, http://www.euro.who.int/__data/assets/pdf_file/0017/43316/E92845.pdf, accessed 23 May 2013.

Wundt, Wilhelm. 1902. *Grundzüge der Physiologischen Psychologie.* Leipzig: Wilhelm Engelmann.

Yablon, Nick. 2007. "Echoes of the City: Spacing Sound, Sounding Space, 1888–1916." *American Literary History* 19 (3): 629–660.

Zittoun, Philippe. 2007. "La carte parisienne du bruit. La fabrique d'un nouvel énoncé de politique publique." *Politix* 20 (78): 157–178.

Archived Material

Bundesarchiv Berlin. 1975. *DQ* 1/13583, [Bestand Ministerium für Gesundheitswesen, Abteilung Hygiene], Bereich, Kommunaler Lärmschutz in der DDR im Jahre 1974, o.D. (1975): 7.

———. 1976. *DQ* 1/13583, [Bestand Ministerium für Gesundheitswesen, Abteilung Hygiene] Rat des Bezirkes Erfurt, Bezirks-Hygiene-Inspektion und Bezirks-Hygiene-Institut Erfurt, Leiter Medizinalrat Dr. Ullmann, Teilbericht über die Situation auf dem Gebiet des kommunalen Lärms im Bezirk Erfurt im Jahre 1975, o.D. (1976): 1–5.

———. 1977a. *DQ* 1/13583, [Bestand Ministerium für Gesundheitswesen, Abteilung Hygiene] Rat des Bezirkes Erfurt, Bezirks-Hygiene-Inspektion und Bezirks-Hygiene-Institut Erfurt, Leiter Medizinalrat Dr. Ullmann, Teilbericht über die Situation auf dem Gebiet des kommunalen Lärms im Bezirk Erfurt im Jahre 1976, Erfurt (12.03.1977): 1–6.

———. 1977b. *DQ* 1/13583, Ministerium für Gesundheitswesen, Bereich Kommunalhygiene, Kommunaler Lärmschutz in der DDR im Jahr 1976, o. D. (1977): Bl. 79–89, Bl. 80.

———. 1978a. *DQ* 1/13583, Teilbericht kommunaler Lärm im Bezirk Erfurt im Jahre 1976, Erfurt (12.03.1978): 3.

———. 1978b. *DQ* 1/13583, Rat des Bezirkes Erfurt, Bezirks-Hygieneinspektion und Bezirks-Hygiene Institut Erfurt, Leiter Medizinalrat Dr. Ullmann, 4. Teilbericht über die Situation auf dem Gebiet des kommunalen Lärms im Bezirk Erfurt im Jahre 1977, Erfurt (12.03.1978): 1–6.

Stadtarchiv Erfurt. 1967. 5/968 B, box 24, folder 210 B, IAKH, MAE, Dipl.-Ing. Günther Engler, Neue Lärmbekämpfungsmaßnahmen im Automobilbau (Referat, Lärmtagung Erfurt 1967): 1.

———. 1970. 1–5/1100–14, [Akten des Oberbürgermeisters der Stadt Erfurt, Scheinpflug] Bezirks-Hygiene-Inspektion des Rates des Bezirkes Erfurt, Kommissarischer Leiter Dr. med. R. Ullmann, an Abteilung Gesundheit und Sozialwesen des Rates des Bezirkes Erfurt, Frau Obermedizinalrätin Dr. Völlkopf, Betr.: Die Lärmsituation in Erfurt, Erfurt (10.6.1970): 1–8.

———. 1971. 1–5/32–4657, Rat der Stadt Erfurt, Abteilung Gesundheits- und Sozialwesen, Kreisärztin, [Obermedizinalrätin Dr. Lachmann] an Herrn Oberbürgermeister [Scheinpflug], Betr.: Ergebnisse der Maßnahmen zur Reinhaltung der Luft und Gewässer sowie der Bekämpfung des Verkehrslärmes, Erfurt (9.3.1971): 1–5.

Chapter 8

Restoration and Redemption

Defending Kultur *and* Heimat *in Eisenach's Cityscape*

JASON JAMES

One evening in early 1997, following a dinner filled with discussion of battles over historic preservation and renewal in the small East German city of Eisenach, Ronald Dieckmann brought out a large illustrated volume with the title *The Fates of German Architectural Monuments in World War II: A Documentation of Damage and Total Losses in the Territory of the German Democratic Republic* (Eckhardt 1978).[1] The second volume of a series published in the German Democratic Republic (GDR), it covered the administrative districts that were reconstituted after unification as the federal states Saxony and Thuringia. As we paged through scores of "before" and "after" images depicting former grandeur and "senseless" devastation—including Eisenach's Luther House and old city hall—Dieckmann's voice became increasingly somber. It was as though we were speaking of deceased family members. After we finished with the book, he went to the window and looked out over the rooftops of the old city toward the autobahn. "Just now we are beginning to repair the damage that Hitler brought upon this country," he remarked wearily, "and it will take many years to finish it."[2]

Dieckmann's comment confirmed what I had come to suspect: the stakes in the many ferocious battles waged over preservation and renewal in Eisenach since unification are much larger and the sentiments involved deeper and more complex than historic preservation, local identity, or political power per se.[3] At first glance the issues appear all too familiar: the preservation and authenticity of historic buildings threatened by renewal; the integration of new structures into the city's historic fabric; and the relative power of citizens, government officials, and developers in determining the future contours of the *Stadtbild* (cityscape).[4] Eisenach's battles can also be read as contestations over fundamental questions faced by East Germans in the wake of national unification: the meaning of democratic citizenship and government, the character of private property and capitalism, and the meaning of locality, all refracted through contests among members of the local *Bildungsbürgertum* (educated bourgeoisie) for control of the cityscape and local identity. But in addition to the obvious economic, political, and social transformations faced by East Germans in years following 1990, these actors also confronted the task of fashioning a sense of belonging in the face of a doubly stigmatized past. With the exception of this brief and private moment in Dieckmann's living room, however, the individuals embroiled in these battles never make explicit what his remark betrayed: that the battles also have everything to do with regret over modern Germany's losses and a longing for redemption.[5]

I argue that Eisenach's cityscape, like that of many other East German towns and cities, has been subject to fierce contention by virtue of its function as a medium for performing national unification as recuperation. Preservation and renewal have served, that is, as a local allegory of national redemption that relies on the "material authority" of the city's historic fabric and cultural landmarks (Till 2005).[6] Historic cityscapes have served as the focus of many East Germans' efforts to grapple with the problem of Germanness because they address the past as a material cultural legacy to be retrieved and protected, rather than as a past to be worked through in the sense of *Vergangenheitsbewältigung* (process of realizing and coming to terms with past mistakes). The nation and its burdened pasts are symbolically domesticated, rendered in seemingly untainted, tangible, at once local and universal guises of cultural heritage and hometown belonging, or *Heimat*.

In Eisenach's conflicts, heritage and *Heimat* serve as talismans of redemption not just because they symbolize a seemingly unspoiled German past, but also because they represent precious but vulnerable objects threatened with disruption, pollution, or destruction by agents located outside the moral boundaries of the hometown and its *bürgerlich* (bourgeois) custodians. In this regard, local preservation activists find validation in official discourse, which has often cast preservation and renewal in East German cities as a ritual of national healing to repair damage inflicted by the communist—as manifested by the governing Socialist Unity Party (SED)—and Nazi regimes. For local preservation activists and many other Eisenachers, however, the unified German order has not only failed to uphold this promise, it has actually repeated the errors of previous regimes, perpetuating a legacy of loss.

Those familiar with the history of preservation and the nineteenth-century *Heimatbewegung* (homeland movement), as well as debates in postwar West Germany will find many echoes of the past in the idioms and actors at work in Eisenach's battles, not to mention the treatment of the local historic cityscape as a locus of redemptive identity.[7] German cityscapes and landmarks have long served as a symbolic arena for engaging issues of national belonging, citizenship, and modernity. One of my aims in this chapter is to scrutinize these apparent continuities by telling the specific story of local preservation activism and conflict in the late GDR and first decades after unification, thereby highlighting the ways heritage and *Heimat* have been recast and mobilized under unique conditions prior to and following unification.

Eisenach's cultural landmarks and historic cityscape join those of other cities and villages as a vital part of Germany's contested landscape of commemoration. The politics of heritage in Germany has been closely documented and analyzed, but with the exception of commentaries on singular projects like the reconstruction of the Frauenkirche (Church of Our Lady) in Dresden and the Stadtschloss (imperial palace) in Berlin, contests over preservation and renewal often do not find a prominent place in discussions of Germany's contemporary politics of memory, which tend to focus on official discourse, monuments, film, literature, and historiography. The reason for this lack of emphasis mirrors the reason preservation has proven so important to Eisenachers; those concerned with collective memory in Germany tend to view cultural heritage as something quite distinct from monuments and sites explicitly connected to the nation's burdened pasts.

Structures of Difference and Desire

Approaching Eisenach's preservation battles from a perspective informed by anthropology and cultural studies facilitates closer attention to the dynamics of identification, symbolism, and desire that fuel them. Studies of conflicts over German cityscapes and landmarks often take these dynamics for granted. Treating *Heimat,* for example, as a dynamic iconography and a nostalgic discourse that locates Germanness in the hometown landscape is quite illuminating, but does not capture the flexibility and power of *Heimat* as a structure of longing and difference that defines national belonging in relation to what it lacks and what it is not (its others).[8] In relation to *Heimat,* cultural heritage, and Germanness, that is, identification is generally treated as a problem of who, what, and when, but not how: we learn about actors and organizations as well as objects of identification and their transformations, but not as much about how deep structures of identification operate and why specific objects of identification attract such intense investment. To understand Germanness at this level requires not just tracing this history of *Heimat* and preservation discourse, but also examining the ways that structures of difference, identification, and desire that define Germanness operate in specific contexts. Applying this approach to the case of Eisenach's battles allows for tracing the deeper interconnections among activists' "fundamentalist" demands for authenticity and harmony, their *bürgerlich* longings for heritage and *Heimat,* and the conundrums raised by postunification attempts to fashion a usable identity.

My argument is thus informed not just by a close reading of Eisenach's conflicts and the history of preservation, nationalism, and *Heimat* discourse in Germany, but also by an understanding of identification and belonging that treats them as inseparable from loss and mourning. This approach draws on but goes beyond notions of invented tradition and imagined community.[9] Some scholars of nationalism, most notably Rudy Koshar in his exhaustive studies of historic preservation in Germany, have criticized these approaches to national and ethnic identity for neglecting continuities and local, concrete practices of identification (1994). The popularity of invented tradition and imagined community as concepts may well have led to their simplistic use in some cases, but neither concept was originally intended to suggest that national belonging is fabricated at will or *ex nihilo.* In fact, Koshar's own insightful—albeit not fully elaborated—claim that we should view preservation as both a ritual performance of Germanness and as the production of an "optic identity of the nation" resonates strongly with these approaches. In fact, the very "substantiality and materiality" of landscapes and landmarks naturalizes them as local touchstones for imagining a national community even though there is nothing intrinsically national about them (Koshar 1994: 20–21; Koshar 1998: 18–19).[10] My interpretation of Eisenach's preservation battles finds limitations in the concepts of imagination and invention too, but in my view their shortcoming lies primarily in their failure to examine closely the investments in belonging and difference that invigorate national imagination and ritual performance, as well as the complex interactions between official discourse and local appropriations of it.

Approaches to identity and nationalism that draw on poststructuralist literary theory and cultural studies have paved the way in theorizing these investments. A compelling example is Eric Santner's probing analysis of Edgar Reitz's miniseries *Heimat* and Hans-Jürgen Syberberg's *Hitler: A Film from Germany* (1990). Santner updates the thesis of Germans' postwar "inability to mourn" using insights from recent Freudian and poststructuralist theory. His emphasis on objects of identification dovetails nicely with a strain of theory in anthropology and cultural studies that views national belonging as a matter of making claims on national belongings. The power of national icons like cultural landmarks becomes more explicable when we recognize that actors appropriate them not just as visible, tangible representations of a national community, but also as exclusive possessions upon which they make competing claims, and as fetish objects that stand in for other "stranded objects" of identification, to borrow Santner's term.

This approach points not only to the bourgeois model of national identity and agency as expressed through possession of property, but also to the centrality of loss in nationalist imaginaries. National belongings are constituted, as Slavoj Žižek explains, by the threat of loss; their significance lies precisely in their vulnerability to being degraded or stolen. In the case of Eisenach's preservation battles, local activists articulate a version of this possessive claim when they accuse various agents of ruining the city's architectural heritage, destroying the opportunity presented by unification to recover a precious cultural legacy. Heritage and *Heimat* are therefore best viewed in this context as structures of difference, identification, and desire that render local and national belonging in material and spatial terms—discrete objects and a defined territory whose symbolic power lies precisely in their potential loss at the hands of others. They are nothing if not threatened. In this way preservation activism maintains a clear distinction between perpetrators and victims, and implicitly identifies German cultural heritage—and by implication its defenders—as a traumatized victim.

Eisenach in Context

Eisenach is not the only East German city to experience numerous battles over its cityscape in the postunification era. Conflicts over preservation, reconstruction, and renewal occurred in many East German cities after unification due to the heightened symbolic weight placed on Eastern cityscapes combined with the sheer speed and intensity of their transformation. The most widely publicized conflicts have occurred, not surprisingly, in more prominent and larger cities, such as Berlin and Dresden. Eisenach's battles share some fundamental qualities with these better-known conflicts but also display some attributes unique to a provincial "hometown" struggling to locate itself along the axes of development and history.

The conflicts in Berlin that share the most in common with those in Eisenach concern critical reconstruction, a neotraditional approach to architecture and planning realized most consistently in the Friedrich-stadt district (around Friedrichstraße) and the battle over the Palast der Republik (Palace of the Republic), the signature structure of the SED regime located on Unter den Linden boulevard. The fate of this structure has been intertwined in complex ways with the proposal to rebuild the Stadtschloss.

Put most simply, critical reconstruction is Berlin's version of new urbanism. With roots in West Berlin's International Building Exhibition (IBA) in the 1980s, it represents a move away from the modernist vision of a city fundamentally remade according to rational principles. Critical reconstruction is conservative in the literal sense: it emphasizes "understanding and preserving the existing, functioning city" (Ladd 1997: 229ff; see also Till 2005: 45ff). In the 1990s, critical reconstructionist plans for redeveloping central districts in the eastern half of Berlin emphasized mixed use, the preservation of existing structures, and urban design regulations intended to revive the street life and sense of belonging associated with the *Kiez* (local designation of a nineteenth-century Berlin neighborhood). Critical reconstructionists view the *Kiez* as a central feature of Berlin's identity and lament its extensive destruction by World War II bombing and postwar reconstruction in both the eastern and western parts of the divided city.

Advocates of critical reconstruction share with Eisenach's preservation activists a desire to recapture urban traditions and restore a lost identity. And, not surprisingly, critical reconstruction has also provoked charges of nostalgia, rigidity, elitism, and impracticality similar to those leveled at Eisenach's activists. Berlin's *Kiez* also bears a strong resemblance to Eisenach's old city *Heimat* as a site of desired belonging that bears on the historical burdens of Germanness without addressing them directly. Most importantly, in both cities the process of renewing the cityscape through preservation and new construction has been similarly presented as a correction of previous mistakes, a healing of wounds inflicted during and after the war.

This allegory of healing is even more pronounced in the reconstruction of the Stadtschloss in Berlin, now in its early phases, as well as the rebuilding of the Frauenkirche in Dresden along with the Neumarkt (New Market) quarter surrounding it. In the case of the Stadtschloss, the symbolic undoing of earlier damage is especially pronounced. The building was damaged by bombs in World War II and later demolished by the socialist regime. Removing the Stadtschloss and building the Palast der Republik in its place thus represented an unequivocal symbolic replacement of Germany's imperial legacy with an ostensibly peaceful and just socialist one. Those who advocated reconstructing the Stadtschloss façade (complete reconstruction of the palace is considered technically and financially infeasible) claimed that the project is necessary to restore proper spatial and aesthetic relations in the heart of Berlin. Critics of the project have characterized it as a falsification of history and as driven by a desire to forget both the GDR and Germany's imperialist past, along with everything that occurred thereafter. At the very least the Stadtschloss façade betrays the desire to restore an earlier identity—in this case by undoing the socialist regime's own undoing of an earlier legacy.

If conflicts over Berlin's cityscape have been especially fierce due to its status as the nation's new-old capital city, struggles in Dresden have been equally so due to the city's status as the quintessential German victim of World War II bombing—a status already well established during the communist era (see Vees-Gulani: 2005; Jarzombek: 2001). Dresden's victim status follows, in turn, from a narrative that characterizes it (misleadingly) as a place not of military or political activity, but only of beauty and cultural traditions (Florence on the Elbe), and therefore of innocence. Like the Berlin Stadtschloss, the reconstruction of the Frauenkirche (completed in 2005) has been framed as the recovery of a lost local identity, but the national symbolism is also unmistakable. In this case the central perpetrator is either the Allies who carried out the bombing, or "Hitler" as the agent who provoked it, although the SED also receives blame for having left the structure a ruin.

Meanwhile, Dresden has initiated something akin to critical reconstruction in the Neumarkt quarter with the stated aim of providing the Frauenkirche with appropriate surroundings. The arguments here echo those surrounding Berlin's neighborhoods and Eisenach's historic cityscape. Members of the Gesellschaft Historischer Neumarkt Dresden (GHND, Society for the Rebuilding of the Historical Neumarkt Dresden) have objected to the city's plan to reconstruct selected *Leitbauten* (principal structures) in the Neumarkt but otherwise allow contemporary architecture that reflects the proportions and materials of missing structures. GHND activists fear that these "experimental" structures will surround the historic reconstructions with "faceless, functional buildings" (GHND 2005). To give Dresden back its old identity and do justice to Germany's national cultural heritage, "the Neumarkt must be rebuilt in its historic image and as a harmonious architectural unity." The GHND states quite clearly that this means restoring "the condition of the Neumarkt on 13 February 1945, before the bombing." Critics have condemned this view as inviting a historical "masquerade" and a "Jurassic Park of the baroque" (Simon 2002; Holzamer 2002). Saxony's state conservator Gerhard Glaser has responded to critics by stating that the relationship between the surrounding baroque structures and the Frauen-kirche simply must be reinstated. Without the appropriate surroundings, the restored Frauenkirche apparently lacks the power to alleviate what Glaser describes as Dresden's "traumatized condition" (Simon 2002).[11]

Struggles over Eisenach's cityscape share important characteristics with these conflicts, but also illustrate just how pervasive such struggles have been in provincial East German towns and cities. Although conflict over historic cityscapes was most intense in the 1990s, similar battles continue to be waged. Controversy erupted recently in another small East German city, Altenburg, for example, over the planned demolition of several historic structures near the main marketplace to make way for a new mixed-use complex. Back in Eisenach, activists are currently en-gaged in protest against a new structure to be built directly across from the main train station. They have voiced their opposition to the project with characteristic wit; the new building will stand at a *Tor* (gate or en-trance) to the city, but in their view its design constitutes an *Eigen-Tor*, referring to the situation in soccer when a team accidentally puts the ball in their own goal and scores for their opponent.

The combination of historical and ethnographic detail made possi-ble by my extended fieldwork in Eisenach allows for a more nuanced understanding of the ways in which local activists have appropriated and responded to discourses of renewal, heritage, and national recovery. Moreover, Eisenach's battles offer a clear example of how preservation battles in a more "average" setting are bound up with questions of na-tional belonging, but framed by activists as distinctly local. Indeed, in Eisenach's church steeples, winding streets, and historic houses, activ-ists see the quintessential image of *Heimat*.

Quo Vadis Eisenach?

Although Eisenach's preservation conflicts closely resemble those in many other East German cities, some of the city's particular features have contributed to their intensity. Most important among these are its close proximity to the West and its uncertain status somewhere between provincial hometown and bustling economic center. The Wartburg Cas-tle, Eisenach's auto factories, the railroad, and the A4 autobahn long have prevented the city from retreating into the sleepy security of a provincial backwater. Yet many residents embrace Eisenach as precisely that, par-ticularly when they focus on its historic center. This is especially true of citizens involved in the Förderkreis zur Erhaltung Eisenachs (Society for the Promotion of the Preservation of Eisenach), an organization formed in 1991 by Eisenachers who engaged in both state-sanctioned and dissident activity surrounding preservation and planning in the 1980s. Most of the association's membership can be classified as belonging to the educated bourgeoisie; the most active members include teachers, museum professionals, artists, doctors, and lawyers, along with local business owners.

In terms of party politics, the Förderkreis bears no specific cast or affiliation, although its support for constraints on private property rights has led some critics to accuse members of having retained a "socialist mentality."[12] More often than not, Förderkreis members express skepticism toward all established political parties and the "democratic" system they inherited from West Germany. Some members have even suggested that the Förderkreis should start its own party. The association has received occasional support, however, from the Greens, Party of Democratic Socialism (PDS), and a local independent party called Bürger für Eisenach (Citizens for Eisenach, a holdover from the *Wende* period). As the two parties that have dominated the city council and mayor's office since unification, the Christian Democratic Union (CDU) and Social Democratic Party (SPD) have been the most frequent targets of Förderkreis attacks. In addition to elected officials and planners, the group's opponents also often include local and regional preservation officials, property owners, developers, and architects.

The Förderkreis also competed during the 1990s with an organization called the Kulturkreis (Cultural Society), formed by the city's director of cultural affairs. Committed to a cosmopolitan vision of the cityscape and local cultural identity, he frequently painted the Förderkreis as provincial and reactionary. The rivalry between these two groups reflects vividly the class dimension of Eisenach's battles; all parties involved are members of the bourgeoisie and assume that one or another faction of that class should serve as custodian of the cityscape and local culture. The vehemence of Förderkreis members' attacks on their opponents and their sense of betrayal toward the unified German order can thus be seen as a result of their thwarted desire to regain a lost dominance in local affairs. Their idealized image of preservation in the nineteenth century assumes the political and cultural hegemony of devoted *Bürger* (citizens) like themselves. Like their predecessors, Eisenach's contemporary activists think of their mission not as a matter of class dominance, however, but rather in the local-universal—and implicitly national—terms of heritage and local identity.

Under both the CDU and SPD, the city government has grappled openly with the pressures of development and preservation, which were especially intense in the years following unification. On the way to

Eisenach's old center one day in March 1996, I happened upon a flyer advertising a public forum on urban planning to be held the next day that captured this ambiguity as well as the immense significance assigned to planning decisions at that time. The theme of the forum was: "Quo Vadis Eisenach? Garden City or Hong Kong?" Today, Eisenach's old center includes buildings that can be read as pointing in both directions: tiny half-timbered houses and larger *Bürgerhäuser* (bourgeois residences) from the seventeenth and eighteenth centuries; a baroque palace; banks and hotels with neoclassical, art nouveau, and pseudo-timbered facades; two- and three-story apartment buildings from the 1930s and 1950s; and a cluster of socialist *Plattenbauten* (GDR-era apartment blocks built in the 1980s), referred to by many Eisenacher as the "Goethe ghetto" (after Goethestraße, the quarter's northern boundary). After unification these apartment blocks received a radical makeover in bright hues—an emphatic contrast to the "gray" that many East Germans associate with socialist architecture. Equally if not more important, however, is the contrast between refurbished historic structures and those not yet restored (see figure 8.1).

Since 1990, a number of four- and five-story structures have been built in the old center as well, some on large plots of land cleared in the late

Figure 8.1. The allegorical cityscape: a refurbished house in Eisenach's old center next to one still awaiting renovation. Photograph by Jason James.

1980s to make way for projects unrealized due to unification. In some cases these new structures cover an entire city block once occupied by many individual buildings. In terms of style, most of the new additions to the cityscape can be described as postmodern; their materials and designs mark them as new, but they also incorporate selected historical materials and motifs and usually conform more or less to the proportions of surrounding structures. Yet activists condemn such structures as *Kulturschanden* (cultural atrocities) and *Bausünden* (literally "architectural sins," eyesores). For the Förderkreis, the architecture of unified Germany as found in Eisenach consists for the most part of "cheap" and "monotonous slabs" (*Klötze*) that disrupt the harmony of Eisenach's old center (see figure 8.2).

Casting new buildings in these terms equates them with socialist *Plattenbau* architecture, which activists also regard as a poor substitute for historic structures. Activists in Eisenach recall that in the 1980s they feared local communist officials would eventually preserve only a small part of the old city and replace the rest with *Plattenbauten*. New structures thus appear to them as an unfortunate repetition of past mistakes, but these mistakes are not attributed solely to the SED. As I discuss

Figure 8.2. The Sophiencenter, one of the structures built in the early 1990s that activists criticized as failing to integrate itself into the existing urban fabric. Photograph by Jason James.

further below, they also claim that the renewal of East German cities has repeated mistakes made in West Germany during the 1960s and 1970s, a view their West German supporters tend to share.

Even more important than the construction of "disruptive" new structures is the destruction of historic ones. Förderkreis activists argue that too many historic buildings are "renovated to death," leaving them with no authentic "historic substance." Activists also condemn such measures, along with outright demolition of vernacular historic buildings, as a "violation" or "rape" of Eisenach's cultural heritage. In addition to wanton destruction of historic substance and disruption of the cityscape, activists accuse officials and other opponents of incompetence, greed, and a lack of devotion to heritage, as well as failure to uphold legal codes, solicit citizen input, and practice transparency. Officials usually respond by painting activists as hopelessly nostalgic, unrealistic "fundamentalists," whose attitude and tactics pose a serious threat to democracy and the city's future development. If activists got their way, the deputy mayor once declared, the whole city would become a museum.

One of the most dramatic of several confrontations in the 1990s erupted over the municipal government's plan to erect a new building for itself on the south side of Eisenach's Marktplatz, its central square (see figure 8.3). While "anonymous investors" were usually blamed for

Figure 8.3. Eisenach's new municipal complex, which closed a gap left by World War II bombing. Its "tolerated appendages" stand on either side; the old town hall is on the left. Photograph by Jason James.

"architectural sin," in this case the city itself was behind what activists condemned as a desecration of the historic cityscape. Municipal officials, in contrast, envisioned the new complex as a clear sign of postunification renewal—and of their instrumental role in it. The complex would close a gap left in the heart of the city by Allied bombs, a hole that GDR officials had left open for forty-five years in the form of a small park called the Rathausgarten (City Hall Garden). With the possible exception of the gap left in another major square by the demolition of the *Gründerzeit* (late nineteenth-century) Tannhäuser Hotel by the state just weeks before the *Wende* began in 1989, this was the most prominent "wound" to be mended in Eisenach (see figure 8.4). But activists' attacks on the building erected to heal this injury suggest that in their eyes it not only failed to heal this wound but actually inflicted more damage.

The municipal government held a design competition for the new complex. The jury included representatives from several local groups, including the Förderkreis. In contrast to city officials and most other jury members, Förderkreis members rejected the winning entry as too "futuristic" and "monotonous." Like so many other new structures erected after unification, its "massive" scale showed "irreverence" toward the

Figure 8.4. The "Tannhäuser gap" in the mid-1990s. A new structure to fill it was completed in 2007. Photograph by Jason James.

buildings surrounding it, disrupting the square's historic contours. They favored instead a design submitted by a local architecture student that in their view integrated itself better with the "historic image" of the Marktplatz.

Exasperated officials responded by framing the new complex as a new contribution to the history of the city. The architecture of the late twentieth century should be more than just an homage to the past, they contended. In any case, the new complex achieved an acceptable balance between old and new. The deputy mayor also suggested in an interview with me that Eisenach's historic cityscape, the Marktplatz included, hardly exhibited the architectural harmony that activists wanted to protect. In fact, he claimed, architectural contrasts introduced over the ages had come to define the city's history and identity. Viewed from this angle, the new complex could be seen as upholding tradition rather than breaking from it.

The winning architect, who had grown up in Eisenach but fled to the West as a teenager, defended the design at the dedication ceremony by framing it as an exercise in tolerance and individuality. "It is like everywhere else in life," he reasoned. "I must acknowledge the existence of others but at the same time allow myself to be my own person." He had attempted to set the new building "in dialogue with its surroundings" instead of "making it a slave to them." It was time, the architect concluded, to stop clinging to notions of piety and *Anstand* (decency). Yet he felt compelled to reassure his audience that he did not wish to come off as a *Besserwessi* (West German know-it-all). On the contrary, he considered it an honor to design a new public building for the city of his birth. Activists, who often claim exceptional *Heimatgefühl* (devotion to the hometown) and accuse others of lacking it, scoffed at the architect's claim to local roots. In their eyes, he was hardly a real Eisenacher and certainly no better than the other West German investors and architects busy disfiguring their city.

Much to the dismay of city officials, an architecture critic later gave strong validation to activists' criticisms by placing a photo of the nearly completed complex at the center of a feature article in the national daily newspaper *Frankfurter Allgemeine Zeitung* (FAZ) lamenting the "architectural miscarriages" plaguing East German cities (Kowa 1996). The photo's caption describes the complex as "overwhelming" the historic buildings surrounding it, degrading them to "tolerated appendages."

While the battle over the municipal complex raged, activists also condemned the city's restoration of the building adjacent to it (see figure 8.3). The same bombing raid that created the gap filled by the municipal complex also damaged the old city hall, and in early 1990 engineers concluded that stabilization measures undertaken after the war were inadequate. As in many other cases, then, both activists and officials treated the project as rectifying damage incurred in World War II and not fully repaired by the socialist regime. Yet, in news reports and interviews with me, activists sharply criticized the renovation as destructive; the use of modern or otherwise inappropriate materials and design features in the interior, they claimed, left the building a mere façade with little authentic substance. Officials responded that updating a structure is actually more "sincere" when original elements are not salvageable, and that most historic structures in Eisenach had been renovated at some point, making the question of originality difficult at best.

Another major conflict that occurred during the time of my field research concerned the proposed rebuilding of two wings of a medieval residence that had been bombed in World War II. Situated next to the famed Luther House, the open area had been made into a small park called the Lutherplatz (Luther's Square). Although the developer was active in preservation and claimed that the project would help restore the old city's medieval fabric, Förderkreis activists dismissed the project as a falsification of the past and just another attempt to extract profit in the name of heritage. At a public forum on the Lutherplatz project, one activist mocked the developer's claim to "restore" the destroyed structures by stating wryly that they probably did not include the underground parking garage that his design called for, while another likened the project to the Sophiencenter, a large structure whose design activists also attributed to an "anonymous investor's" desire for quick profit.

The Förderkreis won a rare clear-cut victory in this case. The Bürgerinitiative ESA (Citizens' Initiative), a coalition led by Förderkreis members, presented the mayor with a petition containing over two thousand signatures opposing the project, and the city council eventually passed a resolution against developing the Lutherplatz.[13] The most prominent subsequent conflicts have focused on the aforementioned structure near the train station; plans to close the "Tannhäuser gap"; the renovation of the Creutznacher House, a Renaissance-era half-timbered structure on the Marktplatz; and a widely publicized project to expand and modernize the museum attached to the famous Bach House, which involved what activists condemn as the illegal demolition of historic structures.

Preservation, the *Wende*, and Unification

In my reading, the municipal complex and other postunification projects represent for local activists stories of failed redemption and the repetition of loss. In their eyes, unified Germany has betrayed what they understood as a promise of cultural recuperation via historic preservation. To fully understand this view, we must look back a bit further and examine the role of cityscapes and preservation in the GDR, particularly during the late 1980s. Cityscapes figured more prominently in popular East German opposition to the SED than is usually acknowledged. Planned or executed demolitions of landmark buildings, entire neighborhoods, and monuments sometimes provoked open protest, while for many East Germans critical of the SED, the decaying urban centers and *Plattenbauten* came to symbolize the failings of the socialist state just as powerfully as the Berlin Wall.

This occurred in spite of a program of restoration and renewal begun by the East German government in the 1970s. Preservation became part of a strategy to recover legitimacy and encourage a stronger sense of national belonging, which also entailed a less equivocal embrace of notions like national heritage and *Heimat*.[14] In 1982, the Ministry for Culture joined with the Zentralkomitee der Nationalen Front des demokratischen Deutschlands (Central Committee of the National Front of Democratic Germany) and the Kulturbund zur demokratischen Erneuerung Deutschlands (Cultural League for the Democratic Renewal of Germany, the state body under which all clubs and associations were subsumed) to call for a mass movement for "the maintenance of landmarks and their surroundings" (Felz 1988: 9). By the time of the 1982 declaration, many history and preservation enthusiasts had already organized their own groups within the Kulturbund. Eisenach's Interessengemeinschaft Denkmalpflege (Interest Group for Preservation) was formed in 1979. The Kulturbund encouraged popular interest in heritage, informants told me, but sought to keep preservation activities within modest, controllable bounds. As former members explained to me, Eisenach's Interessengemeinschaft and others like it were nevertheless quietly critical of state and occasionally clashed openly with officials. As the unified German government would later learn as well, it proved difficult for the East German state to sanctify heritage and encourage an embrace of local and cultural belonging without also providing activists with a foothold for critiquing state activity in those realms.

Preservation enthusiasts found much to criticize in the GDR. Even after the ideological shift of the 1970s, the regime still emphasized new construction over preservation due to the chronic shortage of adequate housing, an issue especially vital to state legitimacy. Preservation efforts therefore were confined mainly to showcase landmarks or sections of old city centers destined to serve as pedestrian shopping zones. Local preservation enthusiasts, architects, and planners worried about the deterioration of Eisenach's historic center came together in 1988 to form the Arbeitsgruppe Stadtsanierung (Working Group for Urban Renewal). As one of the grassroots "citizens' movements" organized in opposition to the regime, the Arbeitsgruppe had a more subversive cast than the Interessengemeinschaft.

In the midst of what would come to be known as the *Wende* of 1989/ 90, local preservation activists charged that neglect and outright destruction by the ruling SED had inflicted more damage on Eisenach's architectural heritage than Allied bombs. In October 1989, participants in Eisenach's largest demonstration against the regime not only made the demands commonly associated with the East German opposition—for freedom of travel, open elections, the dissolution of the secret police, and environmental reforms—but also carried banners reading "Save Our Old City!" and "Rescue the Hellgrevenhof" (an ensemble of medieval buildings associated with Saint Elizabeth). That same eventful month, the party organ *Das Volk* (The People) printed a letter from a resident who would later become one of Eisenach's most tenacious preservation activists. He wrote, "Our cities, having slowly evolved over the centuries, with their wealth of architectural attractions and all their vestiges of craftsmanship, are a part of German culture, and it is shameful how the city fathers and agencies have treated them in the past. Citizens identify strongly with their city, but with such expansive demolition, a piece of our identity is lost." The letter struck a chord: in the following weeks, at least a dozen letters published in *Das Volk* applauded its critique—only one defended the SED.

After the fall of the Berlin Wall, preservation activists found themselves wielding unprecedented power. As participants in the local round table that brought together socialist officials and the leaders of opposition groups, they succeeded not only in halting construction on a new *Plattenbau* near the city center, but also in replacing the party-appointed director of city planning with a member of the Arbeitsgruppe. The end of the GDR came just in time, as they saw it, to save what was left of Eisenach's historic architecture and morphology.

The numerous conflicts over Eisenach's cityscape that began shortly after unification signaled for activists a departure from what appeared in the months just before and after November 1989 as a unanimous commitment to preserve as much of the old city as possible. Eisenach would soon recover its former identity, activists and other residents hoped, in the same way as the nation would and in conjunction with it. With former activists occupying key positions in the city government, the planning office, and the preservation department, they imagined with some justification that this vision would be realized through a "democratic" coordination of grassroots and government efforts. A pamphlet distributed in 1991 by Eisenach's planning office explicitly pledged that the city would again become worthy of identification, in part because planning would no longer occur "over the heads of local citizens."

Nostalgia for the Nation

Local activists received strong encouragement in their commitment to preservation from West German leaders and preservationists, both of whom cast the former GDR as a treasure chest of heritage, a place where cultural time had stood still. While *Ostalgie* (nostalgia for the GDR) has been extensively analyzed, debated, and often ridiculed, the wave of nostalgia focused on cultural heritage and *Heimat* that followed the fall of the Berlin Wall has attracted less commentary. In the early 1990s, many West Germans were swept up in this nostalgia as much as East Germans. On their first visits to the East, many West Germans found what Sebastian Preuss, writing in the FAZ, called a "revelation" (1990). "Where in the [old] Federal Republic," he asked, "can one find so many buildings still preserved in their prewar state down to the last detail?" "In the Eastern states," he concluded, "we rediscover our past" (Preuss 1990). Recalling this early sense of discovery, another FAZ contributor wrote, "This wealth of architectural heritage, admittedly decaying but not yet falsified by ... prosperity and still preserved in every detail, was for the one [Western] side part discovery and part revelation, and for the other [Eastern side] a fund of cultural property they had once given up for lost but that now demanded immediate rescue" (Kowa 1995).

If poverty is the best preservation, as preservationists frequently remark with only a hint of irony, it had left an enormous, "unspoiled" fund of heritage in the GDR deemed in desperate need of rescue.

West Germans' enthusiasm for historic East German cities also followed from the fact that these cities offered planners and architects a chance to redeem themselves from what some had come to see as their "sins of youth"—i.e., their rejection of historic precedents in architecture and planning in the 1960s and 1970s in favor of modernism (Glaeser 2001).[15] It was therefore not uncommon to hear West Germans warning that Eastern cities should at all costs avoid repeating *Westfehler* (mistakes of the West). These "mistakes" had produced cities that Alexander Mitscherlich (1965) characterized in the 1960s as unlivable and another West German derided in 1990 as "schematized Legolands" (Hampel-Zöllner 1990).

The nostalgic gaze that West Germans cast upon Eastern cityscapes thus played a vital role in constituting architectural heritage as an uncontaminated, ahistorical national legacy that local activists felt called upon to defend. For while the GDR was cast as the moral other of the Western (now unified) FRG, East Germans and their "unspoiled" towns represented a romanticized other.[16] The East embodied an older Germanness associated with tradition and *Gemütlichkeit* (homeyness), but also conformity and backwardness—a Germanness that many West Germans felt they had lost or abandoned and wanted to retrieve and revisit, but also wished to keep at a distance.

Official discourse both encouraged and echoed the claims of journalists, activists, and many others in rendering historic structures and cityscapes in the East as precious icons of cultural identity, which, in turn, strengthened activists' demand that the state take responsibility for heritage preservation and exert strict control over cityscapes. In his address to the first session of the unified German parliament, Helmut Kohl announced:

> Among the contributions of the [new eastern] states [to the unified nation] … we should not overlook an invaluable cultural heritage. They include old landscapes rich with tradition that hold unique testaments [*Zeugnisse*] to our history. The palaces in Schwerin and Potsdam, the marvelous form of the Naumburg Cathedral, the Semper Opera in Dresden—they all stand for a single Germany. At the Wartburg, Luther translated the Bible for all Germans, and Weimar has become a worldwide symbol of German classicism. We are pleased that these monuments to our common history and culture are now accessible to all. (1990)

Kohl's statement not only treats national culture as embodied in landmarks, it also associates unification with retrieval; unification made them once again "accessible to all" and by implication returned them to the nation that unification also restored.

Another prime example of making preservation an allegory of unification appears in the booklet *Bürger rettet Eure Städte!* (Citizens, Save Your Cities!), published in celebration of the fifth anniversary of a ZDF television series devoted to profiling "endangered" landmarks and ensembles in the East and raising funds for their restoration (1997).[17] The show's host, Werner von Bergen, entitled his contribution (1997) to the booklet "Zusammen bauen was zusammen gehört" (building together what belongs together), rendering the preservation of landmarks as a material mirror of unification by playing on Willy Brandt's legendary "Jetzt wächst zusammen was zusammen gehört" (what belongs together, now grows together).

The reclamation of national cultural property in the East offered a powerful way for the leaders of the newly unified FRG to enact the return of the German nation. They cast the unified state, that is, as rectifying the cultural damage inflicted by or left unmended by the GDR, thereby continuing in modified form the negative mirroring between East and West established during national division (Borneman 1992: 15ff). Gerhard Schröder's address to the 2000 World Tourism Conference contains a vivid example of this mirroring in relation to heritage. Schröder lamented "how little we all know of the great cultural treasures [in Eastern Germany] that suffered such neglect under the totalitarian regime of the communist party" (2000). This statement replicates a discourse that locates the GDR outside a national imaginary demarcated by cultural patrimony and proper devotion to it. The socialist regime appears as a thief, a vandal, or, at best, an illegitimate custodian from which the nation and its heritage must be reclaimed. If the renovation and reconstruction of older landmarks, along with the removal of GDR monuments and the changing of street names in Eastern cities have functioned as an allegory of renewal, they have done so by casting the legacy of socialism as another instance of damage to be repaired or reversed by the expanded FRG.

Not surprisingly, many Easterners have also adopted the view that their cities are less corrupted by modernity and, therefore, represent a precious historical legacy on the verge of vanishing. Given the stigmatization in unified Germany of the GDR and most East Germans' pre-1990 biographies, architectural heritage offers an important and rare occasion for Easterners to claim a positive contribution to the unified nation. To an extent, it even redeems their relative deprivation under socialism, since the survival of so much "historic substance" now appears as a fortunate (if unintended) effect of the GDR's economic failings.

The bitterness of debates in Eisenach during the 1990s thus followed in part from the fact that activists saw direct justification for their stance in the state's own rhetoric and policies. The official narrative of unification framed it as a retrieval of the nation, selectively deploying a cyclical model of national history that since World War II has served as a basis for framing contemporary events as potential recapitulations of previous errors and the losses they inflicted—National Socialism and the Holocaust, but more recently East German state socialism and postwar West German society. Yet, the story of repetition as retrieval also necessitated casting (re)unified Germany as an exception to this pattern—as capable of finally breaking modern Germany's cycle of loss and failed projects of recovery. The nation's "wounds" would finally be healed.

Yet, activists concluded shortly after unification that the "mistakes" of the West were being repeated in Eastern cities. Having just succeeded in their confrontation with the socialist regime, activists were emboldened by their West German supporters and hopeful that the wealthy country they had just joined would devote extensive resources to preservation. But all too soon they heard ominous warnings. A preservation official from Lübeck, for example, declared that "[East Germans] must appropriate their cities for themselves, otherwise business [interests] will expropriate them" (Baake 1990). It was not long before the *Aufbruchmentalität* (hopeful sense of a new beginning that followed unification) mutated, as one activist put it in an interview, into *Abbruchmentalität* (a mentality of demolition). This charge, like the claim of "expropriation," effectively inverts the value of recapitulation associated with unity; it is not just the unified nation that threatens to return, these writers suggest, but also destruction and injustice associated with the GDR.

The danger of "expropriation" loomed especially large in the early 1990s because Eastern cities like Eisenach were both gold mines and easy prey for speculators. The federal government made large subsidies available for a wide range of projects, while recently installed local officials had little time to draft new planning and preservation ordinances or familiarize themselves with West German legal codes and procedures (Häußermann 1998). Combined with the practical and ideological demands for renewal that accompanied unification, economic conditions during the 1990s also made Eastern cities eager, if not desperate, for investment. Economic stagnation in these cities made redevelopment especially important as a sign of improvement. Local officials, therefore, felt they could not make significant demands on developers. This placed them in a rather vulnerable position with respect to preservation activists, since it appeared that their allegiance had quickly shifted from the hometown and its heritage to "anonymous investors" interested mainly in profit.

By the time Eisenach's municipal complex was completed in 1997, earlier warnings about expropriation and destruction seemed quite prescient in the eyes of Eisenach's preservation activists. Reporting on the anniversary celebration of a preservation association in nearby Erfurt, Brigitte Peukert summed up East German preservation activists' assessment of the situation in the mid 1990s thus: "Before it was the [socialist] functionaries that ruled by decree. Now it is the boundless power of money to which local officials must kowtow—or must they? What neither war nor forty years of the GDR's ruinous economy could destroy is now being liquidated by the 'fashion of architecture' hand-in-hand with the power of money" (1996). The sense of irony and bitterness here is palpable; the promise of unification as both return and transformation has shown itself to be hollow. "Democracy" serves not the people but business interests and facilitates further cultural destruction. Moreover, the use of the term "liquidation" reflects a tendency I noted to paint cultural landmarks as victims, sometimes by comparing them implicitly to victims of the Holocaust. The head of a company specializing in historic restoration who had worked for one of the district preservation offices in the GDR used the phrase "selection on the ramp" in an interview with me to describe the way in which limited resources forced him to let many valuable structures be demolished or left to deteriorate.

In Förderkreis activists' reading of Eisenach's allegorical cityscape, World War II bombings, demolitions by the East German state, and contemporary redevelopment projects are equivalent moments of loss. The demolition of a historic building represents not just an irreverent act to be protested, but also a repetition of previous injuries and broken promises of redemption. Local activists have embraced the dominant narrative of repetition, but in doing so have also recast it by claiming that the retrieval of identity has been trumped by recapitulation—a compulsion to repeat the errors and losses of the past. At the center of battles waged in Eisenach, then, lies a tension between the longing for historical redemption, promised by the state, and the anxiety that it can be thwarted by a repetition of past mistakes and losses—between a longing to recover normalcy and the anxious conviction that it remains unattainable.

Recapitulation, Redemption, and Victimhood

Preservation activists in Eisenach take official rhetoric at its word in looking to the material authority of the historic cityscape and cultural landmarks to provide an untainted, redemptive legacy of national belonging. But in addition to the nation's stigmatized legacies and the shortcomings of renewal in unified Germany, the contradictions and repressions endemic to the category of authenticity and the project of preservation make redemption profoundly elusive. The promise of return expressed in restoration and the fantasy of permanence implied by preservation help to repress the fact that authenticity is not an absolute material quality, that the (origin)al is never truly available.

Activists' desire for redemption, expressed in demands for authenticity and harmony, can also be understood at a deeper level as a problem of modernity. Most cryptically, we might call it the condition of homelessness or the core of loss that makes nostalgia a modern ailment. But, the problem of modernity has weight and contours specific to the German context by virtue of the country's particular history of embracing and rejecting (sometimes radical) visions of the modern. Heritage and *Heimat* have been vital and closely interconnected components of Germans' engagement with modernity since the late nineteenth century.

Since that time, *Heimat* has been "at the center of a German moral—and by extension political—discourse about place, belonging, and identity" (Applegate 1990: 4). Embodied in the landscape of the city and its natural surroundings, *Heimat* has long served as a metaphor that links the local "home" with the region and the German nation. It makes the nation both a local metaphor and a metaphor of the local (Confino 1998). Efforts to beautify, preserve, and celebrate the natural and cultural heritage of one's hometown or region have therefore long functioned as a performance of Germanness. Indeed, *Heimat* has played a vital role in German nationalism because it renders devotion to the hometown as a form of devotion to the nation, and both forms of devotion as something natural to human beings; everyone needs a homeland, just as they need heritage. Heritage and *Heimat* simultaneously localize and universalize national belonging.

The archetypes of *Heimat* community are the traditional village and the historic hometown. One Förderkreis activist described the traditional village as "a product of centuries of human experience ... The residents knew their territory, knew precisely its advantageous and unfavorable qualities, and adapted themselves to them. The knowledge derived from experience was passed on, the positive in it retained with a sense of reverence." Activists view Eisenach as having once possessed a high degree of social harmony and cultural integrity as well. One activist described Eisenach's nineteenth-century bourgeoisie as enjoying a fundamental "cultural unanimity" in its devotion to the hometown. The harmonious cityscape seems to have mirrored the cultural harmony that preserved it.

Yet precisely to the extent that continuity and harmony serve as the defining qualities of *Heimat* community, it is at bottom a structure of difference; *Heimat* is inseparable from its putative opposite, *Fremde*. Like the authenticity assigned to cultural landmarks, the wholeness, harmony, and integrity attributed to *Heimat* depend on the sense that it is not assured—that it is vulnerable, threatened by others. If *Fremde* is "a synonym for hardship, privation, homesickness, and the loss of a sense of belonging," then the forces past and present seen as preventing the recuperation of belonging are a projection of that primary loss (Suhr 1989: 72).[18] *Heimat* has been the focus of such powerful longing in the postwar era, therefore, because it serves as a proxy for what Santner calls Germany's "stranded objects" of identification—the nation's stigmatized legacies (Santner 1990: 26). *Heimat* is ultimately a figure of lack, a struc-ture of desire "drenched in the longing for wholeness, unity, integrity" (Morely and Robins 1990: 4). As such it inspires identification and long-ing only as something absent or endangered.

Preservation activism in Eisenach is thus energized by, indeed depends on, a vision of threatened heritage and *Heimat.* Just as purity cannot be conceived without pollution, the *Heimat* imaginary as intact, harmoni-ous community both enables and depends on its disruption. For Eisen-ach's activists the story of the historic cityscape as an image of *Heimat* is thus one of lost authenticity, of a prior harmony destroyed by the intru-sion of extrinsic elements. The forces blamed for loss are cast as foreign to a naturally integrated whole. As one activist expressed it in one of her many columns in a local newspaper: "'Just tear down the old shack!' How frequently one hears this often thoughtless remark in the cities and now increasingly in the countryside. Construction firms and project develop-ers are everywhere, ready with plans ... These days it seems anything but harmful to business to erect new settlements in the midst of *anmutenden* (charming), *anheimelnden* (homey) old village centers with no regard for whether the new fits into or adapts itself to the old."

It is thus especially fitting—if not exceptional—for activists to dispar-age new structures as *Fremdkörper* (literally "foreign bodies," eyesores). They originate not in the *Heimat,* but rather from "irreverent" investors and officials—moral outsiders. In this sense, *Heimat* not only serves as an allegory of redemption, but also circumscribes a moral interior, a ter-ritory of belonging occupied by the devoted local citizens who anoint themselves its defenders.

If *Heimat* operates through a territorial metaphor of belonging that casts it as a geographically and morally bounded, harmonious home-town community, then heritage is a complementary possessive meta-phor of belonging that frames identity in terms of collective ownership of authentic artifacts. The cultural landmark is the guise of belonging conceived as the possession of sacred cultural objects rather than moral territory. In this way it is identical to what Slavoj Žižek calls the national Thing: "What we conceal by imputing to the Other the theft of enjoy-ment is the traumatic fact that *we never possessed what was allegedly stolen from us*" (emphasis in original; 1990: 54). Heritage and *Heimat* operate as mutually reinforcing allegories of a redemptive Germanness that can remain an object of longing and appear untainted to the same degree that it remains just out of reach, always subject to potential loss or disruption.

Defending heritage renders the possibility of redemption as a matter of material *cum* cultural restoration, and this depends on both translating the story of national loss into one of suffering and transferring it to the realm of *Kultur* (culture). As *Kultur,* heritage appears innocent by virtue of its supposed distance from "the past" and the political, but also by virtue of its trauma. The supposed suffering of cultural landmarks at the hands of the Other allows them to enjoy the vicarious virtue of victimhood and occupy the moral interior of the nation (Buruma 1994). The Nazi and SED regimes thus become something that was not of us but rather happened to us—to our cultural heritage and homeland.

Local activists' focus on injury and loss resonates, if only indirectly, with a recent surge in attention to German suffering in World War II. Indeed, preservation activism maintains a clear distinction between perpetrator and victim—in the allegorical realm of heritage and *Heimat*—that long has structured discussion of National Socialism. It may be that official engagement with the past in Germany has begun to blur productively the formerly dichotomous moral universe of Germany's politics of memory, but it is difficult to gauge whether most Germans have moved in this direction (Moeller 2005; Langenbacher 2008). Discourse about Nazism both within and outside Germany still treats it as fundamentally evil, while at least one recent study has concluded that young Germans view family members who were associated with the National Socialist regime as innocent even when those elders have admitted participating in atrocities (Welzer et. al. 2002). A similar moral dichotomy persists in characterizations of the GDR as an *Unrechtsstaat* (state not ruled by law) and "second German dictatorship." And as I have shown, the perpetrator-victim divide continues to structure local discourse about preservation and renewal. While more open acknowledgment of German suffering in World War II does not necessarily involve a displacement or denial of suffering inflicted on Germany's victims, local activists' defense of—and identification with—victimized heritage perpetuates an established discourse of national victimhood. It remains difficult to embrace this discourse while at the same time acknowledging Germans' complicity in Nazi crimes; German suffering cannot be acknowledged on its own terms but instead tends to appear as a way of changing the moral implications of World War II and the Holocaust. At the very least, narratives of German victimhood as well as preservation activists' embrace of endangered heritage reinforce an essentialist understanding of national belonging. Among activists, Germanness is imagined in terms that not only morally externalize the legacies of the Nazi regime and SED, but that also place a particular kind of culturally devoted citizen at the moral center of the *Heimat.* This vision of community does not take account of the degree to which Germany is now defined in democratic and multiethnic terms—conditions that do not square with fantasies of common origins and cultural consensus.

Notes

This chapter is a revised version of an essay entitled "Retrieving a Redemptive Past: Protecting Heritage and *Heimat* in East German Cities." *German Politics and Society* 27,3 (2009): 1–27.

1. I conducted field research in Eisenach from March 1996 to July 1998, supplemented by follow-up visits in 2001 and 2005 as well as ongoing research using Internet sources. My claims here are based on a combination of direct interviews, observation, contemporary news articles, and archival material. I have used pseudonyms and composite figures throughout to protect the anonymity of informants. In some cases this also necessitates not providing full citations for quoted material where an activist would be directly identified as a result. Funding for various stages of the project was provided by the Deutscher Akademischer Austtausch Dienst (DAAD), the University of California, San Diego (UCSD) Department of Anthropology, and the University of Mary Washington. I would like to thank all of my collaborators in Eisenach, my mentors at UCSD, and my colleagues at Barnard College, Lafayette College, and the University of Mary Washington for their assistance and support.
2. This and all other translations from the German are by the author.
3. Recent ethnographic studies like Mazur-Stommen's study of renewal in Rostock provide valuable insight into the politics of preservation and renewal in East Germany in this sense, but do not read these battles in relation to deeper struggles over German and East German identity (2005).
4. In what follows I use the English term preservation to refer broadly to practices encompassed by the German terms *Denkmalschutz* and *Denkmalpflege*, literally the protection and care of historic landmarks. In doing so I do not intend to capture the technical distinctions made by both English and German between conservation and restoration. My concern lies more with distinctions made by local activists, particularly between the kind of preservation that maintains the "original" character of historic buildings, and renovation (*Sanierung*) that goes too far in introducing modern elements or techniques.
5. The effort to find redemption did not, of course, arise for the first time in the 1990s. In the postwar era, the politics of memory and identity in both East and West Germany were largely about establishing a redemptive identity vis-à-vis National Socialism. As Jeffrey Olick has shown, efforts of this sort began very soon after the end of the war (2005).
6. See also Huyssen (1997) and Ladd (1997).
7. See Koshar's detailed accounts (1994, 1998).

8. The two most important works that approach *Heimat* in this way are Applegate (1990) and Confino (1998). Both authors also highlight *Heimat's* nostalgic aspects and its opposition to *Fremde* (the foreign), but do not delve as deeply as they could into the centrality of difference, desire, and loss in *Heimat*. Blickle addresses these issues more explicitly, but includes less historical and ethnographic detail (2002).

9. The concept of invented tradition is attributed to Hobsbawm and Ranger (1983); the nation as imagined community was originated by Anderson (1983).

10. Hagen makes a similar point in his illuminating case study of Rothenburg ob der Tauber (2006). Hagen rightfully emphasizes the dynamic interaction among preservation, nationalism, and tourism in the production of Rothenburg as a historic, quintessentially German city, but like other studies of this sort does not delve very deeply into the character of identification and longing that inform this production.

11. For a more in-depth analysis of the Frauenkirche and Neumarkt reconstructions, see James (2006).

12. The following characterizations of the Förderkreis and its members are based on a combination of ethnographic interviews and observations as well as archival materials, primarily newspaper articles.

13. That victory has become slightly less clear more recently due to questions about whether the 1997 resolution is truly binding.

14. A discussion of the appropriation of *Heimat* in East Germany can be found in Confino (2006). On the SED's ideological reclamation of the nation, see von Bredow (1983) and Pfeiffer (1993).

15. On the postwar struggle between modernism and traditionalism in Munich, see Rosenfeld (2000).

16. John Borneman has called this the "orientalization" of East Germany (1998: 112). Glaeser has offered a similar assessment cast in temporal rather than spatial terms, referring to the "distemporalization" of Easterners by Westerners, while Ash claims that both the Nazi and SED regimes have been cast as nonmodern others to the FRG (Glaeser 2001: 180; Ash 2001). See also James (2004).

17. The series was produced jointly by the national (originally West German) television network ZDF and the Deutsche Stiftung Denkmalschutz (German Foundation for Historic Preservation).

18. We might add that *Heimat* takes shape in opposition to the *unheimlich*, literally the "unhomely" or uncanny, which for Freud is essentially the return of the repressed in disguise—something familiar but disavowed that makes an appearance as something foreign, but which we at some level recognize.

References

Anderson, Benedict. 1983. *Imagined Communities: Reflections on the Origin and Spread of Nationalism.* London: Verso.

Applegate, Celia. 1990. *A Nation of Provincials: the German Idea of Heimat.* Berkeley: University of California Press.

Ash, Mitchell. 2001. "Becoming Normal, Modern, and German (Again?)." In *The Power of Intellectuals in Contemporary Germany,* edited by Michael Geyer. Chicago: University of Chicago Press.

Baake, Bodo. 1990. "Der Fluch der Platte." *Treff (Wochenendbeilage der Thüringischen Landeszeitung),* 22 September.

Blickle, Peter. 2002. *Heimat: A Critical Theory of the German Idea of Homeland.* Rochester: Camden House.

Borneman, John. 1992. *Belonging in the Two Berlins: Kin, State, Nation.* Cambridge: Cambridge University Press.

————. 1998. *Subversions of International Order: Studies in the Political Anthropology of Culture.* Albany: State University of New York Press.

Buruma, Ian. 1994. *The Wages of Guilt: Memories of War in Germany and Japan.* New York: Farrar, Straus, and Giroux.

Confino, Alon. 1998. *The Nation As a Local Metaphor: Württemberg, Imperial Germany, and National Memory, 1871–1918.* Chapel Hill: University of North Carolina Press.

————. 2006. *Germany as a Culture of Remembrance: Promises and Limits of Writing History.* Chapel Hill: University of North Carolina Press.

Eckhardt, Götz, ed. 1978. *Schicksale deutscher Baudenkmale im zweiten Weltkrieg: Eine Dokumentation der Schäden und Totalverluste auf dem Gebiet der Deutschen Demokratischen Republik.* Vol. 2. *Bezirke Halle, Leipzig, Dresden, Karl-Marx-Stadt, Erfurt, Gera, Suhl.* Berlin: Henschverlag.

Felz, Achim. 1988. *Denkmale: Von uns bewahrt.* Berlin: Henschverlag.

Gesellschaft Historischer Neumarkt Dresden (GHND). 2005. "Wie soll der Neumarkt wiederaufgebaut werden?" http://www.neumarkt-dresden.de, accessed 15 July 2005.

Glaeser, Andreas. 2001. "Conclusion: Why Germany Remains Divided." In *A New Germany in a New Europe,* edited by Todd Herzog and Sander L. Gilman. New York: Routledge.

Hagen, Joshua. 2006. *Preservation, Tourism, Nationalism: The Jewel of the German Past.* Burlington, V.T.: Ashgate.

Hampel-Zöllner, Manfred. 1990. "Laßt Euch nicht kaputt-sanieren!" *Thüringische Landeszeitung,* 26 October.

Hartmut Häußermann. 1998. "Capitalist Futures and Socialist Legacies: Urban Development in East Germany since 1990." *German Politics and Society* 16 (4): 87–102.

Hobsbawm, Eric, and Terence Ranger. 1983. *The Invention of Tradition.* Cambridge: Cambridge University Press.

Holzamer, Hans-Herbert. 2002. "Die schwierige Beseitigung eines Traumas." *Süddeutsche Zeitung,* 19 April.

Huyssen, Andreas. 1997. "The Voids of Berlin." *Critical Inquiry* 24: 57–81.

James, Jason. 2004. "Recovering the German Nation: Heritage Restoration and the Search for Unity." In *Marketing Heritage: Archaeology and the Con-*

sumption of the Past, edited by Yorke Rowan and Uzi Baram. Walnut Creek, C.A.: AltaMira Press.

———. 2006. "Undoing Trauma: Reconstructing the Church of Our Lady in Dresden." *Ethos* 34 (2): 244–272.

Jarzombek, Mark. 2001. *Urban Heterology: Dresden and the Dialectics of Post-Traumatic History.* Lund: Lund University Department of Theoretical and Applied Aesthetics.

Kohl, Helmut. 1990. "Regierungserklärung des Bundeskanzlers der Bundesrepublik Deutschland, Helmut Kohl, über die Grundsätze der Politik der ersten gesamtdeutschen Bundesregierung, abgegeben vor dem Deutschen Bundestag am 4. Oktober 1990 in Berlin." *Europa-Archiv (Dokumente)* 45 (21): D552–564.

Koshar, Rudy. 1994. *Germany's Transient Pasts: Preservation and National Memory in the Twentieth Century.* Chapel Hill: University of North Carolina Press.

———. 1998. *From Monuments to Traces: Artifacts of German Memory, 1870–1990.* Berkeley: University of California Press.

Kowa, Günter. 1995. "Niemand ist eine Insel: Was der ICE Erfurts historischem Bahnhof anzurichten droht." *Frankfurter Allgemeine Zeitung,* 10 October.

———. 1996. "Das taktische Spiel der Denkmalpfleger. Durchbrochene Stadtmauern, verkitschte Fassaden: In Ostdeutschland machen sich architektonische Mißgeburten breit." *Frankfurter Allgemeine Zeitung,* 8 May.

Ladd, Brian. 1997. *The Ghosts of Berlin: Confronting German History in the Urban Landscape.* Chicago: University of Chicago Press.

Langenbacher, Eric. 2008. "Twenty-first Century Memory Regimes in Germany and Poland: An Analysis of Elite Discourses and Public Opinion." *German Politics and Society* 26: 50–81.

Mazur-Stommen, Susan. 2005. *Engines of Ideology: Urban Renewal in Rostock, Germany 1990–2000.* Münster: LIT Verlag.

Mitcherlich, Alexander. 1965. *Die Unwirtlichkeit unserer Städte: Anstiftung zum Unfrieden.* Frankfurt: Suhrkamp Verlag.

Moeller, Robert. 2005. "Germans as Victims? Thoughts on a Post-Cold War History of World War II's Legacies." *History and Memory* 17 (1/2): 147–194.

Morely, David, and Kevin Robins. 1990. "No Place like *Heimat*: Images of Homeland in European Culture." *New Formations* 12: 1–23.

Olick, Jeffrey. 2005. *In the House of the Hangman: The Agonies of German Defeat 1943–1949.* Chicago: University of Chicago Press.

Peukert, Brigitte. 1996. "Die Altstadt vor Schaden bewahren: Erfurts Bürgerinitiative feiert Jubiläum." *Thüringische Landeszeitung/Treffpunkt,* 19 October.

Pfeiffer, Peter C. 1993. "The National Identity of the GDR: Antifascism, Historiography, Literature." In *Cultural Transformations in the New Germany: American and German Perspectives,* edited by Friederike Eigler and Peter C. Pfeiffer. Columbia, S.C.: Camden House.

Preuss, Sebastian. 1990. "Die Rettung Thüringens: Denkmalpfleger aus Ost und West diskutierten in Fulda." *Frankfurter Allgemeine Zeitung,* 26 June.

Rosenfeld, Gavriel. 2000. *Munich and Memory: Architecture, Monuments, and the Legacy of the Third Reich.* Berkeley: University of California Press.

Santner, Eric. 1990. *Stranded Objects: Mourning, Memory, and Film in Postwar Germany.* Ithaca: Cornell University Press.

Schröder, Gerhard. 2000. "Rede des Bundeskanzler Gerhard Schröder anlässlich des Welttourismusgipfels, 27.9 in Hannover," http://www.bundesregierung .de/frameset/index.jsp, accessed 6 June 2002.

Simon, Axel. 2002. "Architektonische Maskerade in Dresden." *Der Tages-Anzeiger,* 10 April.

Suhr, Heidrun. 1989. "*Ausländerliteratur:* Minority Literature in the Federal Republic of Germany." *New German Critique* 46: 72.

Till, Karen. 2005. *The New Berlin: Memory, Politics, Place.* Minneapolis: University of Minnesota Press.

Vees-Gulani, Susanne. 2005. "From Frankfurt's Goethehaus to Dresden's Frauenkirche: Architecture, German Identity, and Historical Memory after 1945." *The Germanic Review* 80 (4): 143–164.

von Bergen, Werner. 1997. "Zusammen bauen was zusammengehört." In *Bürger rettet Eure Städte: 5 Jahre Hilfe für den Denkmalschutz.* Mainz: Zweites Deutsches Fernsehen.

von Bredow, Wilfried. 1983. "Geschichte als Element der deutschen Identität?" In *Die Identität der Deutschen,* edited by Werner Weidenfeld. Munich: Carl Hanser Verlag.

Welzer, Harald, Sabine Moller, and Karoline Tschuggnall. 2002. *Opa war kein Nazi: Nationalsozialismus und Holocaust im Familiengedächtnis.* Frankfurt: Fischer Taschenbuch Verlag.

Žižek, Slavoj. 1990. "Eastern Europe's Republics of Gilead." *New Left Review* 183: 50–62.

Chapter 9

The *Bauwerk* in the Age of its Technical Reproducibility

Historical Reconstruction, Pious Modernism, and Dresden's "süße Krankheit"

ROB MCFARLAND AND ELIZABETH GUTHRIE

Dresden, in den Musennestern / Wohnt die süße Krankheit gestern ...

(Dresden, in the nests of the muses / Dwells that sweet sickness called yesterday)

—Uwe Tellkamp, *Der Turm* (368)[1]

A few years ago, a friend emerged from Dresden's newly rebuilt Frauenkirche (Church of Our Lady), where she met two well-dressed young women singing Reformation-era hymns. She was interested when they stopped their music and began a speech about the "historical lies" that surrounded them on the Neumarkt (New Market) square. The missionary zeal of these young modernists made an impression on her. Over the past few years, we have been reminded of her experience as we have read in feuilletons, blog entries, and newspaper articles about the *Bausünden* (building sins) of Dresden's Neumarkt, the *Schandfleck* (shameful spot) where Berlin's Palast der Republik once stood, and the *Auferstehung* (resurrection) of Halberstadt's town hall (FAZ 2010; Erenz 2010). The discourse surrounding the reconstruction of historical buildings in former East German cities seems to have taken on a distinctly ecclesiastical tone. The arguments in the media usually escalate between tourists, citizens, and representatives of historical societies on one side and investors, city planners, and professional architects on the other side. Interestingly enough, it is not only nostalgic citizens and historical societies who use religious imagery, but also those very architects and city planners who fashion themselves so self-consciously as modernists, and thus as bulwarks of sobriety and science in an unenlightened, Disneyland world (Kulka 2009b).

It is not that the history of architecture has been free from ideological wrangling; long before the moment that Kaiser Franz Joseph pulled closed his Hofburg palace curtains in disgust at the sight of Adolf Loos's provocative new building across Vienna's Michaelerplatz (St. Michael's Square), modern urban architecture had already been a publicly polemic art.[2] But the battle lines drawn between the ideologies have remained consistent. While individual buildings and small historical districts may have been restored, preserved, and set aside from destruction, the builders of the city maintained a clear mandate: new buildings will overcome the past (Nerdinger 2010: 10–11). Even though postmodern architects may have playfully and symbolically returned to ornamental or technical elements from the past, such as scrollwork, arches, or columns, these individual exceptions have only served as "critical" quotations of the past,[3] as carnivalesque digressions that did not seriously call for a return to any historical architectural ideology (Jencks 1987: 9–12).

Standing on the Neumarkt plaza in the shadow of the newly reconstructed Frauenkirche, however, it is clear that there is a sea change in store for contemporary architectural discourse. An entire building has been reproduced by architectural technology, and the copy now casts its shadow across the columns, ornamented windows, and baroque busts of an entire "historic" quarter of Dresden that did not exist five years ago. These historical reconstructions bring up questions that reach far beyond the city's new/old Neumarkt district. In this article we would like to take a closer look at the current ideological discourse surrounding the reconstruction of destroyed historic buildings in Dresden. What seems at first to be a simple culture war between progressive and reactionary city planners, we will argue, is actually a unique historical moment that blurs the dogmatically held ideas of rationality and nostalgia, ornament and function, and high art and kitsch. From the uncanny shadow of a church recently raised from the dead, we will explore the aesthetic and ethical ramifications of architecture in the moment of history that Walter Benjamin might have called the age of its technical reproducibility.

Auferstanden aus Ruinen (Resurrected from the Ruins)

Faced with the gaping holes that remain in cities across the former East Germany, architects, city planners, and cultural critics have been grappling with the same ethical and historical questions that haunt Dresden:

what is the architectural relationship of a city to its past, and how does one properly process the complex history that pervades many of these open spaces? The vast majority of postunification building projects have been approached from the standpoint of contemporary architectural and city-planning practices, creating new buildings that grapple with the past in a myriad of ways. Erick von Egeraat's "contemporary interpretation" of Leipzig's Paulinerkirche (Church of St. Paul), for example, "offers not only a reference to the past, but opens up a vision for the future as well."[4] Haberland Architects, on the other hand, designed a strikingly modern Potsdam Synagogue, "which still manages to fit beautifully into the historic cityscape."[5] In a very few cases, empty places in the cities of the former East Germany have been filled (or are in the process of being filled) with reconstructions of historical edifices, including the aforementioned Town Hall in Halberstadt (1998), the Kommandantenhaus (Commander's House) in the former East Berlin (2003), and Peter Kulka's reconstruction of Potsdam's City Palace. Although the actual number of historical reconstructions is miniscule compared to the total number of construction projects, they have generated a huge amount of discussion because of their symbolic importance. The most famous *Zankapfel* (bone of contention) in the discussion of historical reconstruction in the former East Germany is, of course, Franco Stella's Berliner Stadtschloss (City Palace)/Humboldtforum project on the site of the former Hohenzollern palace, the remains of which were destroyed on the command of East German officials in the 1950s. The surge of reconstructions has spread to the western part of Germany as well; even that modernist *Hochburg* (stronghold) of Frankfurt am Main has torn down its dowdy 1970s Technisches Rathaus (Technical City Hall) and is currently starting the controversial process of replacing it with a collection of historical reconstructions and reinterpretations that the architect Hans Kollhoff has called "careful first steps" toward the correction of the "chaos or bleakness" that has resulted from the excesses of modern architecture (2011).

Dresden's Frauenkirche and the surrounding buildings on the Neumarkt are not only the largest ensemble of postunification historical reconstructions completed to date in Germany, but also the most widely known and among the most popular. The fascination with the church has a long tradition in Dresden. The original Frauenkirche was constructed between 1726 and 1743 by architect Georg Bähr on the site of an earlier Gothic cathedral. The unique sandstone edifice, with its 96-meter-high bellshaped dome, came to be identified as a part of the iconic skyline that the Venetian artist Bernardo Bellotto (aka Canaletto) captured in his celebrated paintings of Dresden from the mid-eighteenth century. The iconic baroque church was a constant in Dresden's changing landscape; it withstood Prussian bombing in 1760, the Seven Years' War, the invasive modernization of the Dresdener Altstadt (old town) during the late nineteenth and early twentieth centuries, and even the first two days of Allied bombing in February of 1945 (Will 2001). It was not until 15 February 1945 that the interior of the church burned, causing the eight columns supporting the structure to give way (Jäger and Burkert 2001: 170–171). The huge dome toppled into the church, leaving only a ruined stump of the northwest tower, a circular fragment of the choir, a toppled chunk of the west gable, and a few more recognizable pieces among a vast pile of rubble (Marek 2009: 9). In spite of the enthusiastic and widereaching urban modernization policies promoted by the GDR's central SED party, Dresden's citizens, art historians, and architects managed to preserve the rubble of the Frauenkirche from repeated plans to raze the site and to integrate it into the evolving modern postwar cityscape (Richter 2011: n.p.; Marek 2009: 30).[6] In 1966, the two standing wall fragments and the surrounding pile of broken stones were designated as a memorial "against imperialist barbarism, for peace and the happiness of the people" (Friedrich 2005: 69).[7] The memorial consisted of the minimally secured ruins and a plaque. Starting in the early 1980s, the memorial became the site for emotional vigils and memorial services on the anniversary of the 1945 bombing.[8] By the time of the German unification, tree saplings and grass had begun to grow on the mound, reclaiming the rubble into the empty, grassy landscape that had once been Dresden's bustling Neumarkt.

The decision to rebuild the Frauenkirche was the culmination of decades of debates, studies, and communal political wrangling. In the first years after the destruction, there were many suggestions for rebuilding the Frauenkirche. After a new city plan for the Neumarkt was instituted in the late 1950s, however, any talk of reconstruction was put on hold. In the late 1970s, historians and interested citizens made suggestions again for the rebuilding of the Frauenkirche and several so-called *Leitbauten*, or historically important buildings on the Neumarkt that would set the architectural tone for other buildings in the area.[9] After the events of 1989, the need to ascertain original property ownership led to a careful investigation of the prewar situation of the individual property parcels around the Neumarkt. Starting in 1990, different architectural theorists, city planners, citizens' groups, historical societies, and representatives of the Lutheran Church in Saxony used popular media to present their ideas for the redevelopment of the area. On 18 March 1991, the Synod of Saxony, to whom the property had been returned, voted to rebuild the church (Marek 2009: 33–36). With the support of many Dresden citizens and a vast international movement of donors, architects, and historians, 180 million Euros were raised for the reconstruction (Friedrich 2005: 87). After archeological work was completed, the reconstruction officially began on 27 May 1993, a date that also marked the 250th anniversary of the dedication of the original edifice (Marek 2009: 9).

Once construction began, a significant shift occurred in the way that the project was discussed. Questions surrounding the technical feasibility of reconstruction began to eclipse the philosophical, moral, and aesthetic quandaries that had dominated discussions about the Frauenkirche (Jäger and Burkert 2001). IBM's computer-assisted imaging program put together three-dimensional images of the 8,425 stones saved from the original church. Architects used electronically generated images to piece together the old stones, blackened by smoke, with the new cream-colored stones (Asch 1999: 2–3). While the goal was to follow Bähr's plans exactly, some changes had to be made so as to comply with contemporary building codes. Even with upgrades such as heating, fire alarms, disability access, security systems, and an elevator, the Frauenkirche is an astonishing replica, a soaring bell of stone that is far removed from anything else currently being designed and constructed (Marek 2009: 10, 13).

The technological breakthroughs of the Frauenkirche project were not only limited to construction. Aided by multiple webcams and video streaming, a worldwide audience watched each time an archeological fragment was lowered into place. These spectacles were testaments to the engineering feats that made them possible. In their construction helmets, talking-head interviewees spoke of lasers, software, and advanced imaging technology. The odd juxtaposition of stone vaults (obsolete since the development of steel construction in the nineteenth century) and the latest computer software gradually became a natural relationship, not only at home in the prolonged construction of Gaudi's Cathedral of the Sagrada Família in Barcelona, but also in the reconstruction of Georg Bähr's Frauenkirche. In her exhaustive discussion of recent German reconstruction projects, Katja Marek sees the broad positive reception of the Frauenkirche as a watershed moment. Marek writes, "The Dresden Frauenkirche has a special meaning for historic preservation. As the first monumental [reconstructed] building with international recognition, it contradicts Georg Dehio's 100-year-old maxim for historic preservationists: 'do not restore, but do preserve.' ... The Frauenkirche provides preservationists with an incentive to start a new discussion about the proper treatment of the architectural witnesses of past epochs" (2009: 138).

The art of historical preservation, as it was practiced for a century, maintained that historical building substance should be preserved in the state that history has left it. To keep a monument from further decaying, conservation efforts could be made, but a monument was not to be restored to any state of former glory. To do so would be to destroy the historical authenticity of the monument. This orthodoxy has been brought into question by the construction of the Frauenkirche, not just because of the quality, speed, and scope of the project, but because of the international attention that accompanied the project from beginning to end.

The new Frauenkirche not only casts a literal shadow across the surrounding Neumarkt area, but a looming metaphorical shadow as well. In 1994, the Planungsgruppe Neumarkt (Planning Group for the New Market) was set up to develop a unified concept for potential investors and builders. Planners decided to restore the block structures, parcel width and building height of the prewar Neumarkt area, and reconstruct several historically significant *Leitbauten* among contemporary buildings (Marek 2009: 23). A citizens' initiative in 2003 gathered 63,000 signatures of Dresdners who demanded that sixty historical *Leitbauten* be included in the plan (Will 2008: 36). Beyond the reconstructions of the Taschenberg Palace (reconstructed from 1992 to 1995 while integrating the surviving façade-shell, located across from Dresden's Royal Residence Palace) and the Coselpalais (nothing but two gate houses survived, and the entire palace, located directly to the northeast of the Frauenkirche, was reconstructed from 1998 to 2000), eight further sections of the Neumarkt were designated as sites for significant reconstruction. Each section, or *Quartier,* includes a number of reconstructed *Leitbauten* and a mixture of other historical, modern, and neutral façades. Some projects, such as the first phase of Quartier 4 (completed in 2005), were driven by investors instead of historians, leading to the complete razing of the Quartier's surviving historical cellars and foundations. The entire block in Quartier 4/1 (Hotel de Saxe on the southeast side of the Neumarkt) is one monolithic building made to look like multiple buildings through the use of different historical and modern façades. Others, like the Heinrich Schütz Haus in Quartier 5 on the southwest side of the Neumarkt (completed in 2008), the Britisches Hotel on Landhausstraße in Quartier 4/2 (completed in 2010), and several of the buildings in Quartier 8 between the restored Residential Palace and the Johanneum, have integrated the historical cellars and foundations into the reconstruction process or completed their façades with surviving pieces of ornamentation from the destroyed original buildings. The Gesellschaft Historischer Neumarkt Dresden (GHND; Society for the Historical New Market of Dresden) set an example for other developers with its reconstruction of a *Bürgerhaus* (bourgeois residence) on the

Rampische Straße in Quartier 2 (completed in 2010). The GHND not only reconstructed the façade, but also the entire historical footprint of the building, and carefully reconstructed the house's walls, stairwells, and courtyard spaces using traditional brick construction techniques. The resulting Neumarkt area, inspired by the Frauenkirche, is a colorful mishmash of approaches, from the half-hearted attempts to historicize modern edifices to the historically correct reconstruction of specific buildings, following the sensibilities of the church that they surround.

Modern Mythology

In Uwe Tellkamp's *Der Turm: Geschichte aus einem versunkenen Land* (The Tower: Tale from a Sunken Country), set in Dresden in the last years of the GDR, scholar and editor Meno Rohde writes down his impressions of an evening spent with other members of the *Bildungsbürgertum* (educated middle class) in the crumbling Belle-Epoche neighborhood where he lives (2008). In his narrative, Rohde reflects upon the obsession of his fellow Dresdeners: "I wondered how it could be possible that someone could live so completely in the past, how they could wipe away the present with some interior swipe of the hand" (362). After the requisite liqueur and *Eierschecke* (traditional cake of Dresden) served on Meißener porcelain, his hostess Witwe Fiebig (Widow Fiebig) lays out a lace tablecloth, pulls a picture book titled *Das alte Dresden* (Old Dresden) from the bookshelf, gathers some Dresden recordings of Wagner, and announces in her Saxon dialect: "ßo. Unt jet-zt KOMMEN wir. Zur Kuhl-tuhr" (SSo. And no-ow it's TIME. For cul-ture.) (367). Amid dusty books, old vinyl records, and antique furniture, the group liturgically murmurs a quotation from Gerhardt Hauptmann and mourns the wartime bombing and the subsequent postwar destruction of Dresden's architectural heritage: "'Whoever has lost the ability to cry will learn it again at the demise of Dresden.' ... Everything was different back then. That which is, is not what once was. No comparison. No, No. Today: Dresdengrad ... Ruins have stood for decades ... drafty prefab skyscraper tracts, fifteen-story wonders, rammed like coarse blocks into the famous, now gapridden Canaletto silhouette. And back then: 'We were a royal residence. A residence! Yeah, back then'" (368).

Tellkamp's fictional author Rohde composes his narrative like a hymn, compressing the evening into an ironically lyrical series of well-recited memories of Dresden's past glory, framed by the repetition of the chorus quoted at the beginning of this article:

> They sighed. Photos were brought out. View from the Brühlisch Terrace to the Frauenkirche, a lantern with pointed light rays in the Münzgasse. The incantations begin, the Dresden longing for a utopia, for a fairytale city. The city of niches, of Goethe quotations, of salon music looks sadly toward yesterday; a pitiful, hollowed-out reality is fleshed out with dreams: Shadow-Dresden, illusion behind the truth (and heard the chimes in the clock: Dresden, in the nests of the muses/ dwells that sweet sickness called yesterday), ... and the splintered glass over the photo of the old Frauenkirche. (368)

Ensconced in the muses' nests, these Dresdners indulge in their own sweet sickness; they conjure up images of the past, mourning again what has been lost, and, like Faust, tremble at the ghosts that they have summoned, especially the ghost of Dresden's lost Frauenkirche. The preserved, hollowed-out ruins of the church, as the most tangible symbol of "pitiful, hollowed-out reality" become the distillation point of Dresden's shadowy dream-city.

Tellkamp's characters illustrate the mythical significance that Dresden's citizens projected upon the iconic church that had come to represent the "longing for a utopia, for a fairy-tale city," like no other building. As Susanne Vees-Gulani has argued, the Frauenkirche became mythologized before the dust had settled on the church's bombed-out remains. The collapsing fascist government established a mythical status of old Dresden as a strategically unimportant target, a defenseless city of pure culture that was barbarously attacked in order to destroy Germany's culture. The pain and anguish of the bombing effectively turned Dresden from a political Nazi stronghold into an ideologically pure space, a city of innocent victims buried among ruined masterpieces (Vees-Gulani 2008). The trauma of the bombings, as Peter Richter describes it, became a "collective pain that transcends generations" and the ruined Dresdner Altstadt became the focus of this pain. Despite the best architectural efforts of the proponents of *Licht-Luft-Sonne Sozialismus*, (Light-Air-Sunshine socialism) Richter explains, the *residenzstädtisches Beamtenbürgertum* (middle-class bureaucratic caste of the formal royal residence) was able to join forces with a "phalanx of historical preservationists" and keep vast stretches of the Altstadt undeveloped for decades: "a green space crossed by the traces of the old streets—building space that carried the promise of reconstruction through all of its years as a parking lot or a lawn" (Richter 2001: 19). While the denizens of Tellkamp's "nest of the muses" would only have known the GDR-era ruins of the Frauenkirche, the author actually created the characters and the scene long after the church had already been rebuilt. His portrayal thus not only pokes fun at postwar *Bildungsbürger* as they keep Dresden's mythos alive during socialism, but also serves as a critique of a twenty-first-century city still obsessed with its own mythical past.

Meno's middle-class muses are not the only Dresdeners who mythologize their lost city. Many other heated discussions surrounding architectural reconstructions include rhetorical excursions into the mythic realm. It is not hard to imagine how the incomprehensible science behind the Frauenkirche project led to discussions of the miraculous circumstances of the church's return from the dead.[10] However, as we mentioned at the beginning of this essay, the use of ecclesiastical terms is not limited to the large number of people who followed the reconstruction of the Frauenkirche with such anticipation. As the two architectural missionaries demonstrated with their aesthetic street revival, even the most rational of institutions can cross over into the realm of mythos. Dresden-born architect Peter Kulka, for example, passed a vehement moral judgment when he decried the way that the mythology surrounding Dresden's lost Altstadt has turned "into an existential lie, into a dogma." He coined the phrase that has become an oft-quoted motto of antireconstructionists: "reinventing that which has been lost is as deceptive as a fake hairdo."[11] Andreas Ruby satirically describes a historical "resurrection" that threatens to replace Dresden's iconic Le-Corbusier-style shopping boulevard: "They also want to resurrect what was once the most important shopping street in the city, Prager Straße" (2000). Ruby also uses imagery from the Old Testament as he bemoans the fate of GDR-era buildings; the fact that they are standing on the rubble of an unrestored layer of Dresden automatically means that they should be torn down in the tradition of "an eye for an eye, a tooth for a tooth" (Ruby 2000).

These examples of ecclesiastical language are, of course, provocative overstatements used consciously by architectural critics to make a rhetorical point. But these facetious statements are also based in mythical concepts found at the very heart of the architectural doctrines of modernism. In "Ornament und Verbrechen" (Ornament and Crime), one of the canonical texts of modern architectural discourse, Adolf Loos imagines an architecture that has transcended ornamentation, and the city that such an architecture could produce: "Behold, the greatness of our epoch can be seen in the fact that it is incapable of producing a new ornament. We have overcome ornament, We have achieved a state of ornamentlessness. Behold, the time is near. Fulfillment awaits us. Soon the streets of the city shall gleam like white walls. Like Zion, the holy city, the heavenly city. Then shall fulfillment be nigh!" (Loos 2009a: 44).

Again, Loos's use of archaic scriptural language is a rhetorical flourish, but he uses it to underscore his basic belief in the moral necessity of new architectural doctrines. In his architectural history titled *Todsünden gegen die Architektur* (Mortal Sins Against Architecture), Herbert Weisskamp explores the Calvinistic impulses that drove early modernists such as Loos, Mies van der Rohe, and Frank Lloyd Wright. Turning modernist rationality against itself, he shows how architectural doctrines have come to inhabit a blurred space between Humanist ethics and religious morality (Weisskamp 1986). Wolfgang Schäche argues that critics of historical reconstruction have inherited this metaphysical foundation, and are trapped in the "religious concept, aggressively charged through the centuries, of the singularity of earthly life," in which a building's life should follow that of a human life: "Just as death stands at the end of life and seems irrevocable, so the physical obliteration of a building is considered to be irreversible" (2000).

In the last decade, one particularly religiously laden architectural doctrine has received a lot of time in the discussion of the reconstructions in Dresden: the commandment that architecture shall be "ehrlich," or honest, or, to use an equally fraught but less religiously loaded term, authentic. This idea has its roots in the texts that laid the foundation for the contemporary architectural theorists who criticize reconstruction. Writing about the highly ornamented architecture on Vienna's Ringstraße, Loos criticizes the "Potemkin'sche Stadt," (Potemkin's city) and is disappointed that "only a small circle of people has the feeling that something immoral is going on here, a swindle" (Loos 2009b: 7). Contemporary critics of Dresden's reconstructions continue Loos's work to decry any sort of "swindle" perpetuated by the historical practices of ornamentation. When approaching the architectural history of the Neumarkt, Thomas Will urges readers to focus not only on the baroque buildings that once stood there, but on the later influences of French classicism that were models of "economy" and a "striving for architectural clarity and simplicity" (Will 2001). This version of the Neumarkt history, Will argues, should serve as the model for contemporary architects who are faced with the problem of building around the Frauenkirche, because classicist values prefigured the values of modern architecture: "But similar efforts are also a part of the foundations of modern architecture, quintessentially visible in the works of an Adolf Loos, a Bruno Taut, or a J.J.P. Oud: striving for constructive clarity and honest expression of content ... simplicity and economy as an expression of aesthetic asceticism" (Will 2001).

Just as classicism corrected the excesses of the Neumarkt's baroque architecture, modernism becomes the ultimate corrective to all other architectural movements, replacing criminal ornament with an "honest expression of content" and countering wasteful mythical forms with a morally superior asceticism. This rejection of tradition, Ivan Reimann suggests, endows contemporary architecture with an authority and authenticity that must interrupt any longing for historical styles on the Neumarkt: "The modern architectural vernacular, based upon a rejection of the historical canon of form, will always have a disturbing effect in those situations where contradiction is not appropriate, for the modern architectural vernacular consciously seeks out and integrates contradiction into its very identity. The problem cannot be solved, for we do not possess any other authentic vernacular" (2007). Contemporary architects enjoy the unimpeachable position of moral superiority, Reimann argues, because they have the exclusive claim to an *authentic* architectural vernacular.

Because reconstructions are by definition not authentic, contemporary architectural critics see the Frauenkirche and the Neumarkt not only as morally dishonest, but counterproductive. A modern copy of a building, Will explains, does not serve to represent the urban historical process. Instead, the reproduction actually obscures history: "On another level one must consider the authority of buildings as witnesses to history. Here, as opposed to the aesthetic level, one cannot get any closer to the truth through copies. Quite the opposite: where reproductions try to imitate the historical model too closely, their reference to 'the' past can only seem misguided, for they actually conceal the very history they claim to reveal" (2008: 31).

The more successful the copy, Will argues, the more useless it becomes as a potential contributor to the city's interaction with history. This argument is a keystone in the broader critique of reconstructions. In her 2009 novel *The Winter Vault*, Canadian author Anne Michaels's characters discuss the historical significance of the dismantling and relocating of Egypt's Temple of Abu Simbel, which was moved because it was threatened by the Aswan Dam project. At the dedication of the structure, the head engineer and his wife are dismayed at what they have done to history: "The gargantuan temple before their eyes—with all the lines of the saw now invisible—was irrefutable proof that the events ... had not happened. That the temple's purpose now had become this forgetting" (Michaels 2009: 179). The manifesto of the initiative to stop the reconstruction of the Berliner Stadtschloss, titled "Kein Schloss in meinem Namen" (No Palace in My Name), also criticizes the planned reproduction as a "Vergessensmaschine" (forgetting machine) and an "idealized structure ... that suppresses all of the upheavals and changes of German history and, after creating a new tabula rasa, then showcases

an intact tradition that is fictitious" (Kein Schloss). Will argues that reconstructions on the Neumarkt will be devoid of the attributes of a true
architectural monument and will represent libertine ideals: "[T]he historical authority that finds its expression in surviving works of art, epe-
cially in works of architecture, cannot be misappropriated by artificial
replicas. This point must necessarily shatter any illusions that may arise
under the libertine notion that anything is possible these days" (Will
2008: 31).

According to Will, an architectural monument possesses historical
authority because of its authenticity. No copy—no matter how technically perfect—can reproduce this authority. In fact, several critics of
reconstruction claim that such projects erode the authenticity of "authentic" buildings. Reinhard Seiß reports that historians are worried
about the effect that the reproductions might have upon Dresden's surviving historical architecture: "When you feel like you can start blithely
copying preeminent works of history, you could be seen as depreciat-
ing the value of all authentic architectural monuments—also those in
Dresden" (2005). Peter Kulka sees an even darker future: the Neumarkt
reconstructions will not only undermine the authority of Dresden's built
history, but they will serve as the beginning of an ongoing assault on
the authenticity of all architecture: "Its (the Neumarkt's –RM/EG) buildings have very little in common with the historical buildings and their
erstwhile functions ... what is authentic in Germany anymore? In a few
years no one will be able to tell the difference between what is authentic
and what has been reconstructed" (2011). Continuing Kulka's pessimis-
tic train of thought, Will maintains that because the buildings on the
Neumarkt are devoid of the authority of authentic edifices, they are not
only deceitful, but potentially harmful to the "Rest der Aura" (remnant
of Aura) that remains in truly historical architecture (Will 2008: 31). As
he uses the term "Aura," Will tips the careful reader off to the mythical
underpinnings of the idea of authenticity in architecture, a mythology
not that different from the mythical "Kuhl-tuhr" that Witwe Fiebig and
her fellow Dresdener "muses" conjure up in Tellkamp's *Der Turm*.

Aura and Authenticity

In their decrying of the immorality of the Frauenkirche and other buildings on the Neumarkt as "lies" and "artificial replicas," critics have perpetuated an outmoded tradition in art criticism that places authenticity
as one of the most important attributes of great art. In his canonical essay "Das Kunstwerk im Zeitalter seiner Reproduzierbarkeit" (The Work

of Art in the Age of its Mechanical Reproducibility), Walter Benjamin investigates the relationship between an "authentic" work of art and a technically produced reproduction of the same work. An original work of art possesses a singularity that endows the work with its "aura," its unique, mystical relationship to history and tradition. Only direct contact with the original can convey this aura: "Even the most perfect reproduction of a work of art is lacking in one element: its presence in time and space, its unique existence at the place where it happens to be. This unique existence of the work of art determined the history to which it was subject throughout the time of its existence.... The presence of the original is the prerequisite to the concept of authenticity" (Benjamin 1968: 220).

As a unique artifact, the work of art becomes a constellation point for history, bringing the lost past into the present as a part of its own here-and-now. Going back to the earliest works of human art, Benjamin illustrates how the aura of artworks is embedded in the ritual practices of magic and religion. The authenticity of art is integral to its status as a cult object: "In other words, the unique value of the authentic work of art has its basis in ritual, the location of its original use value. This ritualistic basis, however remote, is still recognizable as secularized ritual even in the most profane forms of the cult of beauty" (Benjamin 1968: 224).

Thus, when art historians speak of their "pilgrimages" to Dresden's Galerie Alte Meister (Gallery of Old Masters) to stand before the original painting of the Sistine Madonna by Raphael, they are revealing the role of the museum as the heir of the church. Uwe Tellkamp's caricature of the "nest of the muses" in *Der Turm* highlights the ritual nature of the art worship of Dresden's *Bildungsbürgertum,* with their well-worn liturgical recitations woven into a sacred chorale in Meno Rohde's ironic text inside a text.

Benjamin speaks of a watershed moment in the history of art when the ability to make and multiply copies of art reached a level of technical sophistication that affected the privileged position of an authentic work of art. With the advent of photography and especially with the development of film, copies became more than imitations: "Around 1900 technical reproduction had reached a standard that not only permitted it to reproduce all transmitted works of art and thus to cause the most profound change in their impact upon the public, it also captured a place of its own among the artistic processes" (Benjamin 1968: 219–220).

Like any good Freudian doppelganger, reproductions can turn maliciously upon their original works of art, bringing elements of the original to light—by means of enlargement, slow-motion, etc.—that would have been previously unattainable (Benjamin 1991b: 476). Even though the original work of art still exists separately from its many reproductions, the mass production of the copies has an irreversible effect upon the authentic work: "That which withers in the age of mechanical reproduction is the aura of the work of art ... The technique of reproduction detaches the reproduced object from the domain of tradition" (Benjamin 1968: 221). Not only are individual works of art potential targets of this process; Benjamin imagines the positive force of technological reproduction as it works toward its destructive, cathartic goal, "the liquidation of the traditional value of the cultural heritage" (1968: 221). Like his contemporary Siegfried Kracauer, Benjamin sees mass production as a way of exposing the mythical nature of institutions that are supposedly dedicated to the project of rationalization (Kracauer 1995: 79–83).

Although his "Kunstwerk" essay is best known for its extensive discussion of film, Benjamin also gives a privileged position to architecture. In the final section of his essay, he explains how the very nature of human interaction with art changes when the interaction becomes a mass phenomenon: "The mass is a matrix from which all traditional behavior toward works of art issues today in a new form ... A man who concentrates before a work of art is absorbed by it. He enters into this work of art the way legend tells of the Chinese painter when he viewed his finished painting. In contrast, the distracted mass absorbs the work of art" (Benjamin 1968: 239).

The mystical power no longer belongs to the work of art: whereas a painting or sculpture previously engulfed the individual viewer, the masses—now themselves unleashing their own mythic power—drown the work of art themselves. Claiming that this power of the masses vis-à-vis art has always been present in architecture, as opposed to other artistic media, Benjamin writes, "This is most obvious with regard to buildings. Architecture has always represented the prototype of a work of art the reception of which is consummated by a collectivity in a state of distraction. ... Buildings are appropriated in a twofold manner: by use and by perception—or rather, by touch and by sight" (Benjamin 1968: 240).

The aura of a building is a different thing altogether from that of a painting or a sculpture. Because humans have an inherent, habitual, tactile relationship to the buildings that shelter them all of their lives, they are not so easily lulled into the kind of mystical state of "contemplation" brought about by a purely optical artwork. As Benjamin describes it, "Such appropriation cannot be understood in terms of the attentive concentration of a tourist before a famous building. On the tactile side there is no counterpart to contemplation on the optical side. Tactile appropriation is accomplished not so much by attention as by habit. As regards architecture, habit determines to a large extent even optical reception. The latter, too, occurs much less through rapt attention than by noticing the object in incidental fashion" (1968: 240).

Although architecture can also be experienced optically, humans have to work against their own nature to turn their scattered, habitual *bemerken* (noticing) into the kind of focused *aufmerken* (attending to) needed to truly lose oneself in a work of art. While the final version of Benjamin's essay sees film as the "true means of exercise" (Benjamin 1968: 240) of this kind of scattered, unfocused vision (*Zerstreuung*), an earlier draft of his essay still gives that distinction to architecture. Following the assignment of *Zerstreuung* to film, he qualifies that it is "more primordially at home in architecture" (Benjamin 1991a: 466). In one of his most memorable lines in the "Kunstwerk" essay, Benjamin famously states that in the moment where the measure of authenticity of a work of art is rendered irrelevant, the whole social function of art turns from a function of ritual to a function of politics (Benjamin 1991b: 482).

Medial Architecture

For a project that is in so many ways founded in uncritical, visceral invocations of nostalgia and beauty, the political ramifications of historical reconstruction seem to be ambiguous at best and reactionary at worst. Far more damning than the critique of the inauthenticity of the Frauenkirche and the Neumarkt or their role as "Vergessensmaschinen" is the claim that the reconstructions distract attention away from the historical context that brought about the destruction—and, much more importantly, the human losses—of 13 February 1945. Vees-Gulani has very convincingly demonstrated, for instance, that the Frauenkirche—first as a ruin and then as a reconstruction—has served as a location for a narrative of victimhood (2008: 30). The rhetoric and building programs of the Nazis, the East German government, and now city planners in post-unification Dresden all ignore the destruction of the Dresden Synagogue in 1938 at the hands of Nazi groups made up of Dresden citizens. The destruction of the synagogue is swallowed up in the story of the bombings of 1945, where innocent Dresdners suffered needlessly because of external fascist and imperialist forces. Vees-Guliani goes so far as to contrast the synagogue as a place of remembering and the Frauenkirche as a place of forgetting (Vees-Gulani 2008: 32–36, 42–43). Jason James warns that the Frauenkirche creates a fantasy narrative that all suffering and destruction—even death—can be undone, rendering Nazi Dresden and the whole existence of East Germany as correctable aberrations (2006: 252–260).

While the new Dresden Synagogue—with its fascinating integration of the lost historical caesura of the old synagogue—successfully represents the power of contemporary architecture to represent history, Vees-Gulani's and James's absolute alignment of modernism with memory and reconstruction with forgetting deserves critical attention.[12] The problem with this argument, as Richter explains, is that any work of architecture—no matter what style—has the potential to turn into a forgetting machine, and that modernism cannot uncritically label itself as the de facto architecture of *Vergangenheitsbewältigung* (overcoming the past):

> The accusation—that historical reconstruction wants to use aesthetics and politics to make it seem like wartime destruction and postwar modernism never happened—is faced with a problem: modernism could come to be misunderstood as a kind of deserved punishment. Moreover, since the innercity architectural ensembles once built for the "New Socialist Man" had, by the early 1990s, become what would later be referred to euphamistically as a "National liberated zone" [a zone where Neo-Nazi violence had succeeded in clearing the streets of foreigners], one cannot be criticized for doubting that even a total historical reconstruction of a city could possibly result in something more blind to the past [than the existing modern German cityscape dominated by Neo-Nazi violence]. (Richter)

Those same modernist buildings built by socialists to repeal the historical threat of fascism, in other words, became the scene of the ultimate historical amnesia. Whether reconstructions or modern interpretations, any kind of architecture built on historically significant sites has the potential not only to obscure or contort the past, but, as Vees-Guliani has forcefully shown, to serve as a distraction from alternate histories that deserve equal or greater attention. How, then, can historical reconstructions serve to commemorate the very destruction that they heal over?

If a mechanically perfect reproduction of a work of art reduces the cult value of the original, then the technically perfect reproduction of a building could potentially have the same effect on the cultural practices that cast a work of architecture into its assumed mystical role as an authentic temple of history. In Benjamin's "Kunstwerk" essay, the cult value of a copied work of art is eventually replaced by its *Ausstellungswert,* its value as a mass experience. As works of art are made more and more available to the public, they are alienated ever further from the context of their cult value. Benjamin posits that the sheer volume of mechanical reproductions can so drastically favor the *Ausstellungswert* of art over its cult value that a critical mass can been reached, a point where the very nature of art itself can be changed: "This is comparable to the situation of the work of art in prehistoric times when, by the absolute emphasis on its cult value, it was, first and foremost, an instrument of magic.... In the same way today, by the absolute emphasis on its exhibition value the work of art becomes a creation with entirely new functions, among which the one we are conscious of, the artistic function, later may be recognized as incidental" (Benjamin 1968: 225).

What could these potential functions be for a reconstructed church? Liberally appropriating Benjamin's argument, one could see architectural copies as having the potential to counteract the unconscious use of mythology in the political and aesthetic discourse of historical construction. More than mere "Vergessensmaschinen," historical reconstructions undermine the very idea that buildings can or should have a metaphysical connection to an idealized time, place, or person. As discussed earlier, critics of the Frauenkirche and the historical reconstructions on the Neumarkt see the projects as destructive to every authentic architectural monument across Germany. The reconstructed Frauenkirche, as Marek has pointed out, has not been designated as a monument, because it does not fulfill the traditional definition of such a structure (2009: 135). Instead of existing as a concrete location of history, the reconstructed building becomes a part of a more ephemeral "media-driven architecture" (Marek 2009: 157). This media-driven architecture, as Marek explains, exists first as pictures of the destroyed building, architectural renderings of the reproduction, and digitally manipulated images showing the virtual building inserted into the context of the real cityscape. These initial images are mass-consumed on the Internet, in newspapers, on television, and on large advertising billboards, allowing them to be "effectively publicized and marketed to the public" (Marek 2009: 157). After the media images successfully sway public opinion in favor of the reconstruction project, more images are proliferated during construction—on webcams, for example, or at the traditional German *Richtfest* (topping-out ceremony). The image of the completed building then becomes further proliferated as a part of advertising campaigns, tourist brochures, etc. The resulting edifice "is the result of various media; it is an architecture that has come about through the media and can, in this sense, be termed as an architecture of media-driven reconstruction"

(Marek 2009: 158). While a so-called authentic building officially recognized as an architectural monument certainly has its own media-driven presence as a visually recognizable icon and a tourist attraction, it also represents the kind of historical aura that transcends the indignity of advertising and tourism. Reproductions, on the other hand, are conceived, funded, and created in and through the media, and even in their built reality they maintain something of a transitory nature.

This is because, as Benjamin states, the copy slowly eats away at the focused, optical cult value of the work of art and replaces it with a new, distracted, tactile *Ausstellungswert.* The copy is bound to earn the scorn of those who want to defend the aura of the original work. Critics of the Frauenkirche and the Neumarkt illustrate the current vehemence of this scorn as they derisively point to the fact that these projects are conceived, financed, and built for the express purpose of attracting masses of tourists to Dresden and then making money by feeding and housing them. Seiß derides the vulgarity of this inferior purpose: "Besides all of the nostalgia, there were massive economic reasons for the city repair movement. Even as a construction site, the Frauenkirche was already an outstanding vehicle for advertising Dresden in the arena of international urban marketing ... Donations were even collected in the USA, and Japanese television crews regularly reported about the progress of the construction" (2005).

The duties of an "authentic" building as an architectural monument, as an accurate, solemn witness of historical truth, are replaced by the media circus of the reproduction. Craven publicity campaigns attract— gasp—the Americans and the Japanese, who—characteristically, to assume from Seiß's choice of nations—downgrade the true, local identity of Dresden into a tourist trap: "The dedication of the church on October 30th will certainly be the high point of the media's interest in the City on the Elbe, but it will not mark the end of it. For by now the reconstruction of Dresden has become an event that is being closely followed across the world, and it is actually helping the city to develop a new identity, at least in a touristic sense" (Seiß 2005). Authentic buildings beget authentic identity, but the reproduced Frauenkirche, Seiß predicts, will only create the kind of touristic identity conjured up by his choice of such words as *Marketing* and *Event,* intrusive English terms indicative of the monotonous projects of globalization long derided by Stefan Zweig and many other defenders of "authentic" European culture (Zweig 1925).

Beyond their ephemeral existence as media-driven architecture, Dresden's historically reconstructed buildings function in a filmic way that resonates with Benjamin's ideal of a reproducible work of art. With the oft-repeated derision of the Neumarkt as *Kulissen* (theatrical back-drops), critics bring attention to the connections between historical reconstructions and the medium of film.[13] Ruby laments the status of Dresden as "a city obsessed with backdrops" (2000: n.p.). Ivan Rei-mann sees the façades of the Neumarkt as signs of a new "dictatorship of the economy," where "only the now, only the image, the surface, a photographable backdrop count anymore" (2007: 92). Kulka sees the Neumarkt as a cinematic space: "Historical façades and ornaments are projected onto the concrete cubes of these buildings as if onto a movie screen" (2010: 15). The most important filmic attribute of the Neumarkt, however, is the distracted gaze that is brought about by the square's permanent state of transience, so different from the mythical, eternal status of the ideal old city. Reimann identifies the façades of the Neumarkt's hotels, the historicized restaurants, and the glass entry-way to an underground garage as classic examples of what Marc Augé calls "non-lieus," the placeless spaces of modernity. Reimann sees the Neumarkt and its buildings as "places of the ephemeral, of the transi-tory, of passing through; places that cannot be lived, only experienced, only seen; places that are consumed in passing. ... It is a peculiarity of non-places that they can be reduced to a postcard image, a travel guide entry, an advertising jingle. Even more: the reduction of a place ... into an image creates a strange distance between the city ... and the traveler who visits it, and who will never arrive at the place as it truly is, or was" (2008: 91).

The Neumarkt is useless as a monument, for it is not conducive to the kind of concentrated, time-intensive interaction that one might seek in a historically authentic space. Instead of being deeply *erlebt* (experi-enced), it is only superficially *gesehen* (seen). It is a place of distraction, of passing—not a place at all. The traveler is perpetually separated from the reality of the place, and must stand outside and watch. In short, the Neumarkt's visitor is the perfect modern viewing subject. Benjamin de-scribes this modern interaction with space in his essay "Loggien" from his collection *Berliner Kindheit um 1900*. Standing in the courtyard of a building he knew as a child, he reflects upon the past, the present, and his own position as a viewer: "In the years since I was a child, the loggias have changed less than other places. This is not the only reason they stay with me. It is much more on account of the solace that lies in their uninhabitability for one who himself no longer has a proper abode" (Benjamin 2002: 346).

Although time and space come together in this personally meaning-ful space, the courtyard and the balcony are both still uninhabitable for him, for they are places caught in a past from which he is hopelessly alienated. In other words, this uninhabitable place is a perfect habitation for the modern subject, and the perfect screen on which to cast the transient modern gaze.

A recent example of the Frauenkirche and the Neumarkt in their proper function as non-places can be found in the Dresden author Ingo Schulze's essay "Einem aus dem Ort gefallenen" (To One Who has Fallen out of Place). Schulze gives a nostalgic look back on the ruins of the Frauenkirche, which for his childhood self—and for the adults he describes—served the same purpose as they did for the "muses" in Uwe Tellkamp's novel: it was the centralized location for their "süße Krankheit Gestern," the altar for their worship, the phantasmagoric dreamscape where their mythos Dresden could be conjured up. The first time Schulze sees the new Frauenkirche and the Neumarkt around it, he is startled and sickened at the way that the buildings serve as false backdrops devoid of any real history. First, he fixes his gaze upon the dark stones of the Frauenkirche, holding onto something that had actual historical meaning. But then his gaze "slides off" of the dark stones, onto the slippery surface of the creamy new sandstone; the inauthenticity of the buildings do not allow him to fix his gaze upon anything real or historical, thus detaching him from any sense of place:

> The nearer I got to the Frauenkirche, the more it seemed to evolve until, seen from the Neumarkt, it froze into a wax figure of itself. I circumnavigated the church, looked into the Cosel Palace, the first "Leitbau" next to the Frauenkirche, built between 1998 and 2000. Back out in the open, I could only see stage scenery! Backdrops that were playing the role of old buildings from centuries past ... Here you feel as if you have fallen out of time, and fallen out of place. What kind of mind wants to make a fairy tale out of Dresden, and damns the city to an existence with no face and no past? (Schulze 2006)

In Schulze's narrative, the reproduced Frauenkirche has lost its function as the heart of Dresden; it is a simulacrum of itself, as creepy and lifelike as a wax figure. He is repelled by the flatness, the kitschy, colorful flatness of the likenesses of the old buildings on the huge sheets of synthetic material that cover the scaffolding. But more horrifying than the images on the sheets are the real buildings: *Kulissen,* backdrops, stage sets, filmscreens upon which the past is projected for the fleeting, superficial consumption by crowds of tourists. In other words, the Neumarkt has become cinema. Just like a film, here is no original copy; it is a flat projection space for an ethereal veneer of history. It is created for consumption by a neverending series of audiences that are looking for historical spectacle to divert and move them before they move on. Mere tourists might swoon at the beauty of baroque Dresden, but those serious thinkers in search of the city's heart will search in vain.

The search for the authentic baroque city is, of course, an oxymoronic errand. The neo-retro edifices at Dresden's heart conjure up practices that were much more at home in the baroque city than they are in our solemn, serious contemporary urban landscapes. Whereas being called *kulissenhaft* (like a backdrop) is the ultimate offense in an architecture based upon metaphorical ecclesiastical values such as "honesty," the baroque, as Thomas Kantschew reminds us, reveled in an "exceedingly refined sense of entertainment and sophisticated, illusory masquerades complete with the most elaborate effects. There was no dearth of fantastic tricks: brilliant deceptions, mindnumbing backdrops and dazzling visual effects. The new office buildings and hotels on the Neumarkt will now join in a play of 'authenticity' and 'lies' for a discerning European—even global—leisure crowd. But we observers are a part of this game ... it is a game that is fit for an era that already fluctuates between the virtual world and reality" (Kantschew 2005). To fill the vacuum left by the rejection of postmodernism in German cities, it seems that the baroque must rise from the dead to fulfill a sweet-sick need for embellishment and theatricality that modernism has tried so hard to eradicate.

For now, Dresden's "süße Krankheit" is happy with a diet of baroque reconstructions, those fascinating anachronisms that seem to outrage the pious modernists who for so long have thumped their copies of "Ornament and Crime" like a preacher at a revival. But, if technically enhanced baroque buildings can return to Dresden to challenge modernity's sacred birthright to authentic architecture, then the ghosts of ages past are now at the beck and call of German city planners. How long it will take before someone actually dares to reconstruct an ornament-laden historicist building, that ultimate bugaboo that modernism has repressed for over a century with its minimalist manifestos? Such a copy will be seen as madness, as hysteria, and as a provocation. The supposedly untenable position of such religiously loaded dogmas as honesty, asceticism, truth, etc. will be faced with the most heretical sinner yet: a long-killed-off architectural freakshow raised from the dead by technology, a Wilhelminian cyberzombie in a prom dress. The aura-worship of puritanical modernism is still safe for now, but in film, and now in architecture, there can always be a sequel.

Notes

1. All translations are by Rob McFarland except for Zohn's translation of Benjamin's "The Work of Art in the Age of Mechanical Reproduction" and Jephcott's translation of "Loggias."

2. For a history of the reception of Loos's building on Michaelerplatz, see Muscheler (2007).
3. For a discussion of the term "critical reconstruction," see Kleihues.
4. http://www.dezeen.com/2008/10/22/new-building-for-the-university-of-leipzig-by-erick-van-egeraat/
5. http://www.synagoge-potsdam.de/, accessed 24 February 2011.
6. For an insider's introduction to the SED's urban development ideology, see Korn and Weise, (1985).
7. Friedrich (2005: 65–70).
8. Ten Dyke (2001: 24–25) demonstrates the cathartic nature of these memorial vigils.
9. For a discussion of the development of the idea of the "Leitbauten" in Dresden, see Marek (2009: 21–24).
10. For examples of ecclesiastical language from the blogosphere, see Guthrie (2010: 13–15).
11. Quoted in Seiß (2005).
12. Mark Jarzombek shows the problematic context of the modernist synagogue that resembles nearby buildings from the National Socialist and East German socialist periods (2004: 61–63).
13. See, for example, Jäger (2006).

References

Asch, Kenneth. 1999. "Rebuilding Dresden." *History Today* 49 (10): 2–3.
Benjamin, Walter. 1968. "The Work of Art in the Age of Mechanical Reproduction." In *Illuminations: Essays and Reflections*, by Walter Benjamin, edited by Hannah Arendt, translated by Harry Zohn. New York: Schocken Books.
———. 1991. "Das Kunstwerk im Zeitalter seiner technischen Reproduzierbarkeit." 1st ed. In *Walter Benjamin. Gesammelte Schriften: Abhandlungen*, vol. 1, part 2, 431–469 Frankfurt: Suhrkamp.
———. 1991. "Das Kunstwerk im Zeitalter seiner technischen Reproduzierbarkeit." 3rd ed. In *Walter Benjamin. Gesammelte Schriften: Abhandlungen*, vol. 1, part 2, 471–508. Frankfurt: Suhrkamp.
———. 1991. "Loggien." In *Berliner Kindheit um 1900*. In *Gesammelte Schriften: Kleine Prosa. Baudelaire Übertragungen*. vol. 4, part 1, 294–296. Frankfurt: Suhrkamp.
———. 2002. "Loggias." In *Berlin Kindheit um 1900*. In *Walter Benjamin. Selected Writings*, edited by Michael W. Jennings, translated by Edmund Jephcott, Howard Eiland, et al., vol. 3, 346. Cambridge: Belknap Press.
Erenz, Benedikt. 2003. "Glück des Eigensinns." *Zeit Online.* http://www.zeit.de/2003/17/Halberstadt, accessed 10 August 2010.
Frankfurter Allgemeine Zeitung (FAZ). 2005. "Dieser Schandfleck muss verschwinden" (20 August). http://berliner-schloss.de/de/Pressespiegel/Dieser-Schandfleck-muss-verschwinden.htm, accessed 10 August 2010.
Friedrich, Andreas. 2005. *The Frauenkirche in Dresden: History and Rebuilding.* Translated by Rosemarie Nitschke. Dresden: Michael Sandstein Verlag.

Fröbe, Turit. 2008. "Disneyland des Grauens." *Rheinischer Merkur* 31: 9.

Guthrie, Elizabeth. 2010. *The Work of Architecture in the Age of its Technological Reproducibility.* Master's thesis: Brigham Young University.

Jäger, Falk. 2006. "Mit voller Kraft zum Mittelmaß." *Sächsische Zeitung,* 22 December.

Jäger, Wolfram, H. Bergander, and Frank Pohle. 2003. "The Reconstruction of the Sandstone Dome of the Frauenkirche." *Construction and Building Materials* 17 (8): 679–686.

Jäger, Wolfram and T. Burkert. 2001. "The Reconstruction of the Frauenkirche in Dresden." In *Historical Constructions,* edited by Paulo B. Lourenço and Pere Roca. Guimarães: University of Minho Press.

James, Jason. 2006. "Undoing Trauma: Reconstructing the Church of our Lady in Dresden." *Ethos* 34 (2): 244–272.

Jarzombek, Mark. 2004. "Disguised Visibilities: Dresden/'Dresden.'" In *Memory and Architecture,* edited by Eleni Bastea. Albuquerque: University of New Mexico Press.

Jencks, Charles A. 1987. "The Death of Modern Architecture." In *The Language of Post-Modern Architecture,* 9-12. London: Academy Editions.

Kantschew, Thomas. 2005. "Vom Sehen, Schein und Sein" (April). http://www .neumarkt-dresden.de/, accessed May 2014.

Kein Schloss in meinem Namen. n.d. "Begründung." http://www.kein-schloss-in-meinem-namen.de/index.php?id=7, accessed February 2011.

Kleihues, Josef Paul. 1996–2001. Berlin Babylon. "Gespräche ohne Kamera." http://www.berlinbabylon.de/Media.Sumo/Kleihues.pdf, accessed February 2011.

Kollhoff, Hans. 2011. "Was ist zeitgemäßes Bauen?" *Frankfurter Allgemeine Zeitung,* 12 May. http://www.faz.net/artikel/C30351/frankfurter-altstadt-was-ist-zeitgemaesses-bauen-30336733.html, accessed 14 June 2011.

Korn, Roland, and Klaus Weise. 1985. *Berlin. Bauten unserer Tage.* Berlin: Berlin-Information.

Kracauer, Siegfried. 1995. "The Mass Ornament." In *The Mass Ornament. Weimar Essays,* translated, edited, and introduction by Thomas Y. Levin. Cambridge, M.A.: Harvard University Press.

Kulka, Peter. 2009. "Architekt Peter Kulka. 'Wir machen dort kein Disneyland.'" *Tagesspiegel,* 3 September.

———. 2009. "Landarchitekt Peter Kulka über falsche Seligkeit und Dresdner Fehler." *Märkische Allgemeine,* 3 September.

———. 2010. "Dresdner Rede." http://www.peterkulka.de/likecms/media/pub lic/100228_Dresdner_Rede.pdf?kulkasess=p5a6lr9nihfmeuvc4ngj4af427, accessed 19 January 2012.

———. 2010. "Peter Kulka zum Thema Identität. Identität und Rekonstruktion." http://www.brillux.de/service/fort-undweiterbildung/architektenforum, accessed 19 May 2014.

Loos, Adolf. 2009a. "Ornament und Verbrechen." In *Warum Architektur keine Kunst ist: Fundamentales über scheinbar Funktionales.* Vienna: Metroverlag.

———. 2009b. "Die Potemkin'sche Stadt." In *Warum Architektur keine Kunst ist: Fundamentales über scheinbar Funktionales.* Vienna: Metroverlag.

Marek, Katja. 2009. *Rekonstruktion und Kulturgesellschaft: Stadtbildreparatur in Dresden, Frankfurt am Main und Berlin als Ausdruck der zeitgenössischen Suche nach Identität.* Dissertation: Universität Kassel.

Michaels, Anne. 2009. *The Winter Vault.* New York: Knopf.

Muscheler, Ursula. 2007. *Haus ohne Augenbrauen: Architekturgeschichten aus dem 20. Jahrhundert.* Munich: Beck.

Nerdinger, Winfried. 2010. "Zur Einführung—Konstruktion und Rekonstruktion historischer Kontinuität." In *Geschichte der Rekonstruktion. Reconstruktion der Geschichte,* edited by Winfried Nerdinger. Munich: Technische Universität München.

Reimann, Ivan. 2008. "Ein unlösbares Dilemma." In *Historisch contra Modern? Erfindung oder Rekonstruktion der historischen Stadt am Beispiel des Dresdner Neumarkts,* edited by Ingrid Sonntag, 89–93. Dresden: Sächsische Akademie der Künste.

Richter, Peter. 2001. "Wo der Blick zurück Tradition hat." *Süddeutsche Zeitung,* 14 March, 19.

Ruby, Andreas. 2000. "Las Vegas an der Elbe." *Zeit.de* 46. http://zeit.de, accessed 8 August 2001.

Schäche, Wolfgang. 2000. "Für ein Recht auf Rekonstruktion." *Berliner Zeitung,* 5/6 February.

Schulze, Ingo. 2006. "Ich war ein begeisterter Dresdner. Zum Auftakt der 800-Jahr Feier der sächsischen Hauptstadt—Nachtgedanken eines aus dem Ort Gefallenen." *Süddeutsche Zeitung,* 31 March.

Seiß, Reinhard. 2005. "Vorwärts in die Vergangenheit." *Wiener Zeitung,* 28 October.

Tellkamp, Uwe. 2008. *Der Turm: Geschichte aus einem versunkenen Land.* Frankfurt: Suhrkamp.

Ten Dyke, Elizabeth. 2001. *Dresden: Paradoxes of Memory in History.* New York: Routledge.

Vees-Gulani, Susanne. 2008. "The Politics of New Beginnings: The Continued Exclusion of the Nazi Past in Dresden's Cityscape." In *Beyond Berlin: Twelve German Cities Confront the Nazi Past,* edited by Gavriel D. Rosenfeld and Paul B. Jaskot, 25–47. Ann Arbor: The University of Michigan Press.

Weisskamp, Herbert. 1986. *Todsünden gegen die Architektur.* Düsseldorf: ECON Verlag.

Will, Thomas. 2001. "Rekonstruktion der europäischen Stadt? Zur Diskussion um den Dresdner Neumarkt. *deutsche bauzeitung* 3.

———. 2008. "Städtebau als Dialog. Zur Wiederbebauung des Dresdner Neumarkts." In *Historisch contra Modern? Erfindung oder Reconstruktion der historischen Stadt am Beispiel des Dresdner Neumarkts.* Dresden: Sächsischen Akademie der Künste und dem Stadtplanungsamt der Landeshauptstadt Dresden.

Zweig, Stefan. 1925. "Die Monotonisierung der Welt." *Neue Freie Presse,* 1 January.

Afterword

ROLF J. GOEBEL

It is commonplace that cultural studies, like any scholarly paradigm, does not simply analyze pre-existing phenomena, but constructs them as signifying subjects according to specific theoretical assumptions, mechanisms of selection, and interpretive procedures. Nowhere, perhaps, is this more visible than in the privileged scholarly status enjoyed for many years by Berlin. The city is not only united Germany's old-new capital, but also the seemingly uncontested site of a diverse (and sometimes disunited) German Studies enterprise, which has especially focused on Berlin's twentieth-century fate as the center of the Wilhelminian empire, the playground of the artistic and intellectual avant-garde in the 1920s, the despised capital of National Socialism, the divided hotspot of the Cold War era, and, finally, the site of the fall of the Wall and the consolidation of government power, multicultural immigration, global consumer capitalism, and the international tourist industry in the eastern part of the country. Proverbially in continual flux of self-invention, rebuilding, and self-marketing, Berlin is a city where historical reconstruction and postmodern simulation, authenticity and phantasmagoria, high art and commercial kitsch, serious commemoration and the Disneyfication of the past, the real and the imaginary often slide seamlessly into one another. Examples are the partial reconstruction of the Stadtschloss (City Palace) on the site of the razed GDR Palast der Republik (Palace of the Republic); the museal incorporation of ghostly ruins from the Esplanade Hotel into the futuristic design of the Sony Center; or the former Checkpoint Charlie, combining open-air political information displays with actors posing as allied military police officers for photo-ops with tourists. Right next to it, visitors can see Yadegar Asisi's stunning Berlin Wall panorama showing, in high-definition details, a condensed assemblage of typical sites from both sides of the edifice, such as the death zone, a GDR border guard watch tower, a West Berlin viewing platform, a trailer settlement, and other markers important for commemorating daily life in the shadow of the Wall. Enjoying a spectacular presence in the public imagination as well as in scholarly circles, Berlin has assumed a kind of benign hegemony over other cities and regions in Germany, which may actually be more representative than the capital of the postunification country's quest of "normalcy" after the political perversities of the past (Koepnick 2001).

But as with any type of hegemony, the more it is asserted, the more it opens itself to being challenged, subverted, and deconstructed. While focusing on some areas of Berlin but mainly concentrating on *other* cities in the former East Germany, the essays in this collection resolutely de-center Berlin as a privileged subject of cultural studies, reconstructing the social histories, architectural rebuilding efforts, and other issues marking the transition from the former GDR to postunification in Dresden, Erfurt, Hoyerswerda, Frankfurt (Oder), and elsewhere. As a result, these cities and towns lose their reputation for being located on the periphery (of the German territory and the analytic map of cultural studies) and move into the new limelight of a different critical attention. Beyond and underneath the *Realpolitik* of urban planning politics, citizens' interests, and commercial viability, these cities seem to stage a veritable metaphysics of urban fate in postunification Germany, captured in the binary terms of loss and redemption, authenticity and replication, nostalgia and futuristic vision, historical memory and the renewed quest for *Heimat* or "Germanness," the contemplation of ruins and the aggressive efforts to rebuild for the future. In this way, cities in the East capture poignant issues of national identity formation that go far beyond the local but appear especially sharply edged in its seemingly "provincial" context.

There is another dimension in which cities in the East prove to be a fertile ground for thinking about urbanity generally; they motivate us to question the established theoretical notion of city space as "text." Harking back to the *topos*, developed during the Latin Middle Ages and the Renaissance, of the world as the infinitely readable book of nature written by God (see Curtius 1954: 323–329), this concept has gained new prominence through hermeneutic turns in cultural ethnography and poststructuralist notions of generalized "writing" as a potentially infinite network of differential signification. Several contributors to the present volume profitably rely on this textual metaphor. Thus Gwyneth Cliver's chapter identifies "a number of voids in the urban 'text' of Hoyerswerda" and considers "the[ir] literary, historical, social, and cultural significance." Similarly, Christopher Jones notes that for the detective in Buddy Giovinazzo's crime novel *Potsdamer Platz*, "the sheer scale of the Potsdamer Platz project, with its constantly mutating layout," makes it impossible "to establish any sense of understanding or familiarity with

his new temporary home; he can neither read nor write this 'urban text.'"
The notion of the city as text that often subverts its own readability is
associated with the concept of the palimpsest as a multilayered com-
pilation of writing traces that are superimposed upon one another and
that remain only partially legible, thus reflecting the historicity not only
of what is written down but also the act of writing itself. In this sense,
Sebastian Heiduschke, even while focusing on cinematic, i.e., predominantly visual, representations, argues that "the sleek, modern skyline
of Frankfurt turns out to be a palimpsest of Germany, reinscribed with
postunification problems of high unemployment and difficulty adjusting
to a new social system."

Such conceptualizations of the city as text certainly allow us to for-
mulate many interpretive insights into the cities' history, social life, built
environment, and cultural values. But, it seems to me, they also raise the
question whether the notions of the cultural text, palimpsest, and writing are still sufficient to account for the multiplicity of urban phenomena
in the age of global capitalism. In Jacques Derrida's *Of Grammatology*,
the generalized notion of writing takes on truly hegemonic power over
other media. "Writing," he notes, nowadays stands metonymically "for
all that gives rise to an inscription in general, whether it is literal or not
and even if what it distributes in space is alien to the order of the voice:
cinematography, choreography, of course, but also pictorial, musical,
sculptural 'writing'" (Derrida 1976: 9). But as the slightly defensive "of
course" indicates, Derrida's deconstructive notion self-deconstructs because "of course" it cannot really account for the material media differences that separate written signifiers from visual, auditory, tactile, or
olfactory ones. In his seminal essay on "The Voids of Berlin," Andreas
Huyssen, who has done important work in promoting the notion of the
city as text or palimpsest (and who is cited in this collection), has aptly
noted a shift away from the centrality of these concepts in the age of
visual computer technologies: "The notion of the city as sign ... is as
pertinent as before, though perhaps more now in a pictorial and imag-
istic rather than a textual sense" (2003: 50). This shift, Huyssen argues,
is due to, or accompanied by, a sociopolitical change, since the 1970s,
from the critical discourse of architects, literary critics, theorists, and
philosophers to the promotion of the city as image by urban developers
and revenue-conscious politicians focusing on mass tourism, cultural
consumption, and visual spectacles (2003: 50). Even though the notion
of the city as text or palimpsest is employed figuratively rather than literally, its predominant association with written signs may be too restrictive to account for the visual, aural, olfactory, and tactile signifiers of the
modern city, for these overdetermined signs often exceed the textual

and scriptural. But rather than deleting the concept of the urban text or palimpsest from the critical vocabulary, I am arguing for redefining it as one manifestation among others in an (urban) field of intermedial affiliations. As Friedrich A. Kittler has argued, modern cities can be understood as media because in the age of information technologies, they mark the transition from a territory that could be surveyed with the blank eye by someone standing on a cathedral spire or palace tower to a "network made from all kinds of networks" that stretches from the center to the periphery, encompassing the transfer of information through the telephone, radio, and television, or energy through systems of water supply, electricity, or highways (Kittler 2013: 182). Especially the textual, visual, and sonic opportunities of the Internet, of course, with its seemingly infinite modes of interconnectivity and immediate access across geographic expanses, have dramatically redefined the positions of its users as subjects of communication, self-articulation, and social practice in the actual localities of metropolitan life (Kittler 2013: 188–190). Since the modern city, as Kittler argues, is shaped by many overlapping media, the notion of culture as text or palimpsest, it seems to me, retains only limited validity, because the writing and rewriting of signs that are partially erased and partially still legible cannot fully account for the many sensory data and nonsensory values that produce the city today. What I propose, then, is to think of the city not only as a textual topo-*graphy* (literally: the written locality), but as a topo-*medium,* a spatiotemporal entity that signifies, is sustained by, and made livable for its citizens through an immense variety of textual, visual, tactile, and auditory media technologies that supplement, or compete with one another in complex and often unpredictable ways.

Many contributors to this volume focus indeed on this (inter-)mediality of the *Medienhauptstadt* (media capital) Berlin and cities in the East in multidisciplinary ways, combining literary hermeneutics, film analysis, and the relatively new paradigm of sound studies to account for the transpalimpsestic surplus represented by urban spaces. For instance, Susanna Miller, Jennifer Hosek, et al. trace figures of spatial movement, transportation technologies, and the visual consumption of city life through the figure of the flâneur in avant-garde films portraying the "village" aspects of the old-new capital. This essay's primarily visual focus is supplemented by Heiner Stahl's analysis of traffic policies and public transport in Erfurt before and after the *Wende,* foregrounding the auditory perspective on the city's soundscape in the cultural history of people's technological mobility in public spaces. In Erika Nelson's essay on the Toskana Therme and the Liquid Sound temple in the ancient/futuristic spa town of Bad Sulza, a multimedia experience of bathing in technological displays of phantasmagoric sound, light, and video projection evokes the literary traditions of Orphic myth and dream worlds cultivated by the works of Rainer Maria Rilke, Paul Scheerbart, Bruno Taut, and Sigmund Freud.

These are but three examples from this fascinating and insightful collection of essays, but they show that thinking of cities not as topographies but intermedial sites has several advantages for cultural studies. First, we understand that cities are not merely built environments sustained by a functional infrastructure in which people carry out their lives as autonomous subjects. Rather, cities as media produce urban subjects by providing the technological conduits that allow people to make sense of their (urbanized) existence through the production of visual images, auditory sensations, and textual artifacts that demand continual interpretation, critique, and revision. Secondly, cities as media provide the channels of transmission—akin to Hans-Georg Gadamer's hermeneutic notions of *Überlieferungsgeschehen* (tradition-as-event) and *Wirkungsgeschichte* (effective-history) but going beyond their textual horizon—for collective histories, shared or contested values, multiple forms of aesthetic articulations, and other sociocultural processes (1975: 277; 284–290). Thirdly, cities as media, like any other medium, continually draw self-reflexive attention, not only to the content of what is being mediated, but to the very mechanisms of mediation themselves: their technological apparatuses, their ideologies, their pragmatic purposes, and so forth (Urbich 2011: 113–128).

As the interdisciplinary field of sound studies gains more prominence in German studies, we come to a better understanding of cities as spaces of multisensory experiences other than visual and textual ones (Sterne 2012). Through the modernist paradigm of *flânerie*, inherited from theorists such as Walter Benjamin, Franz Hessel, and Siegfried Kracauer, we have come to conceptualize the city primarily as a site of the mobility of visual consumption, for which buildings, streets, people, and traffic may serve as surface signifiers evoking the memory of half-forgotten or marginalized traces of collective history (Gleber 1999). But this paradigm, as Michael Bull has shown, seems insufficient for the postmodern iPod user, whose imagination is stimulated, not by the visual otherness of the events unfolding in public spaces but rather by phenomena that are aesthetically reinterpreted according the emotional moods evoked by the musical sounds in the user's ear (Bull 2012). Thus, we need to conceptualize cities as media that, through a range of competing technologies, emerge as conglomerates of narrative discourses, visual surfaces, and soundscapes. Of course, it depends not only on each individual city itself, but on its larger surroundings—the region, the nation, the political alliances—how these (re-)presentational modes are acted out in the lived experiences of actual people, institutions, and lifestyles. That is why each city discussed in the present volume mediates—represents, promotes, copes with—the transition of East Germany from the former GDR to the postunification *Neue Länder* (new federal states) according to its own timeline and spatial configurations, which overlap only partially with those of its neighbors in historically uneven ways. Because of these differences playing out in a comparatively small region, East German cities provide a highly diverse, yet sharply edged grounds for investigating how urban space mediates historical change, social processes, and material culture today.

References

Bull, Michael. 2012. "The Audio-Visual iPod." In *The Sound Studies Reader*, edited by Jonathan Sterne, 197–208. London and New York: Routledge.

Curtius, Ernst Robert. 1954. *Europäische Literatur und Lateinisches Mittelalter.* 2nd ed. Bern: Francke.

Derrida, Jacques. 1976. *Of Grammatology.* Translated by Gayatri Chakravorty Spivak. Baltimore and London: The Johns Hopkins University Press.

Gadamer, Hans-Georg. 1975. *Wahrheit und Methode.* 4th ed. Tübingen: J.C.B. Mohr (Paul Siebeck).

Gleber, Anke. 1999. *The Art of Taking a Walk: Flanerie, Literature, and Film in Weimar Culture.* Princeton, N.J.: Princeton University Press.

Huyssen, Andreas. 2003. "The Voids of Berlin." In *Present Pasts: Urban Palimpsests and the Politics of Memory*, 49–71. Stanford: Stanford University Press.

Kittler, Friedrich A. 2013. "Die Stadt ist ein Medium." In *Die Wahrheit der technischen Welt: Essay zur Genealogie der Gegenwart*, edited by Hans Ulrich Gumbrecht, 181–197. Frankfurt: Suhrkamp.

Koepnick, Lutz. 2001. "Forget Berlin." *The German Quarterly* 74 (4): 343–354.

Sterne, Jonathan. 2012. *The Sound Studies Reader.* London and New York: Routledge.

Urbich, Jan. 2011. *Literarische Ästhetik.* Cologne, Weimar, and Vienna: Böhlau/ UTB.

Contributors

Heike Alberts received her M.A. in geography from the Free University Berlin (Germany) in 1998 and her Ph.D. in geography from the University of Minnesota in 2003. Since 2003 she has been teaching a wide range of different geography classes at the University of Wisconsin Oshkosh, where she is now an Associate Professor. Her research focuses on highly skilled migrations as well as on urban development in North America and Europe.

Trevor Blakeney earned a bachelor's degree in German at Queen's University. His area of focus was the Eastern identity and the portrayal of nostalgia in film.

Gwyneth Cliver is Assistant Professor of German at the University of Nebraska at Omaha. She completed her Ph.D. in 2008 from Washington University in St. Louis and has also taught at Guilford College in North Carolina and Ball State University. Previous research has studied the integration of mathematics and mathematical philosophy in the writings of Robert Musil and Hermann Broch and the modernist interest in infinity.

Rolf J. Goebel is Professor of German and Chair of the Deptment of Foreign Languages and Literatures at the University of Alabama in Huntsville. His areas of research include: German modernism; representations of metropolitan space; and intermediality, media competition, and media transfer. In addition to numerous articles and conference papers, he has published three books: *Kritik und Revision: Kafkas Rezeption mythologischer, biblischer und historischer Traditionen* (1986); *Constructing China: Kafka's Orientalist Discourse* (1997), and *Benjamin heute: Großstadtdiskurs, Postkolonialität und Flanerie zwischen den Kulturen* (2001). He is also a co-author of *A Franz Kafka Encyclopedia* (2005) and has edited *A Companion to the Works of Walter Benjamin* (2009).

Elizabeth Guthrie completed a master's thesis on the Dresdner Frauenkirche, architectural reconstruction, and the media. She received her

M.A. degree from Brigham Young University in 2010. She has also col-laborated on several projects for *Sophie: A Digital Library of Works by German-Speaking Women* (http://sophie.byu.edu/), including an up-coming critical edition of the works of Elisa von der Recke.

Sebastian Heiduschke is Associate Professor of German in the School of Language, Culture, and Society and affiliate faculty in the School of Writing, Literature, and Film at Oregon State University. He is the au-thor of *East German Cinema: DEFA and Film History* (Palgrave, 2013) and the co-editor of *Re-imagining DEFA: East German Cinema in its National and Transnational Context* (Berghahn, 2015). His essays on cinema have appeared in *A New History of German Cinema, Monats-hefte, German Studies Review, Colloquia Germanica*, Seminar, and *In the Peanut Gallery with Mystery Science Theater 3000.*

Jude Hirman received a bachelor of arts (honors) with a dual major in history and German. She works with the Canadian Forces as a Naval Communicator, sailing the east coast of the United States and Canada and up into the Arctic Circle. Her work focused on the interplay of sex-uality and space within the films.

Jennifer Ruth Hosek is Associate Professor in the Department of Lan-guages, Literatures, and Cultures at Queen's University. Dr. Hosek works on twentieth- and twenty-first-century Germany in transnational con-text, notably *Sun, Sex and Socialism: Cuba in the German Imaginary* (University of Toronto Press, 2012). She has also published on literature, film, critical theory and neuroscience, information technology, and the women's movement. Her current large projects include a monograph on urban motion and cinema under late capitalism and http://www .linguaelive.ca, a free, educational web platform that facilitates language exchange among students worldwide. "Berlin Through the Lens" is a col-laborative, interdisciplinary, real-time research project that grew out of a winter 2010 seminar entitled "Approaches to the Urban," led by Dr. Hosek.

Jason James has taught anthropology at the University of Mary Wash-ington since 2005. After receiving his Ph.D. from the University of Cal-ifornia, San Diego in 2001, he was a Mellon Postdoctoral Fellow in the Humanities at Barnard College in New York, New York, and taught at Lafayette College in Easton, Pennsylvania. His book *Preservation and National Belonging in Eastern Germany* was published in 2012. He is currently conducting research on the commemoration of slavery and the Civil War in Richmond, Virginia.

Christopher Jones is Senior Lecturer in German in the Department of Languages at Manchester Metropolitan University (UK), where he teaches German language, literature, and culture. Although his Ph.D. was devoted to a study of influences on the work of Peter Handke, his current research interests are in the field of German popular culture. Recent work has included an examination of ideals of beauty in the romance novels of Hedwig Courths-Mahler; an analysis of the attitudes to cultural identity in Swiss-German detective fiction; and several studies looking at contemporary German-language, female-authored crime fiction. In this latter work, authors have included Pieke Biermann, Sabine Deitmer, and Thea Dorn.

Heidi Manicke graduated from Queen's University with an M.A. in German written under Dr. Hosek. Her thesis as well as her contribution to the chapter "Berlin Through the Lens" centered on the topic of transportation and how it shapes interpersonal relationships within cities. She is currently pursuing a degree in Geological Engineering at the University of British Columbia.

Rob McFarland is Associate Professor of German and head of the German Section at Brigham Young University. His research interests include cultural studies, film, and urban history and literature (especially literary and film portrayals of Berlin and Vienna). He is also associate director of *Sophie: A Digital Library of Works by German-Speaking Women* (http://sophie.byu.edu/). He is currently completing a book manuscript titled *Red Vienna, White Socialism and the Blues: Ann Tizia Leitich's Amerika* about the writings of the American correspondent for Vienna's *Neue Freie Presse* during the 1920s and 1930s.

Susanna Miller graduated with a bachelor's degree from Queen's University in linguistics with a minor in German. She is currently pursuing a master's of early childhood studies at Ryerson University in Toronto. Ms. Miller is particularly interested in the treatment of and rifts between insiders and outsiders in modern day Berlin. She, along with the other authors in "Berlin Through the Lens," presented as part of Dr. Hosek's conference entitled "Globalization & (Dis)Unification: Europe's Berlin Republic Turns 20."

Tamara Nadolny received a bachelor's degree in film studies and German from Queen's University and an M.A. in media studies from the New School in New York City. She has a special interest in the use of the traditional "flâneur" in modern film and how voyeurism or the act of being watched changes how film is interpreted.

Erika M. Nelson is Associate Professor at Union College, where she teaches German language, literature, and culture courses. Her doctoral research, completed at the University of Texas at Austin, focused on issues of identity construction and sound in Rainer Maria Rilke's Orphic poetry and was published as a book entitled *Reading Rilke's Orphic Identity* (2005). She has published on various transnational poets and filmmakers, including Zafer Şenocak, Andrea Štaka, and Dragica Rajčić, as well as on transnational identity and poetics, German spa culture, and modern renditions of mythic figures in literature and film.

Carrie Smith-Prei is Associate Professor of German Studies at the University of Alberta. She has written articles on post–1960 German culture, is the author of *Revolting Families: Toxic Intimacy, Private Politics, and Literary Realism in the German Sixties* (University of Toronto Press, 2013), co-editor of two special journal issues (*Germanistik in Ireland*, 2010; *Feminist Media Studies*, forthcoming 2015), and holds a major grant from the Social Sciences and Humanities Research Council of Canada for research on popfeminist activism (with Maria Stehle). She is co-founder of *Imaginations: Journal of Cross-Cultural Image Studies* and is currently co-editor of the *Women in German Yearbook* (2014–2017).

Heiner Stahl has been working since October 2013 as a Lecturer in modern and contemporary German history in the Department of History at the University of Siegen (Germany), focusing on subjects like environmental history, youth culture, and migration in Germany. From 2009 on he has been a post-doctoral researcher in the Department of Communication Studies at the University of Siegen (Germany), working on public, political, and academic discourses about sound, noise, and environment in the twentieth century. His Ph.D. project, conducted at the Potsdam Centre for Research in Contemporary History e.V. (ZZF), was published in autumn 2010 under the title *Youth Radio Programmes in Cold War Berlin. Berlin as a Soundscape of Pop (1962–1973)*.

Flavia Zaka graduated from Queen's University with a degree in politics and studied law at University of Victoria. Since graduation she has worked at an international NGO based in Hamburg as a media and communications associate. In the future she hopes to receive her master's in health, community, and development from the London School of Economics. Her particular area of interest centers on how capital flows in late modernity impact equitable distribution of resources.

Index